ALSO BY IRA KATZNELSON

ion and Enlightenment: Political Knowledge After
otal War, Totalitarianism, and the Holocaust

alism's Crooked Circle: Letters to Adam Michnik

Marxism and the City

oling for All: Class, Race, and the Decline of the Democratic Ideal (with Margaret Weir)

nches: Urban Politics and the Patterning of Class in the United States

Men, White Cities: Race, Politics, and the Migration
United States, 1900–1930, and Britain, 1948–1968

AFFIRMA

WA

Desola

Libe

Sch

City Tr

Black
in the

WHEN AFFIRMATIVE ACTION WAS WHITE

An Untold History of Racial Inequality in Twentieth-Century America

IRA KATZNELSON

W. W. Norton & Company
New York London

Printed in the United States of America
First Edition

Manufacturing by The Maple-Vail Book Manufacturing Group
Book design by Rhea Bravnstein
Production manager: Andrew Marasia

Library of Congress Cataloging-in-Publication Data
Katznelson, Ira.
When affirmative action was white : an untold history of racial inequality in twentieth-century America / Ira Katznelson.
p. cm.
Summary: "A work that exposes the twisted origins of affirmativeaction" —Provided by publisher.
Includes bibliographical references and index.
ISBN 0-393-05213-3 (hardcover)
1. African Americans—Civil rights—History--20th century. 2. Affirmative action programs—United States—History—20th century. 3. African Americans—Legal status, laws, etc. —History—20th century. 4. African Americans—Economic conditions—20th century. 5. Race discrimination—United States—History—20th century. 6. Johnson, Lyndon B. (Lyndon Baines), 1908–1973—Political and social views. 7. Whites—Civil rights—United States—History—20th century. 8. United States—Race relations. 9. United States —Politics and government—1945–1989. I. Title.
E185.61.K354 2005
323.1197'073'00904—dc22

2004024359

W. W. Norton & Company, Inc., 500 Fifth Avenue, New York, N.Y. 10110
www.wwnorton.com

W. W. Norton & Company Ltd., Castle House, 75/76 Wells Street, London W1T 3QT

1 2 3 4 5 6 7 8 9 0

For Leah,
Who designs and beautifies

CONTENTS

Preface: Du Bois's Paradox

"No more critical situation ever faced the Negroes of America than that of today—not in 1830, nor in 1861, nor in 1867. More than ever the appeal of the Negro for elementary justice falls on deaf ears. Three-fourths of us are disenfranchised; yet no writer on democratic reform says a word about Negroes."[1] When I chanced upon these sentences in an essay by W. E. B. Du Bois, I was astonished to learn it had been written in 1935, a time of great achievement for President Franklin Roosevelt's New Deal. That year, the president and Congress looked beyond the nation's economic desolation and hoped to find more than temporary measures to relieve mass hardship. Joining forces, they created Social Security and assured workers they could band together in industrial unions. More broadly, they sought to demonstrate that the globe's leading democracy could fashion an alternative to the appeal of Soviet and German dictatorships.

These new initiatives coincided with a historic political shift, in which a majority of black Americans had begun to turn away from Lincoln's Republican Party to offer their votes, when they could vote, to Roosevelt's Democratic Party, despite the presence within the New Deal coalition of southern Democrats who fiercely protected Jim Crow. Keenly aware that this shift hardly was ideal, Du Bois was in no mood to celebrate. Black America, he understood, was mired in difficulty despite any bounty offered by the New Deal:

> Negro children are systematically denied education; when the National Education Association asks for federal aid to education it permits discrimination to be perpetuated by the present local authorities. Once or twice a month Negroes convicted of no crime are openly and publicly lynched, and even burned; yet a National Crime Convention is brought to perfunctory and unwilling notice of this only by mass picketing and all but illegal agitation. When a man with every qualification is refused a position simply because his great-grandfather was black there is not a ripple of comment or protest.[2]

The contrast between the extraordinary policy advances of 1935 and Du Bois's mordant appraisal of the pervasiveness of racism at the height of the New Deal unsettled my conventional understanding. I soon launched a research program to ask how the achievements of Presidents Franklin Roosevelt and Harry Truman had been shaped by the pivotal role southern Democrats still were able to play as guardians of racial segregation. I also set out to identify the consequences of these ties between social and racial policy on American politics and society today.

When Affirmative Action Was White is one result of this endeavor. It reveals how policy decisions dealing with welfare, work, and war during Jim Crow's last hurrah in the 1930s and 1940s excluded, or differentially treated, the vast majority of African Americans. It also traces how inequality, in fact, increased at the insistence of southern representatives in Congress, while their other congressional colleagues were complicit. As a result of the legislation they passed, blacks became even more significantly disadvantaged when a modern American middle class was fashioned during and after the Second World War. Public policy, including affirmative action, has insufficiently taken this troubling legacy into account.

My goal in developing these arguments and proposing guidelines for new policies is not to write yet another history or analysis of affirmative action. The number of articles and books on this subject is considerable.

Policy historians have taught us how the origins of affirmative action as federal public policy in the 1960s and 1970s were byproducts of other intentions. For more than three decades, justices of the Supreme Court have gauged the legal status of affirmative action. Many scholarly and popular onlookers have disputed how affirmative action has shaped our schools, workplaces, and government, civil and military. Advocates and detractors have developed powerful arguments about key moral, constitutional, and practical issues. These, by now, are familiar.

I remark on these conflicting understandings and patterns, but this commentary neither is my main theme nor my central purpose. Writing as a historian, I want to set the record straight. As a political scientist, I would like to understand the mechanisms that produced these outcomes. As a citizen, I wish to present these understandings in order to alter our misconceptions and reposition the direction of how we think, talk, and act about affirmative action. Rather than limit attention to successful programs that have made our elite institutions more racially integrated, I propose that affirmative action focus on antidotes to specific harms that date back to national policies in the 1930s and 1940s as remedies for the deep, even chronic dispossession that continues to afflict a large percentage of black America.

Above all, I want to shift our focus in three primary ways. The first alteration I propose is a change in our historical attention span. Discussions about affirmative action—whether historical, philosophical, sociological, economic, or political—usually begin with events and debates that took place four, rather than seven, decades ago. This I believe to be a mistake, albeit one easy to understand. After all, the language of affirmative action as well as explicit policies carrying that name only were launched in the 1960s. By contrast, I look back as well as forward from the vantage of the mid-1960s. As a result, a mainly neglected earlier history of race and public policy comes into view, allowing us to see, think, and act about affirmative action in fresh ways.

The second modification intends to broaden our understanding of these issues. Today, when we say the words "affirmative action," we almost always think about higher education and top tier jobs. Recently,

I conducted a quick key word electronic search to classify stories about affirmative action in some of the country's leading newspapers (*Atlanta Journal-Constitution, New York Times, Washington Post, USA Today*), news magazines (*Newsweek, Time, U.S. News & World Report*), and the black press (*New York Amsterdam News, Chicago Defender*). In each case, "education" and "college" vastly surpass any other category. Only "jobs" and "employment" are also present in significant numbers. By contrast, the words "poverty," "inequality," and "social justice" show up in the media with far less regularity. By linking the history of affirmative action for blacks since the mid-1960s with the prior record of affirmative action for whites, I hope to refocus public debate on these neglected subjects.[3]

A third shift in this book is placing affirmative action on more secure ground by binding New Deal and Fair Deal history to an argument about when, why, and how history should count in crafting public policies today. I first encountered affirmative action as a young assistant professor. In 1971 I served as the junior faculty representative at Columbia University on a political science search committee. The Department of Labor threatened the university with the loss of $13 million in federal funding unless it hired more women and minorities. Not fair, said my colleagues, who resisted by proposing the appointments of five white men. Struck by the fierceness of opposition to what manifestly seemed fair to me (together with the Department of English, Political Science had functioned for years as a relatively closed gentleman's club for white Protestants), I was distressed by the absence of good grounds for a rejoinder to the senior members of my department, who deployed high-minded talk about color-blindness and merit to reinforce a historical pattern of exclusion.

Ever since, I have been troubled by the inability of advocates of affirmative action to secure their ground and by the narrowness of the policies they have defended. To be sure, a persuasive case has been mounted in favor of diversity in middle and higher management and law firms, in higher education, and in primary and secondary classrooms, police forces, and firefighting companies whose members interact directly with a heterogeneous public. But this type of defense has inadequately shown why remedies for harms based on race should be deployed. Defenders tend either to make very general claims for compensatory policies without clarifying how affirmative action should perform acts of restoration, or they retreat to pragmatic statements to argue that corporations and universities would be more vulnerable to anti-discrimination lawsuits without such policies in place. Those of us who think the work of affirmative action is incomplete need to bolster our case. Set against the principled opposition to affirmative action, both lines of reasoning are inadequate. Instead, I follow a more historical path that connects remedies to very particular public harms, and I try to explain why this approach is persuasive in both analytical and practical terms.

When Affirmative Action Was White, in short, is an attempt to affect the ways we consider this vexing subject. Today, the once contentious color-blind standard of non-discrimination is broadly accepted. So, too, are efforts at outreach and recruitment aimed at increasing the number of applicants for scarce positions in schools and firms. Where agreement stops is where compensatory discrimination starts; that is, where minority individuals are chosen even if white applicants have more appropriate qualifications judged by customary measures like grades and test scores.

"The controversy over affirmative action," Randall Kennedy rightly noted in 1986, "constitutes the most salient current battlefront in the ongoing struggle over the status of the Negro in American life."[4] The question still bites. As American troops were being dispatched to Iraq early in 2003, Robert Bartley observed in his *Wall Street Journal* column that "Second only to the pending war, 'affirmative action' is the issue of the day."[5] Unresolved and unsatisfactory, debate seems almost endless between advocates of reparations and defenders of non-discrimination and equal treatment who often seem blind to the organizing power of race in American life. In effect, broad and often unfocused claims for restoration have competed with anti-racist principles that direct us to racial neutrality. As a result, these disagreements by politicians, activists, philosophers, and jurists tend to yield the high ground to opponents of affirmative action, who claim such policies are wrong because, however well intentioned, they remain trapped within racist assumptions. Like many others, I have been unhappy with these choices. Hoping to move beyond options that downplay racism or reinforce racial divisions, this book offers an alternative, one that plaits history and principle together, as in a braid.

Finally, a word about my subtitle. In what sense is this polemical book "an untold history"? Although many features of my story have been discussed and analyzed by an array of talented social scientists and historians, the various strands in these excellent studies have not been brought together sufficiently. This is regrettable because the wide array of literature from which I draw invites just such an effort. From Robert Lieberman, we know how Social Security left out maids and farmworkers and how the landmark law of 1935 distinguished between social insurance for old age and more constricted, less centralized instruments of social assistance. From Jill Quadagno, we learn about the racial sources and implications of modern social policy. From Michael Brown, we discern the tight set of linkages that connected race and fiscal imperatives to the power of the southern wing of the Democratic Party when the modern American welfare state was shaped. From Suzanne Mettler, we are taught how even apparently universalistic public policies can divide categories of citizens from each other. From Neil Foley, we understand the impact of midcentury social policy on racial groups in the cotton culture South. From Lizabeth Cohen, we experience how, even in the North, the treatment of veterans after the Second World War was significantly differentiated by race. From Daniel Kryder, we comprehend the powerful impact race had on the nation during that global war. From Desmond King, we perceive the role that the federal government played from the 1910s to the early 1950s to secure racial segregation. From Nancy Weiss, we witness how torn black Americans were by the bounty and constraints the New Deal presented. And from William Julius Wilson, we grasp the economic, social, spatial, and political mechanisms that have divided black America between a growing but minority middle class and a far less fortunate and good deal more marginal African American majority.[6] My debt to these exceptional colleagues and to this outstanding body of scholarship is substantial. This book simply could not have been written without these and many other excellent works, some dating back to the New Deal and Fair Deal, which have provided me with guideposts, evidence, ideas, and illumination.

Notwithstanding, my subtitle holds. Despite the work of leading scholars, the American public remains in the dark about the moment not very long ago when affirmative action was white. I mean "untold history" in the sense of a not fully conveyed or altogether disclosed story—one that comes into full view only when its parts are considered together. The various elements of mid-twentieth-century public policy that advantaged whites have been thought about, in the main, one at a time rather than in a single, if complex, configuration. Moreover, these histories, even when thought to be germane to current issues, have only been loosely connected to present reflections and disputes.

Instead, my basic themes—how the cumulative and diverse public policies of the federal government during the 1930s and 1940s shaped affirmative action for whites primarily under the aegis of the South in Congress, and why this history matters for present-day efforts to create a less racially unjust country—have been organized to make two kinds of connections: among a range of policies in the past that usually are considered separately; and between that constellation of initiatives then and the possibilities for a new type of affirmative action now.

That is what I have tried to accomplish, all the while motivated by the historical puzzles and goals enunciated in the address President Lyndon Johnson delivered to graduates and their families at Howard University in June 1965. It was called "To Fulfill These Rights." Four decades later, the challenge confronts us still.

WHEN AFFIRMATIVE ACTION WAS WHITE

1

Doctor of Laws

The sun had begun its downward slope on the evening of June 4, 1965, as President Lyndon Johnson mounted the podium on the main quadrangle of Howard University, the country's most celebrated black center of higher education. The temporary platform erected for the graduation ceremony stood directly in front of Frederick Douglass Memorial Hall, named for the escaped slave who had become the nineteenth century's most important abolitionist and had served as a trustee at Howard. Dressed in academic robes, draped in the hood of the honorary degree of Doctor of Laws he just had received, the president turned to face an audience of some five thousand mostly African American students, parents, and family who had been sitting expectantly in the main quadrangle. Reading in the unhurried manner characteristic of his native Texas, Johnson got underway by saluting the university's president, "Dr. Nabrit, my fellow Americans." Then he opened his leather-bound text and began: "I am delighted at the chance to speak at this important and this historic institution . . . truly a working example of democratic excellence."[1]

At the finish, President Johnson was greeted with applause more rapturous than even a president elected by a landslide seven months earlier might have expected. This, however, was no common occasion.

This was no ordinary American leader. And "To Fulfill These Rights" was no run-of-the-mill speech. With the country still confronting southern resistance, this noteworthy address rightly is recalled as the first moment when a president from any region forcefully and visibly sponsored affirmative action for blacks.

But the speech also should be remembered for how it highlighted a powerful historical question it did not adequately answer. Why did the disparity between white and black Americans widen after the Second World War despite the country's prosperity? The answers Lyndon Johnson offered were less compelling than his discussion about what to do once legal segregation had ended and voting rights had been secured. The missing words that balmy evening might well have attended to the history of affirmative action for whites. Had the president done so, his inspiriting but rather open-ended conclusions might have placed affirmative action for blacks on a different, arguably more secure foundation.

I

JUNE 1965 WAS NO ordinary month. Nearly a year earlier, Congress had passed the Civil Rights Act at the start of July. With segregation in public accommodations now forbidden and discrimination in employment proscribed, the mass civil rights movement turned to voting rights.

By the start of 1965, Martin Luther King, Jr.'s Southern Christian Leadership Conference had begun to focus attention on Selma, Alabama, where local registrars backed by an oppressive police force outfitted with cattle prods and led by Jim Clark, a jowly caricature of a racist sheriff, had managed to keep black voter registration under 1 percent. When demonstrations began in Selma on January 18, repercussions were swift in coming. Sheriff Clark arrested hundreds of campaigners, including a great many children. During the start of a Sunday, March 7, protest walk from Selma to Montgomery, Clark's deputies and state troopers beat the six hundred marchers after they had crossed the

Alabama River, assaulting them with tear gas, whips, and clubs, and trampling them with horses until they retreated to town over the Edmund Pettus Bridge. With seventeen hospitalized at Good Samaritan Hospital for fractured legs, arms, ribs, and heads, and another forty treated for the effects of tear gas and minor wounds in the emergency room, "some 200 troopers and possemen with riot guns, pistols, tear gas guns and nightsticks later chased all the Negro residents of the Browns Chapel Methodist Church area into their apartments and houses."[2] At the mass meeting of some seven hundred people who gathered in Browns Chapel, Hosea Williams—who, in the absence of Dr. King had led the march alongside African American civil rights leader John Lewis—quietly observed: "I had fought in World War II, and I once was captured by the German army, and I want to tell you the Germans never were as inhuman as the state troopers of Alabama."[3]

Played out on national television, the piercing cries of terror and the visible brutality of gas-masked troopers riveted the American public. Much of the nation watched news reports of the second, more multiracial march led by Dr. King two days later. Protected by federal marshals but barred by an injunction from moving on past the Pettus Bridge, the marchers stopped in front of a double line of Alabama troopers and sang the civil rights movement's leading freedom hymn. "If you have never heard 2,000 Negroes and whites sing 'We Shall Overcome,' hands joined and swaying in eight-abreast rows on US 80 just east of the Alabama River," Andrew Kopkind observed,

> there is little that can be said to convey the experience. Civil rights demonstrations are now so old that hardly anyone not actually participating feels the essential drama. But for about 10 minutes, the incredibly complex, overplanned, overreported, and certainly unresolved Selma voting rights campaign was invested with a kind of profound passion that the world of pseudo-events rarely sees. . . . No one could say after Tuesday's march whether a column would ever get through to Montgomery, 50 miles away. But the purpose of the whole campaign—to

convince the federal government of the need for voting rights legislation—had already been accomplished.[4]

Six days later, President Johnson, who even a decade earlier would have been an unlikely crusader for civil rights, addressed a joint session of Congress to insist on a law to protect the right to vote for all citizens. If Reverend King's "I Have a Dream" speech at the August 28, 1963, March on Washington had produced the first rhetorical peak for the civil rights movement, this was the second. Speaking to most members of the Senate and House of Representatives in the House chamber—the Virginia and Mississippi delegations were absent, joined in their boycott by several other southern representatives—Johnson astonished his audience by the extent of his warm embrace of the movement and its goals as he promised to "send Congress a law designed to eliminate illegal barriers to the right to vote." Comparing Selma to Lexington, Concord, and Appomattox, the president identified the black struggle as his, and as the country's own. "Their cause must be our cause, too. Because it is not just Negroes, but really it is all of us, who must overcome the crippling legacy of bigotry and injustice." Pausing, then raising his arms, Johnson proclaimed the anthem of the movement: "And we shall overcome!"

Arguably, those four words represented the most remarkable transformation by any president in the extended history of race relations since Abraham Lincoln embraced abolition. In the early republic, the United States had, of course, possessed the world's most developed system of racial servitude. This long era culminated in civil war, followed by the military occupation of the South, and the passage of the Thirteenth, Fourteenth, and Fifteenth amendments to the Constitution (abolishing slavery, endowing blacks with citizenship, and protecting their right to vote).

If only for a moment, the racial question seemed settled. Soon, however, racial oppression took a new form. By nineteenth century's end, the South had embarked on a thoroughgoing program of legally enforced racial segregation. Dense regulations legislated by state governments sharply restricted the place of African Americans in the public sphere while regulating private, including intimate, relations between blacks and whites. A combination of social conventions, racist ideas, economic compulsion, theological justification, political institutions, and harsh enforcement by police, courts, and prisons, buttressed by private violence, supported the unyielding inequality mandated by Jim Crow.[5] African Americans who lived in the seventeen states that made it illegal for whites or blacks to step outside the boundaries defined by this encompassing social order experienced an authoritarian police state, not a democracy of citizens.[6] In this period, Americans living outside the South—in marked contrast to popular abolitionist sentiment before the Civil War—took on an indifference to southern arrangements combined with their own softer, yet still harsh practices of racial discrimination. This was the age of whiteness.[7]

Though not confined to one part of the country, racism was particularly brutal and pervasive south of the Mason-Dixon line. Even for many African Americans, it is now difficult to fathom the omnipresence of racial hierarchy in the region, not just in "redneck" country but in the South's most "progressive" cities. Emblematically, as the opening of the movie *Gone With the Wind* was celebrated in 1939 at a segregated Junior League ball in Atlanta—a city described only a few years later by Senator Theodore Bilbo of Mississippi as "the hotbed of Southern Negro intelligentsia, Communists, pinks, Reds, and other off-brands of American citizenship"[8]—entertainment was provided by the Ebenezer Baptist Church Choir, in slave costume, for the all-white guests. Among those who sang Negro spirituals was Martin Luther King, Jr., dressed as a pickaninny, then a ten-year-old in the sixty-voice group led by his father.[9]

Not surprisingly, the post–Second World War civil rights revolution in the courts and streets took aim primarily at the various codes and attributes of Jim Crow rather than at the more muted patterns of racial inequality widely present elsewhere. One by one, barriers to civil rights were overcome. The armed forces were desegregated after an executive order issued by President Harry Truman in 1948. That year, the

Democratic Party inserted a civil rights plank into its election platform. A series of landmark Supreme Court decisions culminated, in 1954, in *Brown v. Board of Education*.[10] Then, after a remarkable and largely peaceful mass movement that often was met with derision and naked force, a southern Democratic president induced Congress to pass the landmark Civil Rights Act of 1964 and, later, the Voting Rights Act of 1965, followed by the Open Housing Act of 1968.

Applying a standard of racial neutrality, these new laws brought the corrosive era of Jim Crow to a close. Discrimination by employers and in restaurants, hotels, and other public accommodations was banned. The federal government supported school desegregation and removed the most egregious barriers to fair voting. Bias in the sale or rental of housing became illegal. The Department of Justice and civil rights bureaus in the Departments of Labor, Defense, and Health, Education, and Welfare mobilized to protect racial minorities from racist practices.

Just weeks after Selma and his stirring address to Congress on voting rights, President Johnson was at Howard, the focal point of black intellectual life. Now, he took up a theme proclaimed in his speech in March, when he had noted that "even if we pass this bill, the battle will not be over. What happened in Selma is part of a far larger movement which reaches into every section and state of America. It is the effort of American Negroes to secure for themselves the full blessings of American life." Addressing a still mainly disenfranchised audience in the newly desegregated Washington, D.C. (two more months were to pass before the Voting Rights Act would be signed into law on August 6),[11] Johnson looked beyond "the day when my signature makes this bill, too, the law of this land."

The freedom it would confer, he insisted, like the liberty to come and go in the public arena or the right not to be denied a job on the basis of color, "is not enough." At the heart of the speech lay Johnson's explanation of why civil rights initiatives were insufficient and why something more, transcending equal treatment, was needed. In the part of the speech we rightly remember as the harbinger of official affirmative action, Johnson explained:

> You do not wipe away the scars of centuries by saying: Now you are free to go where you want, and do as you desire, and choose the leaders as you please.
>
> You do not take a person who, for years, has been hobbled by chains and liberate him, bring him up to the starting line of a race and then say, "you are free to compete with all the others," and still justly believe that you have been completely fair.
>
> Thus is it not enough just to open the gates of opportunity. All our citizens must have the ability to walk through those gates.

Declaring this to be "the next and more profound stage of the battle for civil rights," the president shifted ground. "We seek not just freedom but opportunity. We seek not just legal equity but human ability, not just equality as a right and a theory but equality as a fact and equality as a result."

What many in this audience specifically knew was just how far this president had moved in a mere decade and a half. The title of Johnson's Howard speech deliberately echoed the 1947 report of the Committee on Civil Rights that President Harry Truman had created by executive order in December 1946. *To Secure These Rights* chronicled the gap between democratic promises and racist practices. At a moment when ending "the familiar system of racial segregation in both public and private institutions which cuts across the daily lives of southern citizens from cradle to grave" seemed a utopian project, the committee projected segregation's demise. Only the termination of segregation in schools, housing, public accommodations, and the armed forces, and only an end to lynching (there were six episodes in 1946),[12] police brutality, the denial of suffrage, and discrimination at work, in health care, and public services, the writers argued, could make American democracy whole. Even the most equal version of Jim Crow, it urged, "could not alter this basic fact: a law which forbids a group of American citizens to associate with other citizens in the ordinary course of daily living creates inequality by imposing a caste status on the minority group."[13]

Johnson's own personal transformation reflected a sea change many could never have imagined. In 1948, a year after the Committee on Civil Rights advocated a wide-ranging, multifaceted civil rights program geared to achieve "the elimination of segregation, based on race, color, creed, or national origin, from American life,"[14] Congressman Lyndon Johnson of Texas, a staunch New Dealer, was elected to the U.S. Senate. His maiden speech, light-years away in content from either his Voting Rights speech or the Howard University address, was delivered on March 9, 1949. President Truman, after his unexpected reelection and the committee's report, had proposed a civil rights program aimed at easing restrictions on black voting, using federal power to curb lynching, and working against discrimination in the labor market by making permanent the wartime Fair Employment Practices Committee (FEPC). Southern senators mounted a filibuster. Their most eloquent spokesman was the new senator from Texas.

Johnson repeatedly punctuated his long speech in the Senate, lasting one and a half hours, with the phrase "We of the South." Despite his own abhorrence of racial prejudice and instruments of exclusion like the poll tax—views he underlined—he mounted a series of arguments that supported not just this specific pro–Jim Crow filibuster but unlimited debate in the Senate as an instrument of freedom irrespective of its effects. In advancing a vision of southern prerogatives based on a particular view of the Constitution and of federalism rather than on a direct endorsement of racism, Johnson nonetheless disdained anti-discrimination efforts as a form of slavelike compulsion. He also opposed federal intervention in voting rights, he told the Senate, not because he was "against the Negro race" but because "this is not the way to accomplish what so many want to do for the Negro." Imposition from outside the South, he cautioned, might "keep alive the old flames of hate and bigotry." Composed in manner and sensible in tone, Johnson reached into an Orwellian kitbag to explain why a federal commission on fair employment would be tantamount to servitude: "If the law can compel me to employ a Negro, it can compel that Negro to work for me. It might even tell him how long and how hard he would have to work. As I see it, such a law would do nothing more than enslave a minority." Further, he insisted that "the Negro—as a minority group involved in this discussion of civil rights—has more to lose by the adoption of any resolution outlawing free debate in the Senate than he stands to gain by the enactment of the civil rights bills as they are now written."[15]

Senator Johnson thus effectively guarded a social order propped up by racist legislation. For that, he was accepted by his southern colleagues as one of their own.[16] When he had represented a relatively liberal district, with few black residents, in the hill country adjoining Austin and the prairie country extending east toward Houston, Johnson never spoke about racial questions on the House floor, even as he voted against every civil rights bill considered during his tenure. But the Senate was different. Now, he represented Texas, as he explained to his page, Bobby Baker, later a key aide. "I am a Texan and I've got a southern constituency."[17] At the speech's end, the *Lubbock Journal* reported, a "long line" of southern senators "formed to shake his hand," and his mailbox soon filled with hundreds of supportive letters from constituents.[18]

Fifteen years later, the contrast could not have been more stark. No longer constrained by a Texas constituency, his own views and commitments had developed with unexpected vigor. By the time Johnson faced his audience at Howard University's commencement as president of the United States, he had become a revolutionary. Having moved through and beyond the upheaval in civil rights to emerge as a leader of racial change, most of his southern colleagues considered him a turncoat and defector. Now, speaking at the black heart of the nation's capital, he took yet another startling step by promoting an equality of outcomes as the measure of how well the country would cross its still stark divide.

"To Fulfill These Rights" posed two main questions. In the same year that the psychologist Kenneth Clark's landmark study of Harlem spoke of the country's "dark ghettos" as "social, political, educational, and—above all—economic colonies" whose "inhabitants are subject peoples,"[19] President Johnson asked why the gap between blacks and whites actually had grown in the two decades after the end of the Second World War. His description of the "much grimmer story" of black economic and social progress during the postwar years began by observing that "the great majority of Negro Americans . . . still, as we meet here tonight, are another nation. Despite the court orders and the laws, despite the legislative victories and the speeches, for them the walls are rising and the gulf is widening."

What should be done after the end of legal segregation and the imminent passage of voting rights legislation? Johnson inquired. And how could all Americans be accorded the same starting point in the pursuit of opportunity? "To this end," Johnson insisted, "equal opportunity is essential, but not enough, not enough." In a post–civil rights period, with the legal playing field leveled, with color expunged as an officially sanctioned badge of deprivation, when, if at all, should race count in authoritative public decisions?

One of the more remarkable features of this eloquent address is the role it assigned to history. Johnson's playing field metaphor evocatively underscored a compensatory approach to racial justice. As Hugh Davis Graham, a historian of affirmative action, astutely has observed, the president was announcing a theory justifying compensation for past racism that found its "grounding not in the Constitution or statutes or in liberal traditions of equal treatment. Rather the social force that justified the new doctrine of race-conscious affirmative action was *history itself*, in the form of past discrimination."[20]

But which history? The primary shortcoming of Johnson's speech was its surprising neglect of the history of public policy that had acted as a key cause of the distressing outcomes he chronicled. As a result, not only did its historical account remain vague, substituting expressive language for hard-edged analysis, but the repertoire of possible answers Johnson announced was unordered and unspecific, leaving unresolved just how he preferred to remedy the cumulative history of racial disadvantage. The dilemma he raised about what to do next remained an open question. But if the president provided only a first draft of adequate answers, he did pose just the right questions by directing the attention of his audience to past causes and future possibilities.

This book offers a second draft, in the form of an extended commentary, on the main themes in "To Fulfill These Rights": How shall we understand the missed chance to fashion black mobility and create a robust African American middle class in the two decades after the Second World War? And what should we do to address the unequal powers of race even after the legislative work of the civil rights revolution has been accomplished? These two questions can be connected by supplying the history President Johnson did not tell.

Three aspects define my reflections on why black difficulty and disadvantage took root in the generation before the end of Jim Crow and on how, in light of this history, the goal of broadly equal results across racial lines best can be advanced. The first and most fundamental is a historical account of the moment when affirmative action was white. The second is a line of argument about race and affirmative action. The third is an approach to policy today.

Ordinarily, chronicles of affirmative action begin in the early 1960s. They focus on the critical moment between 1963 and 1969 when such policies "moved from obscurity to become the single most important federal policy for dealing with employment discrimination," and extend forward to encompass the four decades when affirmative action was black. Writing about the limited qualities of most such accounts, the historian Thomas Sugrue has cautioned that they ordinarily "substitute a flattened image of the past—one of a colorblind constitution and a golden age of racial cooperation," an image that is historically false, and thus repress "the far more complicated and troubled history of racial liberalism."[21] Such approaches obscure important features of public policy in the earlier decades when affirmative action was white. Without this record, the history of affirmative action is incomplete.

II

THE ISSUE POSED FIRST by Lyndon Johnson was the economic condition of black America, considered both on its own terms and in relationship to the striking advances most whites had experienced in the last two decades. Shortly after the Howard address, the journalist Haynes Johnson visited Alabama to chronicle the aftermath of the marches in Selma. He discovered dire conditions, the kind that had inspired the president to believe that civil rights, however robust, would prove insufficient, even derisory, for those stuck at the bottom:

> Economically, the outlook for the Negro is still bleak. There are few jobs. There are still no street lights in the Negro sections. The housing and plumbing is abysmal. The streets are still unpaved. The wages are still below any reasonable minimum. In Selma, a Negro who earns $50 a week is a wealthy man. Next month when the cotton crop is picked the Negroes who work in the fields will receive $2 a day. A maid in Selma can expect $10 a week. If she works six days in a laundry, she will get $12. At one motel, part of a national chain, a maid earns the top figure of $22.50 a week for an eight hour day. And outside Selma, in the farmland through which the marchers made their way, the conditions are worse.[22]

Soon the country discovered that black despair was not confined to the South. Weeks later, the Watts district of Los Angeles was in flames.

The president, of course, had not predicted the ghetto riots that soon would convulse the country, nor did he forecast the nationalist turn the black movement was soon to take.[23] But his unprecedented talk about the "dark intensity" of prejudice, the limits of the landmark Civil Rights Act of 1964, and the "lacerating hurt" and "uncomprehending pain" of the "special nature of Negro poverty" did provide a realistic account of the country's racial situation, particularly its stark economic disparities.

At the heart of his moving address was a methodical, reasoned, diagnostic core that not only described the grim economic circumstances in black America but offered an analysis of their underlying causes. Johnson focused closely on the depths of racism and the decay of the traditional black family because he wished to do more than describe African American distress. His quest for sources and foundations was impelled by the desire that black disadvantage "must be overcome, if we are ever to reach the time when the only difference between Negroes and whites is the color of their skin."

As Johnson knew, the Second World War had followed an especially dismal period for African Americans, one even more grim than for the population as a whole. During the Great Depression, blacks had experienced sharp downward mobility, losing the economic gains hundreds of thousands had secured by moving northward during the First World War.[24] The principle of "last hired, first fired" placed many migrants who recently had joined the North's labor force at a special disadvantage. The world economy's collapse after 1929, especially as it affected agriculture, deepened the poverty experienced by the vast majority of the South's black workforce. The ruinous economy in the 1930s also closed off the option that earlier had opened up as a result of the robust demand for labor in the North during periods of wartime mobilization and postwar prosperity. Further, the small, fragile black middle classes on both sides of the Mason-Dixon line came under intense pressure, having gained only a very tenuous attachment to stable jobs with regular wage incomes, cultural respectability, and chances for mobility before the depression hit. In all, the period spanning 1929 to December 1941, when American participation in the Second World War began, was one of the bleakest economic periods for black employment since the close of Reconstruction.[25]

Much changed as a result of the Second World War. Unemployment virtually disappeared for both white and black Americans. Black migration to the North resumed, spurred by well-paid and stable jobs in the war production industries, putting pressure on southern as well as northern labor markets. Unionization advanced. By 1945, more than 20 percent of the private workforce in the South belonged to unions, many multiracial, a proportion nearly twice that for the United States as a whole today. Though the military remained racially segregated and offered whites far more access to skilled positions than blacks, the armed forces did offer some African American soldiers occupational and literacy training and presented all who served with the "republican" standing of soldier-citizen. Further, the cultural and political terms of the Second World War as a war against fascism made the most outrageous expressions of racism increasingly suspect. The vibrant period of growth that followed the war offered further economic opportunities.

Even with the sharp upward trend toward better living standards, more urbanization, and greater economic growth, the racial gap widened. Just at the moment the United States developed an increasingly suburban middle-class bulge, and Irish and Italian Catholics and Jews were advancing into mainstream white culture, African Americans remained stuck, in the main, in economically marginal class locations. When President Johnson in 1964 announced a "Great Society" effort to eradicate poverty and complete the New Deal, it was widely understood to be an effort directed at black poverty and the exclusion of African Americans from the middle-class mainstream.

The gulf between white and black Americans was the primary problem the president highlighted at Howard. Citing information provided by Daniel Patrick Moynihan, one of the authors of the Howard speech, Johnson chronicled "the facts of this American failure":

> Thirty-five years ago the rate of unemployment for Negroes and whites was about the same. Tonight, the Negro rate is twice as high.
>
> In 1948 the 8 percent unemployment rate for Negro teenage boys was actually less than that of whites. By last year, that rate had grown to 23 percent, as against 13 percent for whites unemployed.
>
> Between 1949 and 1959, the income of Negro men relative to

white men declined in every section of this country. From 1952 to 1963 the median income of Negro families compared to white actually dropped from 57 percent to 53 percent.

In the years 1955 through 1957, 22 percent of experienced Negro workers were out of work at some time during the year. In 1961 through 1963 that proportion had soared to 29 percent.

Since 1947 the number of white families living in poverty has decreased 27 percent while the number of poorer nonwhite families decreased only 3 percent.

The infant mortality of nonwhites in 1940 was 70 percent greater than whites. Twenty-two years later it was 90 percent greater.

Moreover, the isolation of Negro from white communities is increasing, rather than decreasing as Negroes crowd into the central cities and become a city within a city.

Of course Negro Americans as well as white Americans have shared in our rising national abundance. But the harsh fact of the matter is that in the battle for true equality too many—far too many—are losing ground every day.

The issue, as Johnson saw it, was not that blacks in the mid-1960s were as collectively poor as they had been in the prior generation. Rather, Johnson asked how white and black income and wealth could have grown more, not less, distinct in the postwar golden age. Despite the grimness of these developments, he also recognized what he could see, in microcosm, seated before him, the rise of a black middle class. Indicating that "this graduating class at Howard University is witness to the indomitable determination of the Negro American to win his way in American life," Johnson remarked that the black population in higher education had doubled since 1950, and he saluted "the enormous accomplishments of distinguished individual Negroes—many of them graduates of this institution." But "these proud and impressive achievements . . . tell only the story of a growing middle class minority, steadily narrowing the gap between them and their white counterparts."

What, he inquired, had accounted for these growing disparities despite nearly two decades of unbroken and unprecedented abundance? Why had an unparalleled possibility been missed to include the most downtrodden in the full embrace of postwar prosperity and advance their membership in the country's growing middle class?

With the identification of this growing gap between black and white Americans, the president advanced an uncommonly analytical explanation for a political address. "We are not completely sure," he confessed, "why this is." But among the "complex and subtle" causes, he singled out two for special mention. "First, Negroes are trapped—as many whites are trapped—in inherited, gateless poverty." Such poverty is deeper and more distinctive. "Negro poverty is not white poverty." The differences, he hastened to explain, "are not racial differences. They are solely and simply the consequence of ancient brutality, past injustice, and present prejudice." Unlike blacks, the white poor, many of whom had escaped its shackles, "did not have the heritage of centuries to overcome, and they did not have a cultural tradition which had been twisted and battered by endless years of hatred and hopelessness, nor were they excluded—these others—because of race or color—a feeling whose dark intensity is matched by no other prejudice in our society."

The second cause, embedded in the first, he identified as "the breakdown of the Negro family structure," which he attributed to "centuries of oppression and persecution of the Negro man." Here, of course, the president echoed the findings and arguments published just two months earlier in Moynihan's controversial Department of Labor report, *The Negro Family: The Case for National Action.* A self-perpetuating "tangle of pathology," marked by "the deterioration of the Negro family" and produced by "three centuries of injustice," it had argued, blocked black mobility. For this reason, Moynihan advocated that "a national effort towards the problems of Negro Americans must be directed towards the question of family structure."[26]

Neither of these arguments can be dismissed. The barriers to black advancement indeed were more pervasive and deep as a result of the country's long history of racial oppression. No doubt, too, families with one adult tended to be more poor than those with two. Still, these explanations were insufficient. Other possibilities were ignored. A radical decline in agricultural employment in the South and the start of deindustrialization in the North combined to limit opportunities at the bottom of the economic structure. Lags in skill training, more limited access to higher education, and persistent private discrimination by employers, banks, landlords, and other suppliers of economic opportunity also blocked black mobility.[27] Even the most successful fraction of black America—professionals, small business people, white-collar workers in public life, and industrialized workers in union jobs—faced new stresses. The end of Jim Crow, migration northward, and the start of desegregation in education wore away their insulated niches, and left them with fewer assets and greater insecurities than their white counterparts.[28]

Yet even more important, and entirely absent from the president's account, was the set of causes that will be highlighted in more detail in the chapters below: how the wide array of significant and far-reaching public policies that were shaped and administered during the New Deal and Fair Deal era of the 1930s and 1940s were crafted and administered in a deeply discriminatory manner. This was no accident. Still an era of legal segregation in seventeen American states and Washington, D.C., the southern wing of the Democratic Party was in a position to dictate the contours of Social Security, key labor legislation, the GI Bill, and other landmark laws that helped create a modern white middle class in a manner that also protected what these legislators routinely called "the southern way of life."

III

IRONICALLY, THOUGH NO ONE was in a better position to understand this legislative history than Lyndon Johnson, he left it unspoken at Howard, putting aside what, arguably, was the leading reason the gap between whites and blacks had widened since the Second World War. It was a curious omission, because he was intimately familiar with this history of lawmaking. Before his election as vice president in 1960 and his ascension to the presidency in 1963, Lyndon Johnson had been a remarkably effective legislator, first in the House of Representatives, then, as majority leader, as "master of the Senate."[29] During the course of his presidency, moreover, he continued to bring this unparalleled ability into play to craft and guide groundbreaking legislation through Congress.

And yet, his analysis at Howard avoided discussing the racial consequences of the control exercised over congressional legislation by representatives from the South, a group that included naked and strident racists like Theodore Bilbo and "Cotton Ed" Smith, urbane and publicly moderate guardians of segregation like Richard Russell, and expert non-racist liberals like Claude Pepper and Lyndon Johnson. As Congress acted to regulate labor markets and enhance the powers of employees, provide welfare and social insurance, build a powerful military, and reintegrate soldiers into postwar America, its southern members introduced features to fortify their region's social, economic, and political order.

The exclusion of so many black Americans from the bounty of public policy, and the way in which these important, large-scale national programs were managed, launched new and potent sources of racial inequality. The federal government, though seemingly race-neutral, functioned as a commanding instrument of white privilege. The Jim Crow contingent in the House of Representatives and the Senate—the "We of the South" Johnson had embraced symbolically and substantively in his maiden Senate speech—made it so. Because no bills could be legislated into law without the assent of the members of Congress from that region (a result of the balance of partisanship between Republicans and Democrats, the composition of the Democratic Party, and rules that required filibuster-proof votes in the Senate), public policy had to be tailored to meet their preferences, most notably their desire to protect Jim Crow.

All this the president did not say. His personal record and sense of pride were at odds with the quality of his history. Yet without an appraisal of how the southern wing of the Democratic Party had imposed its preferences on the country, it was impossible for him persuasively to explain the racial contours of postwar American capitalism and the impact of color on the country's class structure. As a result, the account he offered at Howard with such an engaging combination of feeling and factual information missed the chance to come to terms with the most dismal, even exploitative, aspects of the New Deal and the Fair Deal. Such a retrospective assessment, of course—measuring what he and his regional colleagues had accomplished—would have been particularly agonizing for a man so identified with that era's most significant lawmaking.

The Democratic Party that fashioned and superintended the New Deal and Fair Deal combined two different political systems: one that was incorporating new groups and voters, who had arrived from overseas or had migrated from the South; the other still an authoritarian one-party system, still beholden to racial separation. Racism, to be sure, was not confined to the South. Irrespective of where they lived, most white Americans before the civil rights era were indifferent to Jim Crow. Yet only in, and surrounding, the former Confederacy did the formal political system utilize race to exclude adults from citizenship and full access to civil society. Private terror combined with public law and enforcement to make this political system authentically totalitarian. Competitive party politics did not exist. Electoral contests were enacted inside the one dominant party.

Within the South, interparty conflicts were virtually unknown. Struggles between individuals and factions were resolved within the ambit of Democratic Party primaries. As a consequence, representation in Washington was the near-exclusive province of only one of the two great national parties. Further, this electoral arrangement was an integral part of a coherent racial civilization, with a distinctive heritage, economy, social geography, and culture. Within this framework there was in fact a great deal of heterogeneity, as in the differences in political behavior and style of upland whites and Black Belt whites. When engaged in the politics of representation outside the region, virtually all the South's members of Congress, however, stood together to preserve the basic contours of the region's racial regime. This was the premise of southern representation, and accounted for its survival. "Two party competition," V. O. Key, Jr., had observed in his classic study, *Southern Politics in State and Nation* (1949), "would have meant the destruction of southern solidarity in national politics. . . . Unity on the national scene was essential in order that the largest possible bloc could be mobilized to resist any national move toward interference with southern authority to deal with the race question as was desired locally."[30]

Southern seniority was exaggerated by not having to compete in a two-party system. Members from the region thus secured a disproportionate number of committee chairmanships, giving them special gatekeeping powers. Further, the filibuster in the Senate served to advance southern power. These features of southern representation combined to make the preferences and sufferance of the South central to all key features of the New Deal.[31] In effect, the South maintained a legislative veto throughout this formative period. Put more abstractly, the core institutions of America's liberal regime—its pattern of congressional representation and its party system—placed the South's practices at the center of Washington's politics and policymaking.

Once in Washington as elected representatives in the House and Senate, the southern members' undemocratic credentials were sanitized.[32] They were treated as delegates of the people just like any other. Allied as "solid South" Democrats, they affiliated with other Democrats to compose House and Senate majorities during most of the New Deal period. Before 1932, the majority of the Democratic

Party in Congress had been southern.[33] Even after the massive non-southern realignment in 1932 and 1936 that rendered southern representatives a numerical minority within the Democratic Party, the core of its senior members and its leading edge of continuity and legislative influence remained southern.

As the great agent of social policy change in the New Deal and postwar periods, this Democratic Party partnership of "strange bedfellows" produced a series of "strange deals" that, together, constituted a program of affirmative action granting white Americans privileged access to state-sponsored economic mobility.[34] The South used its legislative powers to transfer its priorities about race to Washington. Its leaders imposed them, with little resistance, on New Deal policies. Even at the height of the New Deal, the Democratic Party required southern acquiescence to the national program. Rising to oppose a 1940 anti-lynching bill, Congressman John Rankin of Mississippi cautioned northern Democrats to

> Remember that southern Democrats now have the balance of power in both Houses of Congress. By your conduct you may make it impossible for us to support many of you for important committee assignments, and other positions to which you aspire. . . . You Democrats who are pushing this vicious measure are destroying your usefulness here. . . . The Republicans would be delighted to see you cut President Roosevelt's throat politically, and are therefore voting with you on this vicious measure. . . . They know that if he signs it, it will ruin him in the Southern states; and that if he vetoes it, they can get the benefit of the Negro votes this vicious measure would inflict in the North.[35]

Their advantageous situation made it possible for southern members of Congress to support Democratic Party legislation provided the integrity of the South's matrix would remain unquestioned as a matter of "local option." During the depression and the Second World War, southerners in Congress were forced to embark on a great balancing act. They were reassured by the apparent resemblance between the New Deal and Woodrow Wilson's New Freedom, when Jim Crow had been strengthened, and were enthusiastic about the much-needed bounty federal public spending could provide. Concurrently, they distrusted an enhanced central state because they worried that its agencies would be placed in the hands of administrators from other regions who would possess a great deal of discretion. Further, with the glimmerings of the civil rights protest, early pro–civil rights decisions by the U.S. Supreme Court, and support for civil rights by some leading Democrats, southern anxiety continued to grow throughout the 1930s and 1940s. "Our position is desperate," Georgia's Richard Russell wrote to his fellow senator, Sam Ervin of North Carolina, "for we are hopelessly outnumbered. But we are not going to yield an inch."[36]

They did not. The South's representatives built ramparts within the policy initiatives of the New Deal and the Fair Deal to safeguard their region's social organization. They accomplished this aim by making the most of their disproportionate numbers on committees, by their close acquaintance with legislative rules and procedures, and by exploiting the gap between the intensity of their feeling and the relative indifference of their fellow members of Congress.

They used three mechanisms. First, whenever the nature of the legislation permitted, they sought to leave out as many African Americans as they could. They achieved this not by inscribing race into law but by writing provisions that, in Robert Lieberman's language, were racially laden.[37] The most important instances concerned categories of work in which blacks were heavily overrepresented, notably farmworkers and maids. These groups—constituting more than 60 percent of the black labor force in the 1930s and nearly 75 percent of those who were employed in the South—were excluded from the legislation that created modern unions, from laws that set minimum wages and regulated the hours of work, and from Social Security until the 1950s.

Second, they successfully insisted that the administration of these and other laws, including assistance to the poor and support for veterans, be placed in the hands of local officials who were deeply hostile to black aspirations. Over and over, the bureaucrats who were handed authority by Congress used their capacity to shield the southern system from challenge and disruption.

Third, they prevented Congress from attaching any sort of antidiscrimination provisions to a wide array of social welfare programs such as community health services, school lunches, and hospital construction grants, indeed all the programs that distributed monies to their region.

As a consequence, at the very moment when a wide array of public policies was providing most white Americans with valuable tools to advance their social welfare—insure their old age, get good jobs, acquire economic security, build assets, and gain middle-class status—most black Americans were left behind or left out.

Affirmative action then was white. New national policies enacted in the pre–civil rights, last-gasp era of Jim Crow constituted a massive transfer of quite specific privileges to white Americans. New programs produced economic and social opportunity for favored constituencies and thus widened the gap between white and black Americans in the aftermath of the Second World War. And the effects, as we will see, did not stop even after discriminatory codes were swept aside by the civil rights movement and the legislation it inspired.

IV

"FOR WHAT IS JUSTICE?" Lyndon Johnson asked as he concluded "To Fulfill These Rights." "It is to fill the fair expectations of man." In America, he observed, justice connotes "a nation where each man could be ruled by the common consent of all" and where "all of every station and origin—would be touched equally in obligation and in liberty. Beyond the law," he continued, "lay the land. It was a rich land, glowing with more abundant promise than man had ever seen. Here, unlike any place yet known, all were to share the harvest. And beyond this was the dignity of man. . . ." He paused, then the timbre of his voice—the recordings indicate—increased in resonance as he continued: "This is American justice. We have pursued it faithfully to the edge of our imperfections, and we have failed to find it for the American Negro."

A few sentences later he was done, closing an address that had offered history, analysis, and policy in a strong revivalist cadence[38] by calling, in biblical tones, for Americans to light a "candle of understanding in the heart of all America. And, once lit, it will never go out again." When the reverberating applause calmed, the president remained standing together with the audience filling the main quadrangle as the evening closed with the Howard University Choir singing "We Shall Overcome."

The special atmosphere of that occasion may be long past, but its qualities demand revival. President Johnson's question still haunts. For what, indeed, is justice, when measured against the moment affirmative action was white?

2

Welfare in Black and White

Faced with impossible choices, how could black Americans be anything but ambivalent about the New Deal? W. E. B. Du Bois, for one, while allowing that "the organized race hatred and segregation practices of the South are still powerful and prominent in the Democratic Party," nonetheless endorsed Franklin Roosevelt's reelection in 1944. "I feel without the slightest doubt that Franklin Roosevelt has done more for the uplift and progress of the Negro than any president since Abraham Lincoln." In listing the administration's "notable accomplishments," Du Bois included advances in economic status that had been offered by its programs for economic recovery. He underscored the help for small farmers, mortgage assistance through the Federal Housing Authority ("under which I myself have been able to build a home at a reasonable rate of mortgage interest"), and "the recognition of the right of labor to bargain for better wages and better conditions of work." He also acknowledged anti-discrimination efforts in wartime industries, "the appointment of a high class of colored advisers to administrative officials," and "the courteous social recognition given to colored presidents of Haiti and Liberia and to colored guests in general at the White House."

By contrast, Republicans in the first three decades of the century had offered only abstract solace and reminders of their role in Emancipation and Reconstruction. In fact, the party had withdrawn from southern competition and, by leaving the field, had accommodated to its distinct racial order.[1] Thus, only the Democrats seemed to offer resources coupled to a genuine concern for the well-being of even the most vulnerable Americans.

Realist that he was, Du Bois also recognized that political arithmetic would block efforts by the president to advance black circumstances, even if he were to care deeply about their plight. "Franklin Roosevelt has been hindered by the necessity of not going so far as to lose entirely the support of the South."[2] Du Bois returned to this theme during Harry Truman's presidency, urging the Democrats to "put out of business . . . the Southern oligarchy" and to "work upon the liberal wing of the Democratic party and impress upon them the fact that the reactionary remnant of their party in the South has got to be displaced."[3]

This, of course, proved impossible, at least at the time. Inescapably, as the New Deal's rewards were tightly and inextricably tied to the special advantages and blocking capacity of the southern delegation, black America was deeply torn. Support for the New Deal could not be separated from an implicit willingness to accede to the southern system. Opposition promised the loss of only recently secured gains. As reflected by the vibrant black press during the 1930s and 1940s, the recurring debate in black America oscillated, not surprisingly, between expressions of profound appreciation and equally intense articulations of disenchantment.[4] Reacting to the history of New Deal public policy during President Roosevelt's first two terms, the *Pittsburgh Courier*, which had supported Roosevelt both in 1932 and 1936, endorsed Wendell Willkie. Justifying its support of the Republican candidate in 1940, the paper asserted: "With perhaps the best intentions of the world and with a Northern president in the White House, Washington has become overrun with Southerners and from the time of the NRA to the present we have seen ample evidence of their attitude and handiwork where colored people are concerned." In this climate, the paper observed, "the Southern-dominated administration has worked assiduously to establish color discrimination and segregation as a policy of the Federal government, and to a distressing extent it has succeeded."[5] In the run-up to the election, the *Kansas City Plain Dealer* counseled the administration that it should not take the black vote for granted. If it wished to hold on to their support, the Democrats "must admit the Negroes to the Democratic Primaries in the South and give them an equal opportunity to exercise their franchise free from terrorism just as other Americans." They would also have to usher blacks into local and state government, and stop "giving them patronage in the North and allowing lynchers, Ku Klux, segregation, injustice in the courts, unequal facilities in educational systems, the existence of poll taxes, and the denial of the right to vote in the South."[6]

None of this agenda stood the remotest chance of adoption. Like the *Courier,* other supporters of the New Deal in the first two Roosevelt elections defected. In Baltimore, the *Afro American* explained that the political power of the South made further support impossible. Southern power had rendered the president silent about an anti-lynching bill. He permitted "the navy to exclude us and the army to close every unit but seven," and "we are only assigned to Jim Crow units" led by white officers. The Civilian Conservation Corps's supervisors and managers likewise were all white. And it focused on how large numbers of blacks were excluded from key social policies. Roosevelt, the paper accurately observed, "hasn't brought social security to domestics or farm workers, and over half the colored people are in those two classes." Further, these categories had been intentionally excluded from wage and hours protections. Referring to maids at the spa Roosevelt frequented, the editorial asked: "If he believes in a ceiling for hours and a floor for wages, why does he permit the Georgia Warm Springs . . . pay colored women workers $4.50 a week for long hours?"[7]

Yet there was a more favorable side of the ledger. Writing in the *Chicago Bee* on the eve of the 1940 presidential election, an Ohio black minister summarized how much "Roosevelt has done for us," stressing economic gains from relief, public employment, the right to join unions, and "a minimum wage and a maximum hour law."[8] "Don't bite the hand that feeds you," the *Black Dispatch* of Oklahoma City cautioned readers in its own pro-FDR editorial, literally counting the construction funds that had been allocated to black colleges ($11 million), the monies earned by black youngsters in Civilian Conservation Corps camps ($19 million in clothing; $20 million in food; $21 million to send home to impoverished parents), and the cash paid to black college students by the National Youth Administration ($2.3 million).[9] Four years later, the *Kansas City Plain Dealer* justified black support for President Roosevelt despite Jim Crow by rehearsing yet another list of substantial benefits that had been bestowed on a desperate group.[10]

Others emphasized the recognition blacks had received from the New Deal, ranging from social receptions at the White House to the appointment of advisers on race matters in the administration and a visible role at the Democratic Party Convention of 1940. This included a public address by South Side Chicago congressman Arthur Mitchell, a prayer led by an African American Methodist minister where "hundreds of Negroes . . . sat indiscriminately and unsegregated all over the vast Chicago Stadium," and the presence of "27 delegates and alternates on the floor of the convention. Anybody with half a grain of sense could see that the black man is being rapidly integrated into the Democratic party." All in all, the *Oklahoma City Black Dispatch* concluded, Negroes have been given fairer and more impartial treatment by governmental agencies in recent years than ever before in the history of the Republic."[11]

There was no right choice. Both sides scored winning points. The New Deal, beholden to southern votes, did not, indeed could not, undercut segregation and the ancillary denial of civil and political rights. There would be no anti-lynching law on President Roosevelt's watch; nor would racial hierarchies in the armed forces or federal agencies be disturbed in any basic way. The administration was trapped, just as black voters were, by the pervasive legacy of Jim Crow. Any crusade to break out of its power restraints would have been doomed to fail, even if the president had been willing. Such a campaign would have risked undercutting the wide array of social and economic programs the New Deal advanced. So a trade-off seemed on offer to black America: abjure too strident a claim for civil and political inclusion in exchange for assured and concrete material benefits.

It makes no sense to write a retrospective morality tale condemning politicians and citizens who were imprisoned by Jim Crow. We should not imagine a freedom of action they did not have. During the New Deal, most liberals put other priorities well ahead of civil rights. The commitment to this cause among non-southern New Dealers was very uneven, in part because they lacked the means to lighten the burdens of anti-black discrimination. Even the most committed advocates for black rights, including First Lady Eleanor Roosevelt, Senator Robert Wagner, and Interior Secretary Harold Ickes, were not disposed, as Ickes wrote North Carolina senator Josiah Bailey, to dissipate "my strength against the particular stone wall of segregation."[12]

Yet we also should not minimize the ugly and lasting consequences of this Faustian bargain. The Democratic Party's moratorium on confronting its own southern members extended beyond such civil rights measures as attempts to repeal the poll tax or the use of federal power to combat lynching. In essence, the compromise reached to the core of New Deal. By not including the occupations in which African Americans worked, and by organizing racist patterns of administration, New Deal policies for Social Security, social welfare, and labor market programs restricted black prospects while providing positive economic reinforcement for the great majority of white citizens.

I

"THE ECONOMIC SITUATION of Negroes in America," Gunnar Myrdal's hard-bitten summary of 1944 declared, "is pathological." His landmark study, *An American Dilemma*, concluded that "except for a small minority enjoying upper or middle class status, the masses of American Negroes, in the rural South and in the segregated slum quarters in

Southern and Northern cities, are destitute. They own little property; even their household goods are mostly inadequate and dilapidated. Their incomes are not only low but irregular. They thus live from day to day and have scant security for the future."[13]

In this period, most blacks, some three in four, lived in the South. As a whole, the region was poor, often desperately so, for whites as well as blacks. On the eve of the Great Depression, southerners in all pursuits earned average incomes less than half those received by Americans in the rest of the country. Most, nearly 16 million, worked the land in the 1930s and early 1940s. Farm labor dominated the economy of the South as in no other region of the country. Of all people engaged in agricultural labor nationwide, 53 percent worked in the South in 1930, and 50 percent in 1940. Of this massive southern agricultural labor force, 40 percent of those classified by the U.S. Bureau of the Census as "laborers" were black in 1940, as were 55 percent of the region's sharecroppers.[14]

From today's vantage, it is difficult to convey the extent of black deprivation. Despite the large number of black agricultural workers, just 8 percent of southern farm land was operated by black owners, tenants, and sharecroppers; and only a small proportion of black farmers, about one in ten, owned their own land. Short of capital, limited in their access to banks, and often taxed disproportionately on their holdings, these proprietors, less insulated from adversity, had a tenuous hold on their property. In the 1920s, many barely held on during the epidemic of boll weevil. Overall, black, as well as white, ownership declined. In the 1930s, buttressed by federal agricultural assistance, white ownership trends reversed, increasing sharply, but black ownership again declined. The holdings of black farmers, furthermore, were much smaller than white holdings—63 acres in 1935, compared to 145 on average for whites—and their acreage was worth 20 percent less. Thus the average value of a black farm that year was $1,864 compared to $5,239 for whites.[15]

The vast majority of black farmers were even more marginalized, working in the main on white farms as terribly compensated workers of one kind or another. They were in the greater part tenants or sharecroppers. Of the tenants, a small percentage, not more than 10 percent, rented land and thus, in effect, were independent farmers but not owners. Most tenants were supervised workers, often in work groups, whose "wages, however, are not determined according to supply and demand in a free labor market" because the supply was overwhelming and mobility almost entirely absent. They faced a good deal of intimidation, including beatings and sexual coercion.[16] Sharecroppers were even more dependent and ordinarily immobile. Debt tied them to a particular planter who provided the loans for rent, food, seed, and farm implements without which these farmers could not subsist. Rather than being paid in wages, they received a share of the product, and thus were vulnerable to drops in price for the commodities they farmed. When the year closed with the cropper in debt to the farmer (a calculation based on accounting the cropper had little knowledge of and even less control), he and his family faced long months of acute destitution. Black tenants lived on the edge. The availability of food varied by the season, peaking in the fall when they were paid for their cotton and other crops and in the spring when they were extended credit by their landlords. "During the other four to six months of the year," Allison Davis reported in his classic study, *Deep South* (1941), "most tenant families . . . between 1933 and 1935, lived in semistarvation," subsisting mainly on bread and milk.[17]

In 1937, the average per capita income in the South was $314, contrasting with $604 in the other states; farm income in the South was lower, and out of these earnings expenses had to be paid. Tenants and sharecroppers fared less well. On cotton plantations that year, "the average tenant family received an income of only $73 per person for a year's work. Earnings of sharecroppers ranged from $38 to $87 per person; an income of $38 annually means only a little more than 10 cents a day."[18] Even the highest paid farmworkers, earning an average of $53 each month, brought home one third less than their counterparts elsewhere; while those at the bottom were earning less than 50 percent of what non-boarded agricultural laborers were paid in the rest of the country.[19] The depression proved infernally harsh. Cash receipts for cotton, the region's leading crop, plummeted from $1.4 billion to $550 million in the decade between 1929 and 1939, destroying the livelihoods of many black families.[20]

Belying the national norm that women, especially women with children, stayed out of the wage labor force, two in five black women were officially recorded to be working outside the home, while an uncertain number of others did so but were missed in official records. Although some secured clerical or factory jobs, during the 1930s about 85 percent of black women in the labor force worked either in agriculture or in domestic service, mainly in private households. Of these, nearly 700,000, or seven in ten, were maids. In the South, this job, characterized by a complex and demeaning etiquette of inequality, was nearly exclusively black. In no southern state were more than 15 percent of servants white; in most, only one in twenty. Having hired black household help was nearly universal among middle-class and upper-class whites in the region. Even some one in five relatively poor whites, with family incomes under $1,000 per year, employed black maids during the depression. Working some seventy hours and rarely earning more than $5 per week ("there are even localities where the usual wage is scarcely $2 per week"), this was the most exploited group of workers in the country.[21]

"The most abject of America's rural people . . . were the African Americans who farmed in the South; they lived in the poorest region of the United States and were the poorest people living there," writes the historian James McGovern.[22] In the rural South, where most blacks worked and resided, their average family income was only $565 per year (fully half took home less than $480); poor whites earned nearly three times that much, an average of $1,535.[23] Urban blacks fared better, but not by much. In southern cities, most black incomes reached $635 per family per year, compared to white average earnings of $2,019. In bigger cities like Atlanta, Birmingham, Columbia, and Richmond, blacks earned more, but just an average of $760. In Atlanta, the wealthiest metropolis, only 3 percent earned over $2,000. By contrast, an emergency budget—spending at a very low, subsistence level and assuming a restricted diet and a house (usually an unpainted wood frame structure) without an indoor bathroom—required $903 a year for each family. "The so-called maintenance level ($1,261) appears at present to be completely beyond the means of the general Negro population, particularly in the South," another analyst concluded in the 1940s.[24]

Living conditions were wretched. Not even one in a hundred black farm families had cold or hot water piped into their homes, and only some three in a hundred had hand pumps indoors (compared to about 20 percent of white families who could retrieve water inside). Whereas approximately one in three whites possessed an icebox or mechanical refrigerator, fewer than one in ten blacks did. White homes averaged five rooms, black homes just three. Often, these consisted of one or two poorly ventilated rooms that proved stifling in the heat of summer, and overcrowded and unhygienic all year round. In 1940, 97 percent of black rural dwellings lacked electricity. Urban housing was not much better. A national health survey discovered that just 10 percent of white families in cities lacked an indoor water supply, but 60 percent of blacks did not have water in their kitchens; 75 percent in their bathrooms. In Birmingham, Charleston, and Jackson, more than 90 percent had no facilities of this kind at all. And whereas urban whites in the South cooked with gas or electricity 90 percent of the time, the comparable black figures varied from a low of 1 percent in Jackson to a high of 49 percent in Dallas.[25]

Black health, not surprisingly, reflected a dire state of poverty. The cost of a doctor's visit, usually $3 in the early 1930s, was out of reach for most maids and farmworkers. So, too, was medicine. Most southern hospitals refused to admit African American patients; they were treated in black hospitals, which, in the late 1940s, had about twenty thousand beds. In the South, black patients had access only to a limited number of teaching hospitals and segregated wings of voluntary hospitals. At the time, the national standard stipulated 4.5 beds for each 1,000 people; for blacks, the number hovered between 1.5 and 2.5 in the region's largest, best-equipped cities. In Atlanta, where blacks had access to fewer than four hundred of the city's nearly two thousand beds, some three hundred were in a horribly substandard city hospital for the indigent. The South badly lagged behind the national standard specifying there should be no less than one doctor for every 800–1,000 individuals: Virginia and Louisiana had the best ratios, at 1 for every 1,200; Mississippi the worst, at 1 per 1,800. Nationally, there was only 1 black physician for 3,100 people. But the southern ratio of black doctors to black residents was vastly worse than these averages: 1 to 7,100 in Georgia; 1 to 8,600 in Louisiana; 1 to 12,000 in South Carolina; and an astonishing 1 to 18,000 in Mississippi.

Only a small number of black doctors secured hospital affiliations. Despite a higher birth rate than whites, the size of African American families lagged, the result of often astronomically disproportionate infant and maternal mortality rates. Death rates for blacks remained high across the age range. The records of the Metropolitan Life Insurance Company, which had insured more than 2 million blacks between 1911 and 1935, revealed an excess mortality as compared to whites of more than 40 percent for men and 70 percent for women. Comparing white and black policyholders, the firm discovered that "the death rates are two or more times as high among the colored . . . policyholders in influenza, tuberculosis, syphilis, cerebral hemorrhage, pneumonia, chronic nephritis, and homicide." At birth, the federal government reported, life expectancy for blacks lagged that of whites by ten years in the period between 1939 and 1941. By 1947, the gap had grown to eleven years.[26]

Between the First and the Second World Wars, schooling was widely extended beyond the eight primary grades to kindergartens for five year olds and high schools. The secondary school population quadrupled in this period, from 1.5 to 6 million. In 1944, the American Council on Education ranked the states, based on information from 1939 and 1940, by the amount of additional expenditure that would be required to educate all children between the ages of five and seventeen at the national median level. Of the ten most needy states, nine were southern (Mississippi, Arkansas, Alabama, South Carolina, North

Carolina, Georgia, Kentucky, Tennessee, and Louisiana). Of the fifteen states that spent the least in support for each classroom, fourteen were in the South. In the thirty-one states that did not maintain separate schools for black and white children, the median classroom received just over $2,100 each year; in the seventeen southern states that practiced racial segregation, the sum was under $1,100. In the South, some 1.56 million children were schooled in classrooms whose budget was less than $600. Of these, fully 80 percent were black. Measured differently, the value of school plant equipment for each southern white child in 1940 was $162; for each black $34.[27] Most black schools, a comprehensive study reported, "are usually without comfort, equipment, proper lighting, or sanitation. Most are of the one- or two-teacher type. Here are found the poorest trained and lowest salaried teachers, the shortest terms, the poorest attendance, the crudest buildings, and the most meager equipment and teaching materials."[28] Further, many black children, 16 percent according to the 1930 Census, were in the labor force, compared to 3 percent for whites. In the rural South, farmwork by black children was so customary and "officially countenanced that the public schools as a matter of course expect children of tenants to attend only when they are not required in the fields." Not surprisingly, black achievement was relatively low and illiteracy high. While just over 1 percent of whites were rejected from the military in 1942 for educational deficiencies, 10 percent of blacks were deemed inadequate. In Mississippi, 150 of every 1,000 potential African American inductees were rejected; in Georgia, an astounding 256 of every 1,000. In these two states, one in four registrants signed their Selective Service cards with a mark.[29]

II

UNDER THESE CIRCUMSTANCES, the opportunity for blacks to obtain relief payments and secure other sources of public benefits from the New Deal, limited though they were, could seem miraculous. At a time of little hope that disfranchisement, intimidation, discriminatory justice, job ceilings, wage differentials, or segregation could be remedied, the dramatic growth in federal spending promised feasible assistance. National programs were particularly important when naked discrimination prevailed across the spectrum of public services within the South. Under the misleading rubric of "separate but equal," one in seven public libraries in the South served blacks. Even some roads were segregated. Most black neighborhoods lacked paving and lighting. Public employment and access to local and state programs of relief offered whites and blacks starkly different levels of opportunity and support. With a rising share of such expenditures originating in federal programs during the New Deal, destitute blacks could come into contact for the first time with fairer access than they had experienced before.[30] The federal government offered a panoply of initiatives, including unemployment insurance, public assistance, and work relief. These programs injected funds and prospects where there had been little to none.

As the New Deal unfolded, black and white differences persisted, but they diminished somewhat with the federal government now in play. In all, as Myrdal noted, "Negroes get fewer benefits, in relation to their needs, than do whites. Nevertheless, since they are so much poorer than whites, their representation on the relief rolls usually exceeds their proportion in the population."[31] Before the passage of the Social Security Act in 1935—a multifaceted law providing for old age pensions, benefits for survivors (mostly widows), unemployment compensation, and assistance for the poor and for survivors (mostly widows)—the Federal Emergency Relief Administration (FERA) coordinated virtually all the New Deal's national programs that mitigated the harshest results of the depression. This injection of money made survival possible when, during the depression, many states lost their ability to tax and spend.

Though costs were shared with the states, some 70 percent of FERA grants came from the federal treasury. This proportion climbed to over 90 percent in the South, the nation's most stricken region.

Because they were poorer than other Americans, a higher proportion of the black population (18 percent) received FERA payments in 1933 than whites (10 percent). FERA's rolls crested in the spring of 1935. By then, 22 percent of black families had obtained relief grants, while the total for whites had climbed to 14 percent. In the urban North, blacks did gain access as determined by need. There, they consistently qualified more often than whites, often by wide margins. In New York, blacks composed 22 percent of the caseload; in Chicago, 24 percent; in Detroit, 32 percent; in Philadelphia, 40 percent. These numbers were in far excess of their share of the population (6 percent in New York; 8 in Chicago; 9 in Detroit; 13 in Philadelphia).[32] Unlike their brethren in the South, this client group of African Americans composed a voting bloc, one that shifted decisively in this period toward the Democratic Party.

Despite efforts by some Washington administrators, neither the size of benefits nor the pattern of distribution was standardized across the country. Although the Emergency Relief Act of 1933 furnished considerable powers to Harry Hopkins, the administrator of FERA, he soon discovered that "he had to tailor relief . . . to accommodate the demands of southern plantation owners for cheap farm labor by curtailing [the level of] relief payments to agricultural laborers and sharecroppers."[33] Black relief rates were high in the South, as in the North, but far less consistently. Here, they ranged "from 10 to 47 percent for Negroes in the different states and from 6 to 19 percent for whites. State variations were even more pronounced in southern rural areas, ranging from 2 to 27 percent for both Negroes and whites." By 1935, ten southern states had lower relief rates for rural blacks than whites, representing not actual need "but discrepancies in administrative practices and standards" in situations where there was wide local discretion. In some Georgia counties, for example, federal relief monies excluded all blacks; in Mississippi, relief was limited to under 1 percent. "The lack of uniformity cannot be explained," an early 1940s report found, "by differences in financial resources of the communities as the financial burden was largely carried by the federal government." Where landlords customarily had a paternalistic relationship with their tenants, particularly with sharecroppers, they possessed a strong impulse to prevent "their" black farmers from forging a direct relationship with federal relief.[34]

This combination of unprecedented access to governmental support and powerful discrimination generated by local administration produced racial differences in the size of grants to families in need. To get help, blacks had to be in more distress than whites. Clearly, if uniform treatment had been established, black relief grants would have been higher than white allowances, but just the opposite prevailed. Overall, the South offered its residents comparatively low levels of help. In contrast, New York State, in 1933, proffered an average monthly relief grant of $30.59; by 1935, the sum had increased to $49.06. The national average in these years moved from $15.51 to $29.64. In Virginia, one of the more generous southern states, the 1933 figure was $6.94, rising to $17.65 in 1935. A summary, giving an account of a Works Progress Administration (WPA) review, reported that "the low general averages for the South are due in part to the small benefits given to rural and Negro relief cases." In cotton areas, black relief cases "received from $2 to $6 less than the white families on relief." Further, as blacks were less likely than whites to be offered work relief, "this reduced the average size of all Negro benefits in comparison with those received by whites."[35]

These unequal patterns reflected two powerful features in the southern scene. The first was the low earning power of blacks. Relief payments were calibrated not to undercut the labor market. Recipients were not to receive more money on the dole than they would be earning if they had a job.[36] Because the South remained so poor and its rural and urban workers were paid so little by national standards, relief rates were deliberately kept low.

The second, even more important mechanism was the discretionary power available to state and local officials, virtually all white, to maintain this differentiated system of payments. Though many executive decisions about broad rules and spending decisions lay in Washington, their execution was local, placing federal relief initiatives in the hands of the various states. These, in turn, usually assigned responsibility to the smallest, most local unit of government.[37] By decentralizing authority and fragmenting decision making, national policies could be administered to suit white southern preferences.

Before the New Deal, most of the country's social welfare spending had been in private charitable hands. In 1931, only twelve states made provision for pensions for the elderly. Public responsibility was meager, in the main restricted to individuals in extreme personal duress, such as the orphaned, insane, and blind, who often were placed in institutional care. Though there had been some gains in the 1920s in mothers' pensions, in the public sphere, and community chests, in the private sector, it was only with the New Deal that the public realm extended its reach to welfare broadly conceived. It was this extension, of course, that appealed to many African Americans, who otherwise could find very few sources of support in exceptionally difficult conditions. But this extension never was direct or unmediated by state and local officials, who were left almost totally free to manage programs and dispense largesse as they saw fit.

Southern members of Congress often took the lead in demanding the expansion of federal aid. This campaign began in the Hoover years when Congressman George Huddleson of Alabama insisted on the appropriation of $50 million in federal aid to the unemployed, in part as an effort to stem radical agitation by left-wing unions.[38] During Franklin Roosevelt's first term, this drive for funds proved successful as southern states paid for relief with a higher proportion of national funds than any other region. Whereas federal transfers paid 53 percent of the relief bill in Connecticut and 55 percent in New York, they covered 87 percent of the cost in Virginia, 95 percent in Alabama and Georgia, 98 percent in North Carolina, and nearly 100 percent in Florida.[39] The lowest federal contribution in the South was in Texas, at 73 percent, while it was over 80 percent everywhere else, and over 90 percent in eight southern states.[40] Overall, during the 1930s, the various New Deal relief programs, including the FERA, CWA, and WPA, injected some $2 billion into this very needy section of the country.[41]

The South's political leaders thus had to find a tolerable balance between two sources of tension. The region's poverty impelled them to pursue fresh and significant sources of federal help, especially because their states were unable to add much on their own. But they had to keep payments low and racially differentiated so as not to upset their low-wage economy, anger employers, or unsettle race relations.[42] The key decision was an agreement by the southern supporters of the New Deal not to pay relief at a level higher than prevailing local standards. They also secured such accommodations as excluding agricultural workers from relief rolls at planting and harvesting times. Furthermore, they had to manage the strain that potentially might be placed on local practices by investing authority in federal bureaucracies. "With our local policies dictated by Washington," the *Charleston News and Courier* editorialized in 1934, "we shall not long have the civilization to which we are accustomed."[43] To guard against this outcome, the key mechanism deployed was a separation of the source of funding from decisions about how to spend the new monies.

Southern congressional power ensured that all the various New Deal programs possessed this segmented character. "Once a state had received a grant, it controlled expenditure; state law defined the authority of relief agencies, executive orders were issued by the governor or by the relief director he appointed; the legislature decided what money should be appropriated from state resources."[44] This situation introduced a new set of institutional tensions and potential hostility between the levels of government in the federal system. But the federal government did not exercise its powers by enforcing equal treatment. To the contrary, it franchised authority to the states and their localities, which then were free to administer federal policy as they saw fit. Because the need was so urgent and the funds so national, southern members of Congress had anticipated the potential dangers to Jim Crow and thus the administrative need to forestall them. They would risk receiving federal monies, the legislative record shows, "provided that control of grants remained with the state authorities and no conditions requiring state actions were attached."[45] Their goal was to maximize the flow of federal funds while maintaining local responsibility to ensure the continuing viability of the southern racial order.

This strategy worked. Southern racial patterns were guarded by the individuals who managed the programs. In Virginia, the capable administrator of relief, William Smith, had "the characteristic attitude of the Southern person toward the negro," a federal field representative reported.[46] In Georgia, all federal grants were directly channeled through Governor Eugene Talmadge's office, where relief was administered by Dr. Herman De La Perriere, "the archetype of the rotund, southern politician who had absolutely no knowledge or ability in the fields of either relief or administration."[47]

By keeping temporary relief offered by the federal government in the first phase of the New Deal in local hands, the South's heritage of bigotry was both reflected and reinforced in patterns of spending and administration. When FERA's black director of Negro Affairs in Atlanta, Forrester Washington, reviewed his experience after resigning in 1934, he noted that "the way colored people have suffered under the New Deal . . . is a disgrace that stinks to heaven." The *Atlanta Daily World*, the city's African American newspaper, concluded in 1935 that "Under the FERA the Negro was shown the same place assigned to him at the close of the Civil War, which had for seventy years . . . sealed his illiteracy and poverty."[48]

Nevertheless, these programs did make life a bit easier for those stuck at the bottom, both black and white. However unevenly administered, African Americans were offered some governmental protection against wretched conditions for the first time since Reconstruction. So, while tinged with irony, it was also quite accurate for Gunnar Myrdal to have observed that "the institution of large-scale public relief during the 'thirties [was] the one bright spot in the recent economic history of the Negro."[49] As one black tenant noted, despite the absence of any threat to white supremacy, "the government was helping the poor colored people more than anybody else."[50] The New Deal did indeed stem some of the tides of adversity, but at the cost of accommodation with racial oppression.

III

BEFORE 1935, THE NEW DEAL's mixed record, which combined unprecedented assistance with racist policies, was closely tied to short-term help. There was no lasting set of laws and structures for social welfare. All this changed with the Social Security Act of 1935. In the history of American social policy, no legislative enactment has been more significant, influential, or enduring. Even at the start, when it still was relatively diminutive in scale and started slowly, by the standards of the time it quickly made use of significant managerial and economic resources. After 1935, with FERA disbanded, a new American welfare state with national backing and the potential for real permanence was established. The law's encompassing scope had enormous potential for African Americans. It provided security against the economic hazards of old age at a time when more than one half of all black men, compared with one third of white men, remained in the labor market after the age of seventy-five.[51] It insured against unemployment when 26 percent of black men and 32 percent of black women were out of work—compared to 18 and 24 percent for whites—and it ameliorated poverty by providing old age assistance to the indigent poor and aid to impoverished and dependent children when blacks were less well off in both categories than other potential recipients.

Precisely because they worked longer into old age, were more prone to job layoffs, and disproportionately located at the bottom of the social structure, African Americans who proved eligible did, in fact, gain a great deal from the Social Security Act. In 1940, the year Social Security payments for the elderly began after a sufficient fund had been received, the Social Security Board identified nearly 2.3 million black workers as eligible for old age insurance.[52] To be sure, as with earlier patterns of relief, their benefits tended to be on the low end. The scale of Social Security payments hinged in part on prior wages, which, for blacks, often had been derisory. Still, nothing like this scale of assistance previously had been available to the elderly, white or black. A married couple without children who had earned under $50 a month qualified for a grant of $31.50 each month.[53]

Unfortunately, the great majority of blacks still were left out. Most African Americans, we have seen, were farmworkers or domestics, and people in these categories did not qualify. This feature of the new landmark law contradicted the strongly stated recommendation by President Roosevelt's Committee on Economic Security, whose report became the basis for congressional action. That report explicitly had stated that "We are opposed to exclusions of any specific industries within the Federal act," and it recommended the mandatory inclusion of all workers earning under $250 per month. Further, it explained that "agricultural workers, domestic servants, home workers, and the many self-employed people constitute large groups in the population who have received little attention. In these groups are many who are at the very bottom of the economic scale."[54]

This recommendation did not survive the congressional process. Social Security, as passed and signed by President Roosevelt in August 1935, produced a stark outcome. Across the nation, fully 65 percent of African Americans fell outside the reach of the new program; between 70 and 80 percent in different parts of the South.[55] Of course, this excision also left out many whites; indeed, some 40 percent in a country that still was substantially agrarian. Not until 1954, when Republicans controlled the White House, the Senate, and the House of Representatives, and southern Democrats finally lost their ability to mold legislation, were the occupational exclusions that had kept the large majority of blacks out of the Social Security system eliminated. And even then, African Americans were not able to catch up, since the program required at least five years of contributions before benefits could be received. Thus, for the first quarter century of its existence, Social Security was characterized by a form of policy apartheid, something neither Roosevelt nor his study commission had advocated.

How could this have happened? Why was it that African Americans were attached to this legislation in such harmful, even dismissive fashion? Some leading scholars believe racism had nothing to do with this outcome despite its racial implications. After all, they argue, about half the globe's countries at the time left farmworkers outside the framework of social insurance for the elderly. Further, they contend, some administration officials, including Secretary of the Treasury Henry Morgenthau, thought it would be very difficult to administer the program for these workers and for maids.[56]

This argument is unpersuasive. In the political context defined by the strange bedfellows alliance of the Democratic Party, these exclusions comprised what the political scientist Robert Lieberman aptly has called "discrimination by design" by means of "race-laden" provisions with the capacity and intent "to divide the population along racial lines without saying so in so many words."[57] Unless occupational disabilities were inserted in the legislation, the program's inclusive and national structure would have powerfully undermined the racialized, low-wage economy on which the region still depended and on whose shoulders Jim Crow stood.

As Congress's gatekeepers in control of the key committees, southern members brought their controlling influence to bear on each of the components of the Social Security Act. The bill was mainly considered in the Senate Finance Committee and the House Ways and Means Committee. Of the thirty-three Democrats serving on those committees, seventeen were southerners (nine in the Senate; eight in the House), including the two chairs, Senator Pat Harrison of Mississippi and Robert "Muley" Doughton of North Carolina. These southerners who dominated committee considerations broadly supported Social Security as a source of badly needed help for their poverty-stricken region, but they even more emphatically did not want the federal government to threaten the South's "way of life." At the hearings in the Senate, Harry Byrd, the leader of Virginia's powerful Democratic machine, cautioned that unless adequate protections were introduced, Social Security could become an instrument by which the federal government would interfere with the way white southerners dealt with "the Negro question."[58] At issue was both who would be included in the provisions of the act, especially for old age and unemployment insurance, and how much discretion would be offered the states as they administered the non-social insurance parts of the bill. Accordingly, as Lieberman has observed, southern representatives had two choices when confronted with the administration's recommendation for a largely inclusive and nationally oriented bill: "make it either less inclusive or less national."[59]

They chose both strategies. By fashioning legislation that kept farmworkers and maids out, they made old age insurance—the part of the bill that would be managed by a national bureaucracy—less all-encompassing than what the administration had proposed. In contrast, in the social assistance parts of the bill that created aid to dependent children (ADC) and help for elderly poor people, the primary categorical forms of assistance offered by the Social Security Act, they made the legislation less national. These were federal programs whose costs were to be shared between the federal government and the states; even more important, these policies would be decisively shaped and administered by the individual states, which were granted a great deal of discretion in setting benefit levels.[60] Southern members successfully resisted pressures to nationalize responsibility for ADC. Rather, by eliminating federal "decency and health" clauses in committee hearings, and by guarding against more than a minimal federal role on the floor of the House and Senate, they succeeded in keeping ADC's key contours, organization, and supervision in the hands of state governors, legislators, and bureaucrats. Though they failed to get Congress to agree to pick up the whole bill for the poorest states, the bulk of which were southern, they did manage to pass a program of assistance to poor families that left all its key elements in local hands.[61]

ADC offered grants to families with minor children raised in circumstances where one parent—usually the father—was absent from the home. Because families were more likely to be headed by women and the prevalence of need was more extensive amongst African Americans, ADC was disproportionately black from the start, but not uniformly so. Across the United States, 14 percent of children in the program were black. In the South, however, state governments used their discretion, including provisions that an ADC home be "suitable," to reduce their numbers. In Louisiana, 37 percent of the state's children were black, but 26 percent of ADC clients. In North Carolina, the comparable figures were 30 and 22; in South Carolina, 48 and 29; in Alabama 39 and 24; in Arkansas, 24 and 15. Texas, Kentucky, and Mississippi, in the 1940s, did not choose to participate in ADC, so their states' children did entirely without this source of help.[62]

We should note that ADC overall was less generous than the FERA programs it had replaced, which, despite all their shortcomings, had injected more monies into poor black communities. Consider the situation in Georgia. Of the nearly 24,000 white and 23,000 black children eligible for aid in 1935, the state offered funds to only a small fraction. There was a huge disparity by race. Drawing on both a Social Security survey and an account by the State Department of Public Welfare, Swedish demographer Richard Sterner found that "14.4 per cent of white eligibles but only 1.5 per cent of the Negro eligibles" were funded. Further, more than half of the black cases, as opposed to just 18 percent of the white, could be found in counties with cities of at least 10,000 people. He thus concluded that "while the situation is slightly better in cities, the fact remains that Negro children in Georgia have scarcely benefited from aid to dependent children and have suffered more than white children from the inadequacies of the existing program."[63]

The other main form of categorical help created by the Social Security Act was assistance to the elderly poor, individuals, as most states defined the need, who earned "insufficient income to provide reasonable subsistence compatible with decency and health." Because most blacks were not eligible for old age insurance, this aspect of the new law was vital to their well-being. Here, as with ADC, the states, not the federal government, set benefit levels, ascertained eligibility, and administered the program. Here, too, the staff making these decisions in the South were entirely white. The degree of black need and the exclusion of most African Americans from other benefits put a significant amount of pressure on this program. In the main, southern states managed to contain it, forcing a finding, albeit toothless, by the

Social Security Board in Washington in 1940 that in the prior two years, "the number of Negroes to whom aid was granted . . . was low in proportion to the number who needed assistance."[64]

In the North, blacks were, in fact, represented in higher proportions than their numbers in the population of those over sixty-five, but the rate of acceptance in the South was much lower. So, too, were the monthly benefits. In Massachusetts, New York, Pennsylvania, Indiana, Ohio, Illinois, and California, blacks, who were less well off, received slightly higher grants than whites, ranging from $19 to $34 a month. By contrast, in North Carolina, South Carolina, Texas, West Virginia, Virginia, Oklahoma, Delaware, Louisiana, Florida, Alabama, Mississippi, Tennessee, Kentucky, and Arkansas, white benefits were higher than those paid to blacks. Here, benefits often were very low. In five of these states, benefits to blacks averaged under $8 per month; five more made payments averaging under $10. And yet, in the face of terrible, extreme need, it was not unreasonable for a contemporary observer to conclude that "the old age assistance program has brought about a very considerable improvement in the economic position of the aged Negro."[65]

Unemployment insurance, which composed the third key element of the bill, combined both strategies.[66] Here, the administration plan was rather more to the liking of southern members of Congress than the main alternative, a bill advanced by Ernest Lundeen of Minnesota and sent to the floor by the non-southern-dominated House Labor Committee. Whereas that option would have paid all unemployed workers' benefits drawn from federal funds, Roosevelt's design was considerably more limited. It offered compensation only to unemployed workers whose employers had already made payments on their behalf into an unemployment insurance fund. As a result, unemployment insurance required access to continual and secure work before getting laid off. Further, once shaped by the committees on Ways and Means in the House and Finance in the Senate, the bill excluded domestic and farmworkers from its protective reach, and it located control over eligibility and benefit levels in the hands of the states.[67]

Black workers were big losers. With other maids and farmworkers, but in larger proportions, they had no access to this benefit. Where they worked in industrial and commercial pursuits that were covered, they often were left out because they lacked a history of regular, stable employment. With the defeat of national standards, even when they gained a way in, the benefits tended to be comparatively meager.

Not surprisingly, the leading social welfare initiative of the New Deal was resisted by the country's principal black organizations. The National Association for the Advancement of Colored People (NAACP) testified against the bill, arguing quite correctly that it was "like a sieve with holes just big enough for the majority of Negroes to fall through." The National Urban League strongly advocated the alternative bill proposed by Congressman Lundeen because it included "farmers and domestic workers and personal service workers."[68]

In short, each of the old age, social assistance, and unemployment provisions advanced by the Social Security Act was shaped to racist contours. As in the instance of earlier New Deal relief, blacks gained tangible assets in hard times that they otherwise would not have secured. The improvements provided to many blacks living in wretched circumstances under conditions of widespread desolation should not be gainsaid, of course. Neither, however, should the recognition that the political coalition that had produced these vast initiatives slanted them to offer far more of a boost to whites.

Once the range of New Deal social policies and welfare state spending were put in place, moreover, southern members of Congress continued to hold them hostage to Jim Crow. Federal agencies, including the Social Security Board, even when led by staunch anti-racist administrators, relegated the South's practices of implementation to the second tier of their concern. Taking advantage of the anomalous coalition that held the Democratic Party together, many Republicans persistently raised racial issues to embarrass liberal Democrats, court black votes, and peel away southern votes for progressive legislation by offering anti-discrimination amendments to New Deal, and Fair Deal, proposals. The first of these was an addition to a 1943 bill authorizing $200 million in federal aid to schools stipulating that black and white schools would share equally in the their distribution.

With Republicans wielding this "race card," non-southern Democrats found it impossible simultaneously to fight for an enhanced federal role and against Jim Crow. Even when anti-discrimination amendments were offered by Congressman Adam Clayton Powell, Jr., the black Democrat who represented Harlem, liberal whites understood they had to choose. And they regularly made the first of these aims their top priority. When Powell proposed the first of the many riders he would advance to the School Lunch Act of 1946, which would have banned discrimination and forbidden distribution to segregated schools, "northern liberals convinced him to reword the amendment to avoid mention of schools or separate school systems. The amendment passed in the House, only to be replaced in the Senate by a nondiscrimination provision that would have killed it. The legislation was 'saved' when southern Democrats, with northern votes, changed the nondiscrimination amendment into one that provided school lunch funds even to states that maintained separate school systems as long as they distributed the money equally. 'Separate but equal,' after all, was the law of the land."[69]

Over and over, the southern wing of the Democratic Party took advantage of what its members correctly discerned as the order of concerns held by their party colleagues. Well into the 1950s, non-southern Democrats proved willing to trade local control and the segregated utilization of federal funds in order to win southern support to overcome Republican opposition to liberal welfare state spending and services. Under the terms of this "deal," even federal Veterans' Hospitals in the South remained segregated.

To be sure, in the late 1940s, some liberal and moderate Democrats, embarrassed by southern practices that continued long after blacks had participated in the victories against fascism and Nazism, spoke out for black rights. President Truman broke with the long silence about black rights by his predecessor to become a public advocate for fair employment and anti–poll tax legislation. The 1948 Democratic Convention adopted a civil rights plank passionately introduced by the mayor of Minneapolis, Hubert Humphrey, which fractured the party and produced Strom Thurmond's segregationist States' Rights Party challenge that carried five southern states. But at no time did the liberal wing abandon its social policy alliance with the South or the conditions it imposed on African Americans.

Indeed, after 1948, confronted by a climate of red-baiting that had seized the country, non-southern Democrats in Congress, politicians in the party organization, and leaders of the main liberal pressure groups such as Americans for Democratic Action (ADA) grew more timid. Not only did they weaken the party's commitment to civil rights legislation in the 1952 and 1956 platforms (Adlai Stevenson, their presidential candidate, was far more circumspect about segregation than Truman had been), they sought, almost at any cost after Truman's surprise electoral success, to prevent the party from fracturing anew. Perhaps emblematic of this turn back to the South was the letter sent by Hubert Humphrey, Minnesota's new junior senator, to twenty southern newspaper editors in November 1951, which underscored his "deep affection" for their region. While not retracting his support for civil rights, he reassured them that he did not favor an aggressive federal effort. "I know that we frequently place too much trust in the power of the federal government. . . . My program for civil rights places its main emphasis on community activity, including individual responsibility, education, and moral values, supported by legislative standards."[70] Not long after, Walter White of the NAACP condemned Humphrey for his "abject surrender" when, in the Senate, he joined Majority Leader Lyndon Johnson to convince northern Democrats to call off the attempt to reduce the number of votes it would take to end a filibuster.[71]

IV

When the New Deal began, the large majority of black Americans living in the South lacked the civil and political rights of citizens. Ironically, they achieved some starkly limited social rights to relief and welfare even before the battle against Jim Crow had made significant gains. But it was the absence of citizenship rights that radically curtailed these improvements. Barred from the South's political system by a wide array of exclusionary rules and practices, they could secure no effectual political presence either at home or in Washington. Without black political participation, southern representatives in the House of Representatives and the Senate were utterly free not just to impede but veto the full and fair participation of African Americans in the most important welfare-oriented advances of the 1930s. Black and white southerners stood across a great political divide. Blacks could not achieve civic and political inclusion. They lacked recognition as citizens. They had no standing within the polity. Even their physical presence in the public sphere was limited to specific racially designated zones.

By contrast, southern whites were accorded a privileged access to the political order. Since blacks counted in the numbers reported by the census, their large presence combined with their frequent inability to vote allowed white citizens to gain representation in higher proportions than their population in the House of Representatives. The Senate, with its distribution of two seats for each state, conferred on its seventeen racially segregated states a veto on all legislative enactments they did not like. When this power was deployed, as it was in matters of relief and social insurance, it seriously widened the racial gap. Federal social welfare policy operated, in short, not just as an instrument of racial discrimination but as a perverse formula for affirmative action.

Writing about slavery and its legacies, the political theorist Judith Shklar has taken note of how often its neglect in general histories subsequently helped erase its impact on the consciousness of most white Americans. Europeans, she observed, might use the language of having been enslaved, but Americans have lived with the consequences of "the real thing . . . in pain, guilt, fear, and hatred."[72] This experience has been so profound that we should not be surprised that racism and Jim Crow imposed themselves on the key social policies of the New Deal. But if not surprised, we owe it to ourselves not to forget.

3

Rules for Work[1]

Well into the Eisenhower years, the strategy of offering concessions on issues of race, civil rights, and regional prerogatives worked to keep southern Democrats in the fold as part of a broad progressive coalition. But these representatives proved less willing to stay on board in matters that involved labor unions and benefits for working Americans. In the 1930s, the Democratic Party—northern and southern Democrats working, as we have seen, in a "strange bedfellows" alliance—spearheaded initiatives that transformed the wages, working conditions, and hours of work for millions of Americans. The Democratic majority fashioned a set of rules within which labor unions, including unions in mass production industries like steel and automobile manufacturing, could thrive, and passed laws to regulate the length of a work week and establish the lowest wage a person could be paid on the job. The passage of the National Labor Relations Act in 1935 and the Fair Labor Standards Act in 1938 ushered in what one commentator has called "a working class interlude in American labor history."[2] During the Roosevelt and Truman years, American unions grew rapidly, taking advantage of the safe haven offered by federal rules authorizing, indeed empowering unions to organize. And across a wide swath of workplaces, most of which were not unionized, many of the least well paid workers in the United States had their wages lifted and their hours of work limited.

Together, these bills enacted something of a revolution in the status of most working Americans. The National Labor Relations Act (NLRA), for example, affirmed the rights of wage workers to organize and bargain collectively. The law specified election procedures designed to ensure that employees could freely select their union representatives under the principle of majority rule, and, crucially, it delineated and disallowed as "unfair labor practices" a variety of tactics commonly deployed by employers to subvert unionization. These tactics included interference with such concerted employee activities as striking, picketing, and otherwise protesting working conditions; employer surveillance of union activities; discrimination against employees for union membership or activism; and offers by employers of benefits to employees who agree to cease union activities.[3] The new law also barred employers from providing financial assistance to, or attempting to control, labor organizations, thus striking at the heart of company-dominated unions. Administratively, the act created the National Labor Relations Board (NLRB) as a quasi-judicial expert board to investigate and adjudicate most labor disputes arising under the act.[4]

The federal government began to offer unions a broad legal umbrella under which to shelter. Almost immediately, they expanded at a rapid rate. Both the American Federation of Labor (AFL), which mainly represented skilled craft workers, and the Congress of Industrial Organizations (CIO) quickly thrived. In 1929, the labor movement, fiercely resisted by business and already tainted by charges that it was linked to Bolshevism, possessed fewer than 4 million members. A decade later, despite continuing mass unemployment (more than 9 million Americans still out of work in 1939), the new CIO alone matched this membership, the AFL had grown to more than 4 million members, and more than 1 million other workers had joined independent unions. Even before the wave of union expansion made possible by the Second World War, the NLRA labor regime encouraged dramatic union growth, altering the balance of power between labor and management.[5] In manufacturing, between 1930 and 1940, the proportion of workers in unions rose from 9 to 34 percent; in mining from 21 to 72 percent.[6] By 1948, overall union membership reached 14.2 million. The proportion of the non-farm labor force in unions reached 25 percent by 1940, and topped 30 percent a decade later.[7]

The New Deal also transformed conditions of work. Prodded by President Roosevelt, Congress enacted the landmark Fair Labor Standards Act (FLSA) in 1938 to eradicate "labor conditions detrimental to the maintenance of the minimum standards of living necessary for health, efficiency and well-being of workers." The act established a minimum wage of 25 cents per hour for the first year following passage, 30 cents for the second year, and 40 cents within a period of six years. It also provided for maximum working hours of 44 hours per week in the first year following passage, 42 in the second year, and 40 hours per week thereafter.[8] The FLSA also prohibited child labor in industries engaged in producing goods in interstate commerce.

The great majority of southern members of Congress supported these bills, thus allowing this pivotal New Deal legislation to succeed. When they passed, unions were only a scant presence in the region, hence not much of a threat. At the same time, the status of unions was very important to non-southern Democrats who represented large industrial constituencies. The South was willing to support their wishes provided these statutes did not threaten Jim Crow. So southern members traded their votes for the exclusion of farmworkers and maids, the most widespread black categories of employment, from the protections offered by these statutes. In circumstances where congressional Republicans were adamantly opposed to these laws, the Democratic Party made these racially relevant adjustments to secure a winning coalition that included southern members of the party. As a result, these new arrangements were friendly to labor but unfriendly to the majority of African Americans who lived below the Mason-Dixon line. Without this fine-tuning, a majority of southern blacks might have had access to protections negotiated by unions that would have quite shaken the political economy of segregation. Southern Democrats used their blocking powers to ensure this would not happen. As a result, the majority of African Americans, once again, were left out.

Southern participation in the New Deal coalition on labor issues, in short, had a price. In extracting it from fellow Democrats, southerners shaped and limited key labor laws by winning occupational bans.[9] The terms of this arrangement first appeared when Congress debated the National Industrial Recovery Act (NIRA) in June 1933, at the close of the New Deal's Hundred Days, the period at the start of the Roosevelt administration when it passed law after law the president proposed to jump-start the ailing economy. One feature of the bill was a provision that "employees shall have the right to organize and bargain collectively through representatives of their own choosing, and shall be free from the interference, restraint, or coercion of employers . . . in the designation of such representatives."[10] Further, within the framework of inducing industry-by-industry voluntary agreements to "codes of fair competition" and to regulate numerous aspects of production within industries, each code was directed to put into effect minimum wages and maximum hours as means to combat depression-driven wage cutting and stimulate purchasing power. Soon, once devastated unions like the United Mine Workers and the Ladies Garment Workers managed to rebuild their memberships in aggressively successful organizing efforts.[11] "In the floor debate, southern legislators voiced apprehension that these provisions to help unions might include agricultural labor. In a colloquy between Democratic Senators Huey Long of Louisiana and Joel Clark of Missouri, both complained that the Act failed sufficiently to define 'industry' (the category of activity regulated by the Act), and expressed concern that the term could be construed to apply to agriculture." Senator Robert Wagner, the New York Democrat who was the bill's principal congressional author, responded to such criticism by simply stating that "in the act itself agriculture is specifically excluded."[12]

Once the law was implemented, the National Recovery Administration (NRA) ruled that because the contemporaneously passed Agricultural Adjustment Act was meant to protect the interests of farmers, "Congress did not intend that codes of fair competition under the NIRA be set up for farmers or persons engaged in agricultural production."[13] As a result, farmworkers were denied protection under the NIRA based upon how the agency interpreted the intent of Congress. Not just farming but many agriculturally related industries thus avoided regulation. The South was placated, and had learned an important lesson. Even leading liberals, including pro–civil rights senators like Wagner, were prepared under pressure to jettison the people whose inclusion the South most feared.

An explicit legislative exclusion of agricultural and domestic workers from New Deal labor legislation first appeared in the National Labor Relations Act. To be sure, the original draft of the bill introduced by Senator Wagner contained no such exclusion.[14] In the course of examining a witness in the Senate hearing, Senator David Walsh, a Massachusetts Democrat, observed that as the bill was drafted, "it would permit an organization of employees who work on a farm, and would require the farmer to actually recognize their representatives, and deal with them in the matter of collective bargaining."[15]

This possibility triggered discussion of the issue when the bill was referred to the Committee on Education and Labor. Senators Hugo Black of Alabama, who later would change his views about race and segregation, and Park Trammell of Florida worked closely with three non-southern Democrats representing rural states[16] to report a bill containing the exemption of agricultural and domestic labor in precisely the form that would be included in the final passage of the bill. The committee added a definition of "employee" providing that it "shall not include any individual employed as an agricultural laborer, or in the domestic service of any family or person at his home. . . ." While there was no debate on the Senate floor that explains the motives or purposes behind the exemptions, the committee report suggests that they were a response to the initial bill's coverage of agricultural and domestic labor. In a section entitled "What The Bill Does Not Do," the committee stressed that contrary to "propaganda over the country," "misstatements," and "erroneous ideas," as "now drafted, the bill does not relate to employment as a domestic servant or as an agricultural laborer." The version of the bill introduced in the House of Representatives contained exemptions of agricultural and domestic labor identical to those that had been added by the Senate Committee on Education and Labor. These changes met with a virtually total absence of any criticism by non-southern members of Congress.[17]

The history of the Fair Labor Standards Act proved comparable.[18] In 1937, President Roosevelt sent Congress a message calling for minimum wages and maximum hours legislation that would include both industrial and agricultural workers.[19] Notwithstanding, the original bill contained an agricultural exclusion equivalent to that governing unions, though it delegated authority to an envisioned administrative board to define agriculture.[20] Though not mentioned explicitly, domestic workers were effectively excluded by virtue of the law's narrow embrace only of workers "engaged in commerce or in the production of goods for commerce."[21] By now, these exclusions seem to have been taken for granted as a condition for passage. Representative Fred Hartley, a New Jersey Republican, observed that "the poorest paid labor of all, the farm labor," was excluded from the bill as a matter of "political expediency" because coverage of agricultural labor would have resulted in defeat of the bill in Congress. The same point was made more forcefully, in reference to New Deal legislation more broadly, by Gardner Jackson, chairman of the National Committee on Rural and Social Planning, a labor-oriented advocacy organization. Testifying before Congress on the bill, he stated:

> No purpose will be served by beating around the bush. You, Mr. Chairman, and all your associates on this Committee know as well as I do that agricultural laborers have been explicitly excluded from participation in any of the benefits of New Deal legislation, from the late (but not greatly lamented) N.R.A., down through the A.A.A., the Wagner-Connery Labor

> Relations Act and the Social Security Act, for the simple and effective reason that it has been deemed politically certain that their inclusion would have spelled death of the legislation in Congress. And now, in this proposed Black-Connery wages and hours bill, agricultural laborers are again explicitly excluded.[22]

During the legislative process, southern members aggressively expanded the scope of the original agricultural exemption. They inserted an extensive and detailed definition of agriculture in the act itself to ensure that future administrators would apply the exemption to as wide a range of activities as possible. Of the range of activities that would count as agriculture, the bill reported out of committee provided that the exemption should include any "practice incident to farming." On the Senate floor this immunity was amended to include preparing, packing, and storing fresh fruits or vegetables within the area of production, and their delivery to market.[23] Later, before the bill passed, the exclusion was expanded to include the preparation for market of *all* agricultural products, including agricultural processing in the areas of production, and their delivery to storage, markets, or carriers. Democrats from other regions kept up their end of the bargain, voting overwhelmingly with the southerners in favor of expanding the agricultural exclusion in the five relevant Senate roll calls.[24]

It is not hard to see why southern members were so intensely concerned with this issue and why, in order to get the bill passed, other members were prepared to go along. The status of subaltern black labor in agriculture—a structure that often came close to resembling nineteenth-century conditions under slavery—was a consistent concern for southern members in the 1930s that peaked when this bill was being debated. By setting a floor on wages, it necessarily would have leveling effects that would cut across racial lines in the lowest wage sectors of the South, where there existed wide wage disparities between African American and white wage workers.[25]

Florida representative James Mark Wilcox explained:

> [T]here is another matter of great importance in the South, and that is the problem of our Negro labor. There has always been a difference in the wage scale of white and colored labor. So long as Florida people are permitted to handle the matter, the delicate and perplexing problem can be adjusted; but the Federal Government knows no color line and of necessity it cannot make any distinction between the races. We may rest assured, therefore, that when we turn over to a federal bureau or board the power to fix wages, it will prescribe the same wage for the Negro that it prescribes for the white man. Now, such a plan might work in some sections of the United States but those of us who know the true situation know that it just will not work in the South. You cannot put the Negro and the white man on the same basis and get away with it.

Martin Dies of Texas, later famous for his demagogic investigations of Communist activities, articulated the same concern, stating that a "racial question" was embedded in the bill because under its minimum wage provisions, "what is prescribed for one race must be prescribed for the others, and you cannot prescribe the same wages for the black man as for the white man." Echoing Wilcox and Dies, Edward Cox of Georgia complained that "organized Negro groups of the country are supporting [the FLSA] because it will . . . render easier the elimination and disappearance of racial and social distinctions, and . . . throw into the political field the determination of the standards and the customs which shall determine the relationship of our various groups of people in the South."[26]

Yet other southern legislators condemned the FLSA as racial legislation aimed at the South, claiming it was comparable to anti-lynching legislation. South Carolina's "Cotton Ed" Smith opened his speech in the Senate with an attack on anti-lynching legislation—"Every Senator present knows that the anti-lynching bill is introduced for no reason in the world than a desire to get the votes of a certain race in this country"—pronouncing of the bill at hand that "Any man on this floor who has sense enough to read the English language knows that the main object of this bill is, by human legislation, to overcome the great gift of God to the South."[27]

IV

WITH THE PASSAGE of the Fair Labor Standards Act, all the New Deal legislation concerned with work included occupational provisions that converged with, and sustained, intense southern preferences, thus making possible their acquiescence to statutes and rules that advanced the cause of labor; that is, primarily white labor.[28]

During the Second World War, even this arrangement proved unsettling to the southern wing of the party. Pressed by wartime social change, southern Democrats shifted positions, moving to limit the effect of the labor regime they had helped install. With unemployment eliminated by wartime production, and with many blacks entering the industrial labor force at a time when many white workers were overseas, unions began to organize southern workers, including many blacks. In this context, southern representatives feared that the New Deal rules for labor and work they had helped create would undermine the region's traditional racial order. As a result, they shifted their votes from the pro-labor column to join with Republicans during and after the war to make it more difficult for workers to join unions and to limit their rights at the workplace. The country's system for regulating unions and the labor market took on an even more decidedly racial tilt. Politically, this shift by southern Democrats would radically transform American politics, as well as labor legislation, for decades to come.

The political arrangement that kept farmworkers and maids outside the protective embrace of New Deal labor legislation, while helping unions and securing decent conditions of work for the majority of Americans, did not last. By 1947, it had been superseded by new arrangements, which proved more injurious for black workers and much less friendly to unions. Following an unprecedented strike wave in 1945 and 1946, the 1946 election of a Republican Congress placed labor law reform, intended to weaken unions and their organizing potential, at the top of the domestic policy agenda. "No domestic issue," the economist Orme Phelps observed in 1947 as major changes were being debated, "exceeds in importance and no issue, domestic or foreign, has received more attention since the close of World War II than that of the proper policy to be observed in labor disputes."[29] Though Republican gains in the 1946 elections were impressive, their ability to enact new labor law would have been limited, possibly entirely obstructed, without the support of Democratic Party members, particularly in the Senate, where the Republicans had secured fifty-one seats, far short of a supermajority. With Truman in the White House, the veto threat on contentious labor issues meant that the Republicans needed a substantial number of Democrats to join with them if they were to secure labor law retrenchment. Concurrently, the now minority Democratic Party had grown more dependent on the fidelity of its southern members, who represented a greater proportion of the party in the new Congress than they had in a quarter century.[30]

Southern Democrats thus became the pivotal voters in determining the fate of the labor laws the New Deal had enacted. Moving to join Republicans in an assault on these statutes, southern Democrats offered the decisive votes to undercut legislation they once had backed. By 1947, they rallied to pass the Labor-Management Relations Act (LMRA, or the Taft-Hartley Act) to weaken the National Labor Relations Act over the veto of President Truman, who denounced it as a "slave labor bill," and to approve the Portal to Portal Act, which relaxed the enforcement of minimum wages and maximum hours, thus attenuating the effectiveness of the Fair Labor Standards Act.

The most far-reaching anti-labor measures in Taft-Hartley concerned limitations upon the right of unions to negotiate collective bargaining agreements providing for closed shops and union shops. The act banned closed shop provisions outright requiring union membership as a condition of being hired. Further, it authorized states to pass "right-to-work" laws prohibiting agreements under which unions obtain a "union security clause," obliging all employees to pay union dues as a requirement of employment.[31] Even where no state right-to-work law was in effect, union shop provisions now had to be approved by a majority of the membership in a secret ballot, a condition that applied to very few other types of contract provisions. Open shops undermine effective union organizing by eliminating the principal material incentives for joining a union.[32]

The act also added a list of "unfair labor practices" that obstructed or curtailed important forms of collective action. It barred the use of secondary boycotts, picketing, or strikes, which had targeted entities that did business with an employer with whom the union had a labor dispute, and limited the ability of unions to pressure employers through picketing to gain recognition of a union or to engage in mass picketing that interfered with access to the employer's premises by its employees or by the public. Moreover, union members who engaged in wildcat strikes in violation of a no-strike agreement were subject to employer discipline.

In the case both of prohibited strikes and picketing, the NLRB was required under the act to seek an injunction to prevent or end such activity. Further, the act conferred power upon the U.S. Attorney General to obtain injunctions for an eighty-day "cooling off period" in the event of a strike, or threat of one, deemed to "imperil the national health or safety." While the Norris–LaGuardia Anti-Injunction Act of 1932 had extensively proscribed court injunctions in labor disputes, Taft-Hartley negated portions of that law by fashioning a statutory basis for labor injunctions. With respect to sanctions against unions for engaging in the newly prohibited forms of collective action, employers were authorized to bring legal actions for monetary damages against unions for strikes or work stoppages that transgressed the act.

At the same time that Taft-Hartley increased the National Labor Relations Board's power to issue injunctions against collective action by unions, it diluted the board's authority in respects that were harmful to labor. Most significantly, the NLRB was turned into a purely quasi-judicial institution, as its investigative and prosecutorial functions were segregated and delegated to a newly created General Counsel separate from the board. Advocates of this provision complained that employers had been denied due process by a pro-labor board that commingled fact-finding, prosecutorial, and adjudicative functions.[33] Thus, after Taft-Hartley, the board no longer could initiate investigations and prosecute unfair labor practice charges. Such a statutory division of authority within an agency was unprecedented.[34] The board also was prohibited from appointing personnel for the purpose of "economic analysis," thus preventing it from conducting independent expert studies of the industrial relations problems that it might seek to remedy. Further, Taft-Hartley restricted the board's discretion, in a manner favorable to employers, to determine appropriate bargaining units for purposes of union representation. It contained a provision limiting the weight that the board could give to "the extent to which the employees have organized," a factor that had increased the probability that the union would prevail. The act similarly curbed the board's authority to deny recognition to craft workers wishing to opt out of an existing larger union comprised principally of unskilled and semi-skilled workers, something the board had frequently done before 1947, which was regarded as favoring industrial unions.[35]

In another limitation on the board's authority and an attack upon unions as presumptively suspect and corrupt, certain reporting requirements were imposed upon unions as a precondition to the board recognizing and adjudicating their claims. To qualify for the protections offered by the NLRA, union leaders were compelled to submit affidavits to the Labor Department swearing that they were not members of, or affiliated with, the Communist Party, and they had to file reports disclosing a wide array of information about internal operating procedures, including the election of officials and compensation paid to them, as well as comprehensive financial statements. Similar requirements were not imposed on employers. Taft-Hartley also widened the NLRA's exclusions to eliminate supervisory employees and independent contractors from the definition of employee. The exclusion of supervisory employees was significant because foremen, front-line supervisors, served as an important vehicle by which upper management could control workers, particularly for employers attempting to avoid unionization.[36]

While the NLRA's exclusion of agricultural workers remained unchanged by Taft-Hartley, both the Taft and Hartley bills included detailed and expanded agricultural exclusions meant to place workers in processing and handling activities ancillary to agriculture outside the scope of union protection. Such work previously had been found by the NLRB to be industrial and thus covered. However, in conference, the committee opted to retain the NLRA's original exclusion. It did so on the ground that the NLRB's decision had been effectively reversed in the past several years by attaching an expanded agricultural exclusion to the Appropriations Act for the NLRB, which the conference committee found to be a satisfactory way of dealing with the issue. What was most significant about this episode was that all of the Democrats not from the South serving on the House and Senate committees that reported the bills signed minority reports which attacked the expanded exclusions on the ground that they were too broad and unjustly excluded workers who were engaged in more commercial than farming labor.[37] Only now that southerners had defected on labor matters from the New Deal coalition did non-southern Democrats unite to oppose southern efforts to obtain the broadest possible agricultural exclusions.

In contrast to the 1930s, southern members of Congress no longer were prepared to back pro-labor legislation. This switch reflected one of the most significant political developments of the 1940s. In the Senate and the House, southern Democrats, now stalwart opponents, voted overwhelmingly with Republicans; indeed almost unanimously in the key Senate vote to turn back the President Truman's veto. Taft-Hartley could not have become law without this decision by the South to join with the Republicans to overturn what their colleagues and their president desired.

It was the same with the effort to modify the Fair Labor Standards Act. The Portal to Portal Act also stood on southern shoulders, precipitated by the "portal to portal" pay disputes of the 1940s in which suits were brought under provisions of the FLSA to recover payment for "off the clock" time which, by custom or practice, was not compensated. Common examples included time spent walking from a factory gate to a steel furnace (up to half a mile), sharpening tools, or cleaning a work area before an employee set to work at his or her main task.[38] In the early 1940s, some unions, most in the CIO, encouraged or initiated such wage recovery suits on behalf of large groups of employees.[39] Supporters of the bill devoted much attention to denouncing the escalating volume of FLSA legal action, particularly the CIO's central role in coordinating and managing this litigation.[40]

With respect to past claims, the bill provided that any custom or practice of not paying for certain time, even during the middle of the workday, would be sufficient to defeat portal suits. With respect to future claims, while certain activities "preliminary" and "postliminary" to the employee's "principal activity" would not be compensated (unless they were made explicitly compensable by contract), the amendments clarified that time spent doing tasks "integral" to the principal activity was covered by the FLSA, as was time that an employee was required to spend idly between tasks during the workday, regardless of an employer's past custom or practice.[41]

As a number of opponents of the Portal to Portal Act noted at the time, most of the act went beyond the portal issue and cut into unrelated FLSA rights. Perhaps most important was the insertion of a two-year statute of limitations for all FLSA claims. Under the arrangements of the original act the average applicable limitations period was nearly double this, and all comparable federal statutes had longer limitations periods. The act also limited available damages as compared with the original law. The FLSA had included a compulsory "liquidated damages" provision, which provided that employees would recover damages of double the amount wrongfully withheld, where the purpose of the doubling was to serve as a sanction for violation. The amendments to the FLSA modified this provision to require that liquidated (double) damages would only be available if the evidence indicated that the employer had violated the law in bad faith, a provision that effectively promised to gut enforcement of minimum wages and maximum hours.[42]

Another important change wrought by Portal to Portal was a significant curtailing of the class actions facilitated by FLSA's 1938 section 16(b), which had provided that some named employees could sue on behalf of themselves and other "similarly situated" workers who did not have to be named or consent to the suit. The Portal amendments changed section 16(b) to require that each employee individually file written consent to participate in such a suit.[43] This procedural change was important in wage and hour litigation because it is frequently the case that the aggregate value of claims for a small group of low-wage workers cannot justify the costs of litigation. The larger the group of employees on whose behalf a suit can be brought, the greater the incentive to enforce the law, and to obey it in the first instance.

V

WHY DID SOUTHERN MEMBERS of Congress abandon their support for New Deal labor policies that had been adjusted to suit their preferences? At the core of their near-universal shift to positions geared to make union organizing more difficult and restrict federal intervention in labor markets was a radical transformation in the way in which they understood labor issues. When domestic and agricultural exclusions had been made integral to labor legislation in the 1930s, they had viewed these votes primarily as choices about party loyalty and ideological conviction. By contrast, in the 1940s, labor legislation became an occasion for referenda about the durability of Jim Crow. A combination of dramatic labor union gains in the South brought on by the shortage of workers during the war, and growing national administrative responsibilities for labor markets, made southern representatives much more keenly aware of the racial issues at stake. As labor unions began to enjoy increasing, unexpected success in the South, and as non-southern New Deal liberals pressed to create a more expansive federal administration to advance labor interests without relenting where race intersected with labor, southerners in the House and Senate closed ranks to consider labor questions defensively.

From their standpoint, labor matters no longer were a minor sideshow where they could compromise with other members of the Democratic Party in exchange for regional favors. They now had good reason to fear that labor organizing might fuel civil rights activism. They were concerned that close enforcement of the Fair Labor Standards Act would cause wage leveling along racial lines. They worried that the creation of a fluid national labor market under the auspices of the Department of Labor would induce poor black rural labor to leave the region. They were troubled by the prospect that efforts to increase national administrative authority over unemployment compensation would diminish incentives that had been counted upon to keep these workers in the fields. Zealous bureaucrats might use their administrative discretion, reinforced by wartime anti-discrimination efforts, to confront racially discriminatory practices by state government officials. Having merged indissolubly with race, labor votes now evoked preferences in southern members geared more to guard racism than to distinguish Democrats from Republicans.

When southerners had voted for the Wagner Act in 1935, unions were a trivial force in the South. During the prewar period, the unionization movement had been concentrated in large urban areas in the Northeast and Midwest where mass production industries were situated and in isolated "total" work environments such as lumber camps and mining communities. With the exception of union momentum in New Orleans at the docks and in the packing houses, and at steel mills in Birmingham, the South was largely left out of the union surge of the 1930s. And not just for reasons of industrial location. After all, lumber workers had unionized on the West Coast and textile workers in New England, but neither succeeded in the South, where employer resistance, the absence of union traditions, and a widespread fear that unions would disrupt the political economy of race and harm the low-wage strategy of economic development prevailed. Thus, despite some gains, "the union movement of the South in 1939 . . . lagged markedly behind the Northeast, Midwest, and West coast in reacting to the stimulus of the New Deal."[44]

Labor organizing in the South faced high hurdles. The region was less industrialized than the rest of the country, and its factories, by comparison to other areas, were widely dispersed in small and middle-sized towns where resistance, often relentless, was more intense. Further, the huge supply of extremely poor people in the South both depressed wages and made union efforts very difficult. Most important, the region's racial order partitioned workers by race, rendering divide-and-conquer strategies by employers a ready tool with which to defeat union drives. Many efforts before the New Deal to build southern unions, including a large organizing drive conducted by the AFL in the teeth of the depression, came to naught.[45]

Yet even before the Second World War, the growth of the CIO, shielded by the NLRB, had begun to concern leaders in the South. Some of its national unions quickly developed a presence in major industries such as steel, rubber, automobiles, oil, and mining that included a growing southern, often multiracial membership. During the war, both the AFL and the CIO secured unforeseen gains and planned major campaigns to build on these successes in peacetime. The tight labor market induced by wartime industrial expansion was fueled by large federal investments, by urbanization, and by the substantial development of military bases; this in turn facilitated aggressive union efforts to take advantage of the legal climate that had been created by the Wagner Act but previously had had little effect in the South. In just two years, from Pearl Harbor to late 1943, industrial employment in the South grew from 1.6 million to 2.3 million workers. And many farmers and sharecroppers who experienced military service or worked at war centers were not prepared to tolerate a return to prewar conditions (during the war, one in four farmworkers left the land).[46]

All in all, southern trends were brought more in line with national developments. Between 1938 and 1948, the region's rate of increase in membership, marked by more than a doubling from under 500,000 to more than 1 million, exceeded the growth of 88 percent for the country as a whole. A survey of union membership in the South between 1939 and 1953 found that "For the entire period . . . union membership increased more rapidly in the South than in the rest of the country," noting that most of the growth had come in wartime.[47] Indeed, as the Second World War came to a close, H. F. Douty, the chief labor economist at the Department of Labor, observed that "With respect to the South, the existing situation is different from any existing in the past."[48] Cotton mill unionism, for example, had begun to function, and important collective bargaining agreements had been reached with the major tobacco companies (covering some 90 percent of all workers in the industry) and in the cigar industry (covering about half). Steel unionism became strongly established, and there were important successes in oil, rubber, clothing, and a wide array of war-related industries.

These achievements were pregnant with deep-seated implications for southern race relations.[49] Because "the Negro constitutes a relatively large and permanent part of the southern industrial labor force in such industries as tobacco, lumber, and iron and steel," Douty noted, ". . . successful unionization of such industries require[s] the organization of colored workers," adding that, based on wartime experiences, including experiments with multiracial union locals, there "is evidence to the effect that workers among both races are beginning to realize that economic cooperation is not only possible, but desirable." Assessing future prospects, he concluded in 1946 that "union organization in the South is substantial in character and is no longer restricted in its traditional spheres in railroading, printing, and a few other industries." But, he cautioned presciently, "Much of the present organization, of course, has developed during very recent years, and its stability, in many cases, has yet to be tested."[50]

Seeking to secure their dramatic wartime gains in the South, both the AFL and the CIO (with the dramatic title of "Operation Dixie") announced major recruiting campaigns in the spring of 1946, based in part on the understanding, as a CIO prospectus had declared in 1939, that a relatively unorganized South is "a menace to our organized movement in the north and likewise to northern industries."[51] The campaigns began optimistically in light of the wartime gains and the large number of unorganized workers in industries where there had been a good deal of union success elsewhere (70 percent of textile workers outside the South belonged to unions, compared to just 20 percent in southern states).[52] Both federations made efforts to appeal to black as well as white workers (though the AFL continued to display "easy acceptance of racially segregated locals"),[53] albeit without confronting local practices too directly. By August, the AFL was reporting 100,000 new members; by October, 500,000, a success rate (even discounting the overstatement of organizers) due in part to their claim that they represented the more moderate, and less Communist-influenced, alternative. By the end of 1947, the CIO announced (almost certainly an exaggeration) that it had recruited some 400,000 new southern members. However, these campaigns, meeting intense resistance by local elites and police forces, ambivalent about how much to confront Jim Crow, and increasingly caught up in competitive and internecine battles, soon began to falter. But it was the shifts in the legal climate that most decisively helped bring such efforts to an end. By late 1948, in the aftermath of Taft-Hartley, the AFL, formally, and the CIO, informally, both closed their southern campaigns.[54]

Throughout this period, which began before the war concluded and continued well after war's end, southern legislators moved vigorously to alter the institutional rules within which unions could operate. Three such efforts stand out: the 1939 Smith Committee investigation of the National Labor Relations Board and the bill it produced that passed the House but failed to get to the floor in the Senate; the War Labor Disputes Act (Smith-Connolly Act) of 1943; and the Case bill of 1946, which passed both houses but was vetoed by President Truman. Though only Smith-Connolly became law, each legislative event demonstrated the new preferences and pattern of behavior of the South toward unions, and provided important trial heats for Taft-Hartley.

Voting with Republicans, southern members were instrumental in establishing a committee led by Howard Smith, an anti-union Virginia

Democrat, whose main aim would be to investigate "[w]hether the National Labor Relations Board had been fair and impartial in its conduct, in its decisions, in its interpretation of the law . . . and in its dealings between different labor organizations and its dealings between employer and employee." The primary target was the CIO and the help it had received from the board in jurisdictional disputes with the AFL. During the brief debate, themes soon to be more prominent in southern discourse were articulated by Georgia congressman Edward Cox:

> I have no desire to conceal the opinion that I hold with respect to the [Wagner] act itself. I think it is a vicious law that is wrapped up in high-sounding language to conceal its wicked intent. It is one-sided and has been administered in a one-sided way. The Labor Board has construed it as a mandate to unionize industry and has missed no opportunity in the use of compulsion to bring this about. In its zeal to serve certain labor leaders and to direct the labor movement according to its own notion and its own social and economic theories, the Board has brought itself and the law into thorough disrepute. . . . Preaching economic democracy, the Board has moved steadily toward compulsory unionization in unions chosen by the board. . . . The first mistake that the Board made was in the selection of its personnel. It turned loose upon the country an army of wild young men who proceeded against employers as if their business was to destroy the institution of private property. . . . It has sought to terrorize business and to promote radical labor organizations.[55]

Aspiring to allay the NLRB's putative pro-CIO bias, the bill proposed by the committee adopted the expansive Social Security Act definition of agricultural workers. It also denied the board power to reinstate workers convicted of violence or destruction of property during a strike, and included provisions limiting the authority of the NLRB.[56] Most of these proposals later were incorporated into Taft-Hartley.

As sponsors, Howard Smith in partnership with Senator Tom Connolly of Texas also gave the War Labor Disputes Act a southern pedigree. To bring unions under control, they and their southern colleagues supported increasing federal administrative authority over the labor relationship by giving statutory authority to a War Labor Board, authorizing the president to seize and operate struck plants, requiring a thirty-day notice to the NLRB prior to striking in a labor dispute which might interrupt war production, mandating a secret strike ballot on the thirtieth day if the dispute had not been resolved, and prohibiting labor organizations from making national election political contributions.

The language utilized by the southerners was anxious and inflammatory. Referring to wartime strikes, especially by the CIO and the Mine Workers (who had recently left the CIO), southern members characterized union leaders as criminally corrupt ("racketeers," "goon squads"), lacking in patriotism under conditions of war crisis, and as communistic, fascistic, and dictatorial. "The nefarious and dastardly attempts of the Communist to fool the lower classes, and especially the American Negro, into embracing them as a Savior and Liberator," Congressman John Gibson of Georgia orated, in a floor speech complaining about campaign efforts by AFL and CIO leaders to defeat him, "is so cowardly, so full of deceit, when anyone that has studied the history of their activities in the past must know that all labor, including the classes just mentioned, would be subjected to absolute slavery if and when they force their form of government over this country."[57]

Like Smith-Connolly, the Case bill, sponsored by New Jersey Republican Clifford Case, was directed primarily at strikes, heralding Taft-Hartley by proposing, among other provisions, a sixty-day cooling off period, a prohibition against violence or conspiracy that interfered with the movement of goods in interstate commerce, monetary damages against unions for contract violations, and the proscription of secondary boycotts, amending Norris-LaGuardia to allow for injunctions in such cases. Southerners, voting nearly unanimously with Republicans in the House and Senate, were vocal supporters. In protracted floor debates they made clear that they were concerned especially with the CIO's punitive electoral efforts, with what they considered to be the inordinate power of organized labor to bring the national economy to a grinding halt, and with what they viewed as the criminally corrupt and totalitarian character of labor unions.

We thus can see how the coalition that southern members had begun to fashion with Republicans on labor union issues in 1939 grew to almost unanimous solidarity during and especially just after the Second World War. The motivation for this dramatic shift was a deep concern about union power, its growing role in their region, and its potential impact on the racial order.

VI

THE RESULTS OF THE defection of the South from the Democratic Party coalition on labor issues were devastating for unions and particularly harmful for black workers. The new political arithmetic radically diminished their reach into the South and the chance to organize the region's black workers. It also erased the prospect that the national government might put a floor underneath the treatment of African Americans in the South's labor markets. Business and labor both immediately understood the importance of this counterrevolution, whose centerpiece was Taft-Hartley. "Management has grounds," a spokesperson for the National Association of Manufacturers (NAM) put it, shortly after the bill's passage, "sufficient under the LMRA to swamp our courts with requests for injunctions, suits for violation of contract and damages, and prosecution for unfair labor practices, to appear as a tidal wave compared to labor's portal-to-portal suits." But such action was not necessary, NAM counseled, because a "go-slow" policy should prove more effective by holding these powers in reserve.[58]

Three years later, a *Harvard Law Review* assessment took note of the contrast between the National Labor Relations Act, which "had emphasized the promotion of collective bargaining by encouraging the formation and growth of labor unions," and the Labor-Management

Relations Act, which, "less sympathetic toward organized labor, is designed to afford protection to employers and individual workers as well as unions." Similarly, an account by an economist writing for the Public Affairs Institute assessed these changes as drastic, finding that the law's reaffirmation of the right of labor to organize was counterbalanced by the "equal if not greater importance" now offered to protect the rights of individuals to refrain from bargaining, and by the imposition of restraints both on unions and the NLRB just as restraints on employers were being loosened and the role of courts reinforced.[59] Indeed, the preamble to Taft-Hartley was explicit in stating the goal of shifting the balance of power, aiming, it said, "to equalize legal responsibilities of labor organizations and employers."

The AFL's United Textile Workers of America immediately published a warning to its members that "it DID happen here" in "this anti-union Congress" with a result that "threatens the strength, financial security and freedom of Unions to operate under free collective bargaining."[60] In April 1948, the International Association of Machinists, also in the AFL, issued a detailed fifty-page rebuttal of a pamphlet widely circulated by the National Association of Manufacturers, one of the law's prime advocates. Rejoining point by point, the Machinists chronicled the massive shifts in capability entailed by the act.[61] A year later, the International Typographical Union, the country's oldest continuous trade union, likened the act to Mussolini's compulsory labor standards. Despite this hyperbole, the union quite accurately listed among the effects of the law that it made it difficult for unions to deploy their economic strengths and helped confine the labor movement to current pockets of strength by enabling employers to evade unionization, by making it more difficult for unions to act together, and by putting all unions under a cloud of suspicion.[62] Given the stakes, it is not surprising that "The debate over Taft-Hartley was one of the most intense in legislative history. The AFL pledged a million and a half dollars in advertising for radio and newspaper statements. The CIO held rallies in a dozen cities. . . . By June 18, the Capitol had received 157,000 letters,

460,000 cards, and 23,000 telegrams" generated, to no avail, by the labor movement.[63]

Organized labor, of course, did not disappear. It retained many strengths. But its capabilities had been hedged severely. Unions soon comprehended and adapted to this new reality. Ten years after Taft-Hartley passed, the AFL-CIO's Industrial Union Department, chaired by Walter Reuther, assessed the impact of the act in a series of sober reports. "If Taft-Hartley has been a problem to unions in organized industries," one concluded, "it has been a disaster to those unions whose major organizing job is yet to be done." A carefully written case study of the American Federation of Hosiery Workers demonstrated how the new law had helped frustrate that union's organizing efforts in the South. The union had won the large majority of its certification elections under NLRB jurisdiction prior to Taft-Hartley, almost all producing contracts. By contrast, "in the 10 years following Taft-Hartley, the union was able to sign only 23 new agreements" out of "a total of 117 NLRB representation elections."[64]

Indeed, even in the early years of Taft-Hartley a clear change had taken place in the climate of labor relations, shifting the weight of expectations; this had an especially deleterious impact on union efforts in areas that had been poorly unionized in the past. As a 1951 study observed,

> Unions testify almost universally that organizing became more difficult under Taft-Hartley. The "climate" has changed, resistance by employers is more overt and active, organization of whole communities against the union is even less restrained than before. A stimulus and new weapons have been given to antiunion employers. In the South, the long slow process has been slowed up by which Southern industry gradually moves and must move away from its old paternalistic, sometimes substandard, and often bitterly antiunion practices. . . . Most important, in the South and elsewhere, has been the increased use of the "right of free speech" by employers to intervene

> frankly in elections. When collective bargaining elections are lost, significantly it is said that "the company won" . . . this antiunion campaign is inevitably coercive upon the employees. All this goes much further than was permitted even during the last days of the Wagner Act.[65]

By such means, with labor "constantly thrown on the defensive," as Senator Paul Douglas put it in his memoirs, unions in the South "found it hard to get a foothold in these states, and . . . could not establish themselves in such industries as textiles, tobacco, and chemicals."[66]

The changes that the Portal to Portal Act wrought to the FLSA also diminished the ability of organized labor to utilize legal resources to protect workers' rights. The rules it fashioned are an object lesson in the considerable difference that seemingly modest procedural changes to public policy can make. The year 1947, the last before Portal to Portal regulations came into effect, stands out for the high number of enforcement suits filed in federal court (3,772) demanding compliance with the Fair Labor Standards Act, the most in any single year before or since. This peak reflected a steady rise in such judicial interventionism in the labor market under the aegis of FLSA during the prior three years. Once Congress enacted its amendments making such proceedings more difficult, the number of enforcement actions plummeted, in 1948, by 72 percent, to 1,062. During the decade following enactment the average annual number of suits filed was 754, representing a decline of some 80 percent from the high-water mark of 1947.[67] Further, as the overall legal climate for labor altered and FLSA enforcement declined, the cooperation offered by many states in enforcing minimum wages and maximum hours waned, especially in the South.[68]

When the impact of more limited possibilities became clear to the leaders of organized labor, they opted to make three fateful moves, all rational in this new context and all successful in the short term. First, they reined in their once ambitious efforts, focused on the South, to make the labor movement a genuinely national force. This strategy now had become prohibitively costly. Instead, they opted to focus attention where their strength already was considerable. Second, they concentrated on making collective bargaining a settled, orderly, and productive process, trading off management prerogatives for generous, secure wage settlements indexed to inflation. In so doing, they experimented with long-term contracts (such as the UAW–General Motors five-year agreement in 1950), while limiting their scope of attention almost exclusively to the workplace. Third, rather than continue to fight for a more advanced national welfare state for all Americans, they concentrated on securing private pension and health insurance provisions for their members that would be financed mainly by employers.[69]

Under these circumstances, the South's political, social, and economic structure remained largely unchallenged by organized labor, the one national force that had seemed best poised to do so in the 1940s. In consequence, the emerging judicial strategy and mass movement to secure black enfranchisement and challenge Jim Crow developed independently of a labor movement that looked increasingly inward and minimized its priority of incorporating black workers within its ranks. Two effects stand out. First, the incipient civil rights impulse rarely tackled the economic conundrums of southern black society directly, focusing instead mainly on civic and political, rather than economic, inclusion.[70] Second, the unions' potential to alter the status of the majority of black working people profoundly failed to take hold.

These linked outcomes were the direct result of a shift in southern preferences about labor during the 1940s. Faced with the surprising rise of labor in the region and a continuing attempt by members of the New Deal coalition to create a more expansive federal administration to control labor that might not yield where issues of race intersected with those of employment, southern members of Congress no longer could afford to treat labor issues as a partisan question. With good reason, they feared that labor organizing would blend inexorably with, and fuel, civil rights activism; and they were frightened that an active federal government might level wages across racial lines, create a national labor market, encourage blacks to leave the South, diminish the southern establishment's control over those who stayed, and directly challenge Jim Crow practices. Further, even the older 1930s "deal" which had excluded the occupations in which the majority of southern blacks worked from federal protective legislation now seemed precarious at best.

Distressed by wartime developments, keenly aware of what was at stake, and anxious to find means to maintain control of their racial order, Congress's "solid South" Democrats closed ranks to join Republicans and reshape the institutional regime within which unions and the labor market would operate. For their Republican partners, labor remained an issue of party and ideology. In the mind of the southern legislator, by contrast, labor had become race. This was a tidal shift that would affect midcentury American politics as nothing else.

With this transformation, the majority of American blacks, once again, were left out. The craft unions and industrial unions that sheltered under the umbrella of the National Labor Relations Act lost much of their capacity to recruit large categories of black workers, especially in the South, after the passage of Taft-Hartley. The protections offered by the Fair Labor Standards Act were not extended to the preponderance of African Americans. By contrast, federal work policies boosted white prospects.

4

Divisions in War

THEY WERE MEMBERS OF THE SAME "greatest generation," the age group that fought "the good war."[1] When the United States entered the Second World War, John Hope Franklin was twenty-six years old. Robert Byrd was twenty-four. Franklin, who had just earned his doctorate in history at Harvard University, was starting to teach in Raleigh, North Carolina, at St. Augustine's College, a historically black institution. Byrd, who is currently the senior U.S. senator from West Virginia, was beginning to work as a welder building ships in a construction yard in Baltimore, Maryland.

Neither served in the military. Franklin sought to enlist. Nearly a half century after Pearl Harbor, at the close of a distinguished career that culminated at the University of Chicago and Duke University, he recalled his effort to join up:

> How best to serve became the question uppermost in my mind. The question appeared to have been answered by the United States Navy, which ran a full-page advertisement in the local newspaper. There was a shortage of personnel to handle the crush of paperwork, the navy stated; and men who could type, take shorthand, operate simple business machines, and per-

> form other office chores could look forward to early promotion. I rushed down to the recruitment office and volunteered my services to relieve the navy of its distress.[2]

The offer was not accepted. "The recruiter looked at me with what appeared to be a combination of incredulity and distress. . . . He simply said I was lacking in *one* qualification and that was color." After further nasty experiences, including the refusal of a doctor at a Tulsa induction center to draw his blood, Franklin successfully avoided the draft for the remainder of the war, having concluded that "the United States, however much it was devoted to protecting the freedoms and rights of Europeans, had no respect for me, no interest in my well-being, and not even a desire to utilize my services."[3]

Byrd, who was born in North Carolina and who, two years later, would be elected to the West Virginia House of Delegates, wrote a letter of concern about black demands for racial integration in the military to Theodore Bilbo of Mississippi, the Senate's most outspoken racist, in December 1944. "I am a typical American, a southerner, and 27 years of age," Byrd noted,

> and never in the world will I be convinced that race mixing in any field is good. All the social "do-gooders," the philanthropic "greats" of this day, the reds and the pinks . . . the disciples of Eleanor . . . can never alter my convictions on this question. I am loyal to my country and know but reverence to her flag, BUT I shall never submit to fight beneath that banner with a negro by my side. Rather I should die a thousand times, and see this old glory trampled in the dirt never to rise again, than to see this beloved land of ours become degraded by race mongrels, a throwback to the blackest specimen from the wilds.[4]

Within four years, Byrd's nightmare had become national policy. On July 26, 1948, President Harry Truman signed Executive Order 9981, a critical steppingstone on the pathway to racial equality in the military. Writing as commander in chief, he declared "the policy of the President that there shall be equality of treatment and opportunity for all persons in the armed services without regard to race, color, religion or national origin."[5] By the time the Korean War had ended, all the branches of service were integrated by race, though some all-black infantry regiments remained.[6] By 1956, integration was complete. Today, the military is the country's major institution least marked by racial separation.

Such, of course, was not the case before, during, and just after the Second World War. The Roosevelt administration and its military leaders navigated between black aspirations, like those of Franklin, and white resistance, like that of Byrd. Seeking to forge an effective fighting force, maintain order, and build support in the public and in Congress for its policies, the administration combined mass black participation in the armed services and access to formerly restricted officer positions and leadership roles with an unyielding commitment to racial segregation. Linked in a common military project, the United States, in effect, had two armies—one white, one black. Not entirely separate, they were utterly unequal.

I

THE SECOND WORLD WAR was the last major conflict in which the military policies of the United States accommodated undisguised racism. Though the armed services lessened its force as the war progressed, the racial course of action it still pursued was much closer to the Jim Crow policies of the First World War than to the mostly desegregated practices in the Korean War. When Woodrow Wilson took the country into Europe in 1917, the country's racial order seemed beyond question. Ironically, the massive expansion of the armed services compelled blacks to declare their loyalty at a moment when any hint of heresy was met with repression. But the chance to join the national crusade also seemed to offer African Americans an opening to claim their standing as citizens.

"*First* your Country, *then* your rights," W. E. B. Du Bois responded to critics of his famous "Close Ranks" editorial of July 1918 in *The Crisis*, the NAACP monthly, where he had implored his readers to "forget our special grievances and close our ranks."[7] From one perspective, there was little choice. Of course, a war on behalf of imperial and racist powers fought by a rigidly segregated army hardly struck most African Americans as a battle of good against evil. Still, blacks had little option but to answer the question of political obligation with loyalty. Within the country's charged racial climate, with its incompatible ethnic allegiances and atmosphere of intolerance, any visible black dissent courted danger. Aware that it would be difficult for a downtrodden racial minority to consider a war between white colonial nations a battle for democracy, federal intelligence agents watched leading African Americans during the late 1910s and kept a close eye on the black press. This anxious wartime surveillance often interpreted black skepticism and questioning that stopped well short of opposition, let alone disloyalty, as subversion.[8]

Once the United States joined the war, many blacks, including Du Bois, sought to achieve civic gains as a corollary to their steadfastness. Seeking to turn ambivalence to instrumental advantage, he offered a historical argument. The history of race relations in the United States, Du Bois claimed, demonstrated a republican principle at work. In peacetime, black oppression remained unshaken. By contrast, when blacks suited up as soldiers to join white citizens in a common national project, they actually had gained some rights. It was, he wrote, their surest instrument for advancement:

> Five thousand Negroes fought in the Revolution: the result was the emancipation of slaves in the North and the abolition of the African slave trade. At least three thousand Negro soldiers and sailors fought in the war of 1812; the result was the enfranchisement of the Negro in many Northern states and the beginning of a strong movement for general emancipation. Two hundred thousand Negroes enlisted in the Civil War, and the

> result was the emancipation of four million slaves, and the enfranchisement of the black man. Some ten thousand Negroes fought in the Spanish-American war, and in the twenty years since that war, despite many setbacks, we have doubled or quadrupled our accumulated wealth.[9]

The aftermath of the First World War made Du Bois far more cautious as the Second approached. The world had not been made safe for democracy, certainly not for people of color. The leading Allies of the United States, Britain and France, had tightened their grip on their increasingly restive colonial possessions. Racism at home grew more entrenched. In 1919, President Wilson expressed concern after the war that the reasonable conduct black soldiers had experienced in Europe "has gone to their heads." Earlier, in August 1918, General Pershing's headquarters had issued a request to French officers "not to commend too highly the black American troops in the presence of white Americans."[10] At Versailles, Wilson joined with Britain and Australia to repel the proposal by Japan that the Charter of the League of Nations should include a commitment to the equality of all people regardless of race. There were "too serious objections on the part of some of us." During the war, the very moderate black leader, Emmett Scott, who had worked as Booker T. Washington's private secretary and served in the Wilson administration as the Negro Adviser to the secretary of war, was appalled to discover how an entrenched belief in black inferiority sharply curtailed black training and opportunities.[11]

When the United States went to war, Du Bois was convinced that active black participation might make the armed forces a vehicle for equal citizenship. He was grievously disappointed. Although there were just over 1,500 black junior officers, the 404,000 black troops—11 percent of the Army's total strength—were commanded by white officers in all the senior ranks. Most blacks were slotted into labor duties, nearly all menial. Still, blacks were not entirely confined to quartermaster and stevedore service roles; some forty thousand were dispatched to combat units. Their 92nd and 93rd infantry divisions were sent to France, where the 92nd fought alongside three white divisions of the Second Army in attacking the second Hindenburg line.[12]

At the time, the press was full of reports of black heroism; yet after the war, a disproportionately southern white officer class reported black performance as having been deficient. At the conclusion of hostilities, the most racially progressive view in the Army sought to stop massing black troops separately, arguing instead that black units between the size of a company and a regiment should be placed within white regiments.[13] More typical, however, was the mixture of racism and realism found in Major General Robert Bullard's 1925 memoirs reflecting on his command of the Second Army. "If you need combat soldiers, and especially if you need them in a hurry, don't put your time upon Negroes," he cautioned, because "if there are any white people near . . . the task of making soldiers of them and fighting with them . . . will be swamped in the race question."[14] No one inside the armed forces suggested an end to military Jim Crow.

As the 1920s got underway, blacks were confronted with near-hysterical racism, the acceleration of lynching, the revival of the Klan, and more than twenty major riotous assaults by whites in northern and border cities who rampaged in black neighborhoods, stoned blacks on beaches, and attacked them on main thoroughfares and public transportation. A broader climate of nativism dominated. Public discourse took an ugly turn. "Think of submitting questions involving the very life of the United States to a tribunal on which a nigger from Liberia, a nigger from Honduras, a nigger from India . . . each have votes equal to that of the great United States," Senator James Reed of Missouri remarked about the League. Such talk went unrebuked.[15]

Not surprisingly, disenchantment characterized the mood of black America both at the start of the New Deal and, later, at the end of the 1930s and into the early 1940s when a world war loomed again. In 1934, the dean of Howard University's Law School, Charles Houston, remonstrated to the Army's chief of staff, General Douglas MacArthur, about the military's failure to incorporate black soldiers in the air, field artillery, and tank corps.[16] After MacArthur replied that "I can assure you . . . there has been and will be no discrimination against the colored race in the training of the national forces," Houston responded with a catalogue of specific complaints. They included the observation that "colored army officers . . . seem to get shunted away from regiments into detached service just as soon as they rank high enough to have seniority and control over any number of white officers" and that black regiments functioned not as fighting forces but as "labor battalions." He also noted that the Machine Gun Troops in the Colored Cavalry Detachment lacked "machine gun equipment, drills very little, and does not take part in maneuvers except in the capacity of orderlies," and that black soldiers were not offered access to vacancies in "newer arms of the service." He concluded: "When I note the complete absence of colored men in the Tank Corps, in the Coast Artillery, in the Field Artillery, in the Air Corps, in the Chemical Warfare Service and other newer arms, I must confess your assurances leave me skeptical."[17]

He was not alone. Seven years later, on the eve of American participation in the Second World War, Walter White, the executive secretary of the NAACP, made fighting dictators abroad conditional upon fighting for liberty at home. Reflecting on "bitter green" memories of white betrayal, he pledged that blacks would demand racial equality as their just reward. "It is tragic," he later remarked in the midst of the conflagration, "that the Civil War should be fought again while we are fighting a World War to save civilization."[18] Soon, much of black America was caught up in a "Double V" campaign, for "victory over our enemies at home and victory over our enemies on the battlefields abroad."[19]

Du Bois was even more forceful, more skeptical. He had become an exceedingly reluctant warrior. As the country entered the Second World War, he rallied black America very grudgingly. "We close ranks again, but only, now as then, to fight for democracy not only for white folk, but for yellow, brown, and black. We fight not in joy," he continued, "but in sorrow with no feeling of uplift. . . . Whatever all our mixed emotions are, we are going to play the game."[20]

Before Pearl Harbor, he had been disinclined to back American participation. Despite his loathing for Nazism, Du Bois had been appalled by racist depictions of the Japanese and by the manifest double standard of Western imperial powers fighting for democracy. Contrasting the West's fierce response to the Soviet Union's incursion in Finland with the moderate reaction that had been displayed to the 1935 invasion of Ethiopia by Italy and to the long history of colonialism, Du Bois tartly observed that "the world is astonished, aghast, and angry! But why? . . . England has been seizing land all over the earth for centuries with and without a shadow of rightful claim: India, South Africa, Uganda, Egypt, Nigeria, not to mention Ireland. The United States seized Mexico from a weak and helpless nation in order to bolster slavery. . . . This is the world that has grown suddenly righteous in defense of Finland."[21] Why, he asked, should not he and other African Americans believe that the war, at least in part, was a campaign to deepen white control? After Franklin Roosevelt and Winston Churchill signed the Atlantic Charter in August 1940, a document full of regard for self-government and sovereign rights, Du Bois remarked that this drive for freedom was unlikely to include Nigeria, Zululand, Natal, the Gold Coast,[22] the Dutch West Indies, "and a hundred other lands of the Blacks."[23] How, Walter White wished to know, could the United States "fight a war for freedom" with a segregated army?[24]

Under Du Bois's direction, *The Crisis* gave voice to a wider black campaign to make their support for the war conditional on gains at home. Though "sorry for brutality, blood, and death among the peoples of Europe," the magazine editorialized in July 1940, more than ten months after Germany's invasion of Poland, "just as we are sorry for China and Ethiopia . . . the hysterical cries of the preachers of democracy for Europe leave us cold. We want democracy in Alabama, Arkansas, in Mississippi and Michigan, in the District of Columbia—in the *Senate of the United States.*"[25] This theme remained prominent after Pearl Harbor. "Now is the Time Not to be Silent," the magazine argued. "A lily-white navy cannot fight for a free world. A jim crow army cannot fight for a free world. Jim crow strategy, no matter on how grand a scale, cannot build a free world."[26]

Both before and during the war, blacks campaigned actively to remove the massive contradiction such an armed force represented. One month before the United States entered the war, Roi Ottley reported that "Negro communities are seething with resentment," in large measure in reaction to "the treatment of Negro members of the army" which included "race riots at Fort Oswego; fighting at Camp Davis; discrimination at Fort Devens; jim-crow conditions at Camps Blanding and Lee; stabbings at Fort Huachuca; killings at Fort Bragg; and the edict 'not to shake a nigger's hand' at Camp Upton."[27] They were not put off by the kind of propaganda the Office of War Information issued in 1942. Written by the black publicist Chandler Owen, a widely circulated pamphlet, *Negroes and the War*, contrasted Nazi racism and the insult meted out to Jesse Owens, the black track star, at the Berlin Olympics of 1936 with a U.S. Army that had "two full divisions of Negro soldiers." Stressing that "Negroes serve in all branches" and that "there are Negro officers," the document evoked the image of Joe Louis, "*our* champion," knocking out "the German champion in one round."[28] Composed in an anxious voice, this Office of War Information publication sought to counter the "Double V" campaign by reminding black soldiers that "our future, like the future of all freedom lovers depends upon the triumph of democracy."[29] Nowhere did the document acknowledge the fierce discrimination they faced.[30]

Outside government circles, black leaders and the black press rejected this kind of soft-pedaling of segregation. In 1938, the publisher of the *Pittsburgh Courier*, Robert Vann, organized the Committee for Participation of Negroes in National Defense, a lobby of black World War One veterans. "I need not tell you," he wrote President Roosevelt in an open letter, "that we are expecting a more dignified place in our armed forces during the next war than we occupied during the World War." And in June 1940, on the eve of that year's presidential conventions, Walter White proclaimed that the NAACP would assay candidates by their commitment to end racial discrimination in the armed services. "What point is there in fighting and perhaps dying to save democracy if there is no democracy to save?"[31] "Who wants to fight," Roy Wilkins, editor of

The Crisis, demanded the following year, "for the kind of 'democracy' embodied in the curses, the hair-trigger pistols, and the clubs of the Negro-hating hoodlums in the uniforms of military police?"[32]

II

THE ADMINISTRATION'S OFFICIAL position insisted that the fight against the Axis powers and the challenge of civil rights at home be distinguished, as if the separate-but-equal tentacles of *Plessy v. Ferguson* could extend to the military sphere. In 1942, John J. McCloy, then assistant secretary of war, who headed an Advisory Committee on Negro Troop Policies, thought it reasonable that blacks should suspend their agitation for improvement during the course of the war. Writing in July to William Hastie, the African American civilian aide to the secretary of war, he called for a lessening of emphasis in the black community on discriminatory acts, "irrespective of whether the White or the Colored man is responsible for starting them. Frankly," he added, "I do not think that the basic issues of this war are involved in the question of whether Colored troops serve in segregated or in mixed units, and I doubt that you can convince the people of the United States that the basic issues of freedom are involved in such a question." When the war wound down, Walter Wright, the chief historian of the Army, observed that "As to the segregation of Negroes to special units in the Army, this is simply a reflection of the state of affairs well-known in civilian America today. . . . Since the less favorable treatment characteristic of southern states is less likely to lead to violent protest from powerful white groups, the Army has tended to follow southern rather than northern practices in dealing with racial segregation."[33]

The black campaign for military integration failed dismally. Writing for *The New Republic* in 1944, Lucille Miller accurately summarized the wartime situation:

> The Navy has refused to commission Negroes in any branch of the service—in the Navy proper, the Marine Corps and

> the Coast Guard. While it has admitted Negroes to its fighting ranks, Jim Crowism is practiced in training and in service. The Air Corps has discriminated against Negroes in the most complicated and costly way, building a segregated air base for Negroes when there was room in established training centers over the country. The annual output of Negro pilots was 200 when it could easily have been five times that number. The Army trains and commissions colored and white candidates without discrimination, but Jim Crow rules over every Southern camp. Colored women are excluded from every auxiliary service but the Wacs, and here there is segregation. With the Army calling for thousands of nurses, they have held down the quota of colored nurses to about 200.[34]

Charles Wilson, an African American private, reflected on these circumstances in a long letter he wrote to Franklin Roosevelt in May 1944. Without hyperbole, he criticized military segregation and the exclusion of black troops from active fighting roles in favor of "decidedly menial work, such as BOQ orderlies, janitors, permanent KP's and the like." He then offered a more abstract reflection:

> The picture in our country is marred by one of the strangest paradoxes in our whole fight against world fascism. The United States Armed Forces, to fight for World Democracy, is within itself undemocratic. The undemocratic policy of jim crow and segregation is practiced by our Armed Forces against its Negro members. Totally inadequate opportunities are given to the Negro members of our Armed Forces, nearly one tenth of the whole, to participate with "equality" . . . "regardless of race and color" in the fight for our war aims.[35]

There is a treasure trove of such letters from black soldiers that records their disenchantment in the face of brutal segregation. "We are servant and ditch diggers," Private Jus Hill, at Randolph Field in Texas, wrote to his hometown newspaper, the *Pittsburgh Courier.* "They got us here washing ditches [sic], working around officers houses and waiting on them, instead of trying to win this war they got us in ditches." From Camp Meade in Florida, an anonymous "Negro Soldier" reported that in his third week at the base

> they started us cleaning the white officers rooms, making us they [*sic*] dirty beds and cleaning they latrine and are still doing that right at the present. We cannot go to the church services on the camp . . . the service clubs are off limits to us because a Staff Sgt. went over with some more of our comrades in the Co. to get a couple of sandwiches and were told by a civilian worker we don't serve colored, and Sir this is an Army post. . . . Sir, we sleep in sand floors with no boards or anything to bed. We stand up and eat each meal which they call a meal. . . . The truth, Sir, are we nothing but slaves.

Addressing William Hastie, Private Bert Babaro complained about the indifference of the company commander to segregated theatres and buses and to "barracks located just in front of the camp cess pool." Private Latrophe Jenkins, at Alabama's Camp Rucker, alleged "being driven and down trodden worst than animals in the fields around us. Men losing their lives at the hands of power intoxicated anti-Negro MP's and Nazi minded Southern whites that take us to exercise their animosities on just as the Japs are branded for treating the Chinese." He continued: "We have served faithfully" and "this war will be a Victory for us. But then that leaves us to become terribly bewildered, because if this war is won by us (I mean America), then who's going to help us win ours?" Writing collectively to request a transfer, "We as a group of Negro soldiers, wish to be soldiers in the Army of the United States, not dogs at Jackson Air Base, nor in the State of Mississippi . . . We are treated like wild animals here, like we are unhuman. The word Negro is never used here, all they call us are nigger do this, nigger do that. Even the officers here are calling us nigger. . . . Our food are fixed in such a manner that we can't eat. We never get enough to eat. In the hospital we are mistreated. . . . We don't want no more than to be treated like soldiers." And from Camp Hood in Texas came the complaint that we "are really being treated worse than these German prisoners here."[36]

Of course, not all African Americans had experiences quite so dire. For many, there were opportunities unimagined before the war. After 1942, the Navy accepted blacks for general service and as noncommissioned officers. Black women were allowed to join the WAVES for the first time. The Marine Corps, which had never accepted black recruits, finally did so, if only in segregated units as laborers and ammunition handlers. With the exception of the Air Corps, black officers trained and graduated alongside whites and received commissions in all the services and branches (though they always were assigned to black units and never commanded white troops). When at the start of joint officer training black candidates were nominated in puny numbers (from July 1941, when officer candidate schools opened, to October, only 17 of the 1,997 students were black), the chief of staff, General George Marshall, moved to increase their numbers significantly and defended this experiment in integration against southern opposition.[37] Overseas, black troops played key roles, particularly after D-Day. There were twenty-two black combat units in Europe. One in five engineering units was black. Black pilots took to the air in two combat air units. Skilled black service units built roads and ports in the Pacific. And in exceptions to the rule, a very small number of black sailors were integrated into oceangoing ships; and black platoons of forty men fought in previously all-white companies of approximately two hundred soldiers when American troops reached the Ardennes in the winter months of 1944–45.[38]

The exigencies of war, moreover, did compel military leaders to address black unrest, improve base conditions, and open some doors to training and recognition. In 1943, McCloy's committee, which functioned as the highest-level War Department group concerned with the condition of black troops, sought to eliminate the most egregious violations and develop a coherent approach to training and personnel issues in order to manage the race question effectively. General Marshall, following the committee's lead, distributed a letter to his three major commanders insisting they improve the racial climate. Taking note of disturbances that had been provoked "with real or fancied incidents of discrimination and segregation" and how "disaffection among negro soldiers continues to constitute an immediately serious problem," he directed that "under no circumstances can there be a command attitude which makes allowances for improper conduct of either white or negro soldiers." Concurrently, the War Department ordered base commanders to give blacks greater access to recreational facilities, opening the way to a local option on integrated use by noting that "facilities will be provided without instructions either implicit or implied that certain ones are for the exclusive use of either white or colored personnel."[39] The War Department also instructed the commanders to desegregate transportation on buses and trucks owned by the federal government. The reaction of many southern newspapers and members to this sole breach of Jim Crow was fierce. The *Montgomery Advertiser* maintained that "even Army orders, even armies, even bayonets cannot force impossible and unnatural social race relationships upon us." "Social customs rooted in ancient emotions," the *Birmingham News* cautioned, "can never be changed by fiat." Louisiana's Congressman A. Leonard Allen sent a sharp protest to Secretary of War Henry Stimson, advising that "this is a most unwise step. It is a blow to the Southland and it is a slap at every white man from Dixie wearing the uniform."[40]

Despite some ameliorative steps, the war persistently underscored the second-class status of the great majority of black troops in both symbolic and practical terms. Of the fifty camps housing significant numbers of black troops, fully thirty-eight posts were in the South. Their location was selected in part for the weather, allowing easier all-year outdoor training, but mainly because of their proximity to black population centers and to areas where the Department of War anticipated moderate to low levels of resistance to the presence of so many black soldiers. A corollary, never fully enforced because it proved unworkable, was the policy recommended by military planners that "Insofar as practicable, Negroes inducted in the North be stationed in the North" for fear that they might introduce unacceptable standards into the South. Black officers working alongside white officers to command black units usually were excluded from officer housing and officer clubs, living and eating instead with the enlisted men. When Hastie inquired about the Army's policy on access to various facilities by black officers, he was informed that "The Army has always regarded the officers' quarters and the officers' mess as the home and the private dining room of the officers who reside and eat there."[41] This policy extended even to the two weeks of rest and recreation the Army offered many of its overseas troops. White soldiers were sent to top-tier resorts in Miami Beach, Hot Springs, Santa Barbara, and Lake Placid. Black soldiers had to make do with Chicago's South Side Pershing Hotel and Harlem's Hotel Theresa, thus extending segregation to the North as official policy. These hotels, the secretary of war explained in 1944, were "the best obtainable for the purpose" in keeping with the "War Department's long-standing policy not to force the intermingling of the races."[42]

Recurrently, black soldiers in the South were confronted with local violence aimed at enforcing indigenous racial restrictions. In just the spring and summer of 1941, black soldiers stationed in Arkansas, Louisiana, North Carolina, South Carolina, and Tennessee were attacked by white civilians; and black soldiers at Camps Livingston and Claiborne in Louisiana and Camp Davis in North Carolina fought military police. Daniel Kryder has commented that "the difficulty with which blacks purchased accommodations, tickets, and means in segregated towns and situation . . . contributed to curfew violations, scheduling snafus, and arguments in bus and train stations. Violence often stemmed from interracial contact on commuter buses and trains, which were governed by widely varying but typically strict local laws and customs. Soldiers arriving at their destinations found themselves in towns and cities that might be openly hostile to their presence."[43]

At a December 1941 meeting at the Department of War to discuss this state of affairs, a group of black editors was informed that "The Army cannot change civilian ideas on the Negro."[44] Colonel Eugene Householder, representing the Adjutant General, admonished these molders of black opinion that "The Army cannot be made the means of engendering conflict among the mass of people because of a stand with respect to Negroes which is not compatible with the position attained by Negroes in civil life. . . . The Army is not a sociological laboratory."[45] Both George Marshall, as chief of staff, and Henry Stimson, as secretary of war, shared these views. They turned aside black pleas to consider at least the gradual integration of the military. Marshall was the more sympathetic of the two, but was active in representing the skeptical views of the Army's staff. That month, he explained that as his first task was dealing with the country's enemies, reform would have to wait. "The military would be unable to solve a social problem which has perplexed the American people throughout the history of this nation. The Army cannot accomplish such a solution and should not be charged with the undertaking." Stimson was even more adamant because he was skeptical about the capacity of black soldiers. Mindful that the Army had segregated its units since 1863, in October 1940 he noted in his diary that he had urged FDR not to place "too much responsibility on a race which was not showing initiative in battle." Some fifteen months later, in January 1942, he recorded his anger at Eleanor Roosevelt's "intrusive and impulsive folly" in pushing racial integration.[46]

III

THE KEY DECISIONS about ways to include large numbers of black soldiers in the military without affronting the white South were taken before the onset of the war, and announced by the policy statement issued with President Roosevelt's approval on October 9, 1940. "Negroes," *The American Soldier*, the leading postwar work on the subject, matter-of-factly summarized, "were needed and were not excluded, but neither were they fully integrated or fully accepted."[47] Written at a moment when only one black cadet had graduated from West Point in the last two decades and none from the Naval Academy in Annapolis (the first black graduate finished in 1949), and when there were only five black officers in the entire military, three of whom were chaplains, the document promised that "the services of Negroes will be utilized on a fair and equitable basis."[48] It pledged that "The strength of the Negro personnel of the Army of the United States will be maintained on a general basis of the proportion of the Negro population in the country." It also promised black access to aviation training, reserve commissions, and entry to all branches of the military.

But not without two crucial caveats. The first concerned the assignment of officers: "Negro reserve officers eligible for active duty will be assigned to Negro units officered by colored personnel." The second, even more pivotal, affirmed Jim Crow:

> The policy of the War Department is not to intermingle colored and white enlisted personnel in the same regimental organizations. This policy has been proven satisfactory over a long period of years, and to make changes now would produce situations destructive to morale and detrimental to the preparation for national defense. For similar reasons, the department does not contemplate assigning colored reserve officers other than those of the Medical Corps and chaplains to existing Negro combat units of the Regular Army. These regular units are going concerns, accustomed through many years to the present system. Their morale is splendid, their rate of reenlistment is exceptionally high, and their field training is well advanced. It is the opinion of the War Department that no experiments should be tried with the organizational set-up of these units at this critical time.[49]

This document was confirmed with a presidential "OK."[50]

As they had demanded, blacks now would be inducted on the basis of their share of the population, but they would be assigned exclusively to black units. Such segregation was not a military policy. In fact, the decision to organize the military by the racial patterns mandated by law in seventeen of the forty-eight states imposed high costs: the need to provide separate facilities by race limited opportunities for blacks to serve up to their capacity, impeded the organization for total war, and lowered black morale. It forced blacks who lived outside the South to encounter far more segregation than they had previously experienced. It placed "undertrained black soldiers in units that were often inefficient and sometimes surplus to its needs," and it isolated the best trained black leaders from the most challenging tasks.[51] Its core assumption, albeit an unarguable one, was that any attempt to move beyond the policy of separate black units would be met by resistance of the kind Robert Byrd later articulated. Bearing this social reality in mind, the military, led by a primarily white southern officer corps, concluded the instrumental cost of segregation had to be paid.

In the interwar period, black campaigning had moved in three steps. The primary demand during the 1920s into the early 1930s was for an increase in the number of black troops. Chicago's Congressman Oscar De Priest, for example, complained at the end of this phase, in 1932, in a speech at Howard University, that African Americans made up only some 2 percent of the armed forces.[52] "The United States Army is about to be increased," the *Pittsburgh Courier* noted two years later. "There should be a larger percentage of colored soldiers in it." Noting that the Army was proposing an increase of 47,000 enlisted men and 4,063 officers, it objected that "no provision is being made to include the Negro." Arguing for a 10 percent quota, it observed: "Here is something worth going after."[53]

Second, the black press and political leaders increasingly found fault with the way in which black troops were deployed. The problem was not merely insufficient numbers, but their status as "virtually servants . . . doing menial chores for whites." Blacks in regular Army units had been transformed into "stable boys."[54]

When the *Courier* launched its campaign for the Participation of Negroes in National Defense, it combined both demands. In a February 1938 open letter to President Roosevelt, Robert Vann sought an "opportunity for our men to enter the military and naval service in larger numbers and at the same time to procure enlistment in the higher branches of the services." Observing that "one American citizen in every ten is black, but only one American fighting man in every 33 is black," Vann issued four requests: increased black enlistment; openings in the Air Corps and Navy; "formation of an entire division of Negro combat troops composed of all the customary services"; and "training of Negro officers for such a division."[55]

This visible campaign, stressing black patriotism, loyalty, and Americanism ("We are not Africans"),[56] stopped well short of insisting on an end to racial segregation. Once it became clear that a massive expansion might be just ahead, however, Jim Crow itself, as we have observed, became the central target. Meeting at the White House with the president, Secretary of the Navy Frank Knox, and Assistant Secretary of War Robert Patterson on September 27, 1940, three black leaders—T. Arnold Hill, adviser on Negro Affairs at the National Youth Administration, A. Philip Randolph, the leader of the Brotherhood of Sleeping Car Porters, and Walter White of the NAACP—insisted that only individual ability should restrict the placement of black officers and enlisted men. Segregated units should be closed. African Americans should be integrated as individuals throughout the service. "Existing units of the army and units to be established should be required to accept and select officers," their memorandum for the president insisted, "without regard to race."[57] "Southern Americanism" no longer would be acceptable.[58]

At each stage, the military and the president said no. The Department of War fashioned black manpower policies at three occasions in the interwar period. Finding black performance in the First World War to have been "not discreditable," a 1922 plan called for a modest role for small units of such troops, led primarily by white officers. This design was part of the shift of the Army to a much smaller peacetime basis, and it was characterized by "a definite tightening of segregation."[59] A 1937 plan set the goal of a racially proportionate army to assuage concern by whites that they would be placed disproportionately in harm's way in a future war and apprehension by blacks that they might be excluded from the status of soldier. At the time, the military, including the National Guard, had some 360,000 soldiers, of whom only 6,500, or fewer than 2 percent, were black (by 1940, these numbers had declined to 4,000, or 1.5 percent).[60] But as there were many objections to black soldiers by the various branches, including the Army's Air Corps and Signal Corps, a 1940 mobilization plan limited blacks to under 6 percent of the military (compared to their 10 percent of the population) and channeled them primarily into non-combat roles.[61]

An Army War College training manual to prepare for the influx of black troops summarized the predominant view that underpinned these various decisions:

> As an individual, the negro is docile, tractable, lighthearted, care free, and good natured. If unjustly treated, he is likely to become surly and stubborn, though this is usually a temporary phase. He is careless, shiftless, irresponsible, and secretive. He resents censure and is best handled with praise and by ridicule. He is unmoral, untruthful, and his sense of right doing is relatively inferior. . . . On the other hand, the negro is cheerful, loyal, and usually uncomplaining if reasonably well fed. He has a musical nature and a marked sense of rhythm. His art is primitive. He is religious. With proper direction in mass, negroes are industrious. They are emotional and can be stirred to a high state of enthusiasm. Their emotions are unstable and their reactions uncertain.[62]

With such attitudes predominating in a disproportionately southern-dominated institution, the military was slow to bring African

Americans into the ranks. When the war broke out, blacks sought to enlist in record numbers. Like John Hope Franklin, many were turned back. In numerous regions of the country, not just in the South, initial call-ups under the Selective Training and Service Act of 1940, which required the registration of all men between the ages of twenty-one and thirty-five, filled quotas exclusively with white recruits.

Resembling all New Deal legislation passed by Congress, this statute established national policies, including a prohibition of discrimination based on race and color, but implemented them in decentralized fashion in order to protect southern preferences. Noting this new law and the decision to send black recruits to the South, the *Courier* wryly, but accurately, remarked: "Northern Negroes who vote a Democratic President in office put the South in the saddle. The South runs our Congress, Army and our Navy, and there is not very much left of the country after that."[63]

When a black minister from Memphis wrote to complain about local treatment, the director of the Selective Service, Lieutenant Colonel Lewis Hershey, responded that "this office cannot assist you, since it is the responsibility of the governor of each state to set up the necessary registration machinery and personnel." There were 6,442 local draft boards, with at least three members. Outside the South, some 250 blacks served out of a total of at least 25,000. Within the South, with the exception of a tiny number of individuals in Kentucky, North Carolina, and Kentucky, there were none. Across the country, only eleven blacks appeared on appeals boards, and none in the South. In the early period of the draft, no blacks were called. The draft's national headquarters lacked authority to compel local boards to do so.[64]

As John Hope Franklin discovered, there also was a good deal of resistance to black troops by the military. Though needed, they were not always welcome. Even after blacks were selected, the Army frequently delayed their induction until segregated facilities could be readied. As late as early 1943, when manpower needs had become sufficiently acute that African Americans could not be kept away, some 300,000 potential black soldiers had been selected by the Selective

Service but were still awaiting induction, often after many months. The backlog was so substantial in southern communities that single black men waited while married white men were drafted into service.

Illiteracy also clearly played a part. Throughout the war, gross educational deficiencies continued to be the major reason blacks were accepted for service at a lower rate than whites.[65] The 1940 Census had revealed that some 10 million Americans had not been schooled past the fourth grade, and that one in eight could not read and write. This, primarily, was a southern problem. A higher proportion of blacks living in the North had completed grade school than whites in the South.[66] Three in four potential black inductees rejected for this reason came from the South, compared to one in four whites. In truth, though, "the War Department apparently seized the opportunity to use illiteracy as a tactic to discriminate against blacks while accepting illiterate whites without question."[67] Secretary of War Henry Stimson recorded in his diary that "the Army had adopted rigid requirements for literacy mainly to keep down the number of colored troops."[68] As Hershey conceded in 1944, "what we are doing, of course, is simply transferring discrimination from everyday life into the army. Men who make up the army staff have the same ideas [about blacks] as they had before."[69]

Thus, in the midst of a war defined in large measure as an epochal battle between liberal democracy and Nazi and Fascist totalitarianism, one that distinguished between people on the basis of blood and race, the U.S. military not only engaged in sorting Americans by race but in policing the boundary separating white from black. Because the draft selected individuals to fill quotas to meet the test of a racially proportionate military and because they were assigned to units based on a simple dual racial system, the notion of selective service extended to the assignment of definitive racial tags. The Selective Service system soon found this often was not a simple task. The issue of classification proved particularly vexing in Puerto Rico, where the population was so various racially and where the island's National Guard units had been integrated. Even here, registrants were sorted by race and the National Guard was divided into two sections. The large number of mixed race individuals in the border states, the Creole population of Louisiana, and American Indians offered other challenges, as did ambiguous individual cases almost everywhere. Embarrassingly, the Selective Service fell on blood percentages, using racial guidelines not unlike the country's European enemy, Nazi Germany. Ordinarily, the rule it used was "that 25 percent Negro blood made a person a Negro." Nonetheless, Hershey made clear that it would be unwise for the local board to disrupt "the mode of life which has become so well established" when a draftee in question had been passing as white.[70] After August 1944, the system was sufficiently overwhelmed that he took the decision, at first resisted by Secretary Stimson, to accept the classification an individual claimed for himself when a dispute over a racial assignment came to pass.

IV

THE WAR PROVED TO BE a particularly important junction for white ethnic Americans, chiefly the children of Catholic and Jewish newcomers who had arrived in the United States from the 1880s until the closing of the immigration gates in 1924. Military training, wartime service, postwar benefits, and integration into a common American purpose brought many of these newcomers into their first robust contact with the white and mainly Protestant America from which they had lived at a physical and symbolic distance.

For Jews, in particular, the Second World War produced a shift in standing that was quite radical. On its eve, "Jews were not so confident of their prospects in America."[71] During the period of economic hardship, resurgent anti-Semitism, and grim news from Palestine and above all from the heartland of Europe in the 1930s, American Jews faced quotas on admission to leading universities, markedly to professional schools,[72] and a more widespread restrictive system of anti-Semitic practices that impelled the creation of parallel networks of hotels, country clubs, and other social institutions. Before the First World War, most Jews had not sought to enter crowded labor markets outside their areas of economic specialization, notably in the garment trades. But in the interwar period, as the children of immigrants sought to move beyond these niches, they discovered high walls barring many types of employment, in particular in banking, insurance, and engineering. Public opinion polls revealed a great deal of skepticism and many popular myths about Jews. Anti-Jewish expression often was unguarded and unashamed.[73] Enhanced Jewish visibility in economic and civic life often went hand in hand with heightened apprehension and nervous efforts to limit Jewish prominence, as in the case of the unsuccessful effort in 1938 by the Jewish secretary of the treasury and the Jewish publisher of the *New York Times* to persuade President Roosevelt not to appoint a second Jew to the Supreme Court.[74]

In contrast, by the 1950s, Jewish Americans had achieved remarkable social mobility, high measures of participation in American life, and impressive political incorporation.[75] Anti-Semitism had become unfashionable, at least its open expression. University barriers to entry became more permeable. Mobility from one generation to the next accelerated as access to formerly closed occupations quickened. Housing choices multiplied. Jews entered mass culture on vastly more favorable terms.[76] The war, in short, proved a great engine of group integration and incorporation. Under arms, American Jews became citizens in a full sense at just the moment that Jews virtually everywhere in Europe were being extruded from citizenship. Jews served as officers in the U.S. military as well as enlisted men in higher proportions than their share of the population. After the First World War, they often were classified with blacks as a racial minority.[77] By the 1940s, they were linked with predominantly Catholic groups to compose the category of white ethnics—a grouping that signified the extension of American pluralism and tolerance.[78]

If, for Jews and Catholics, the war marked the first moment of full inclusion via the pathway of military service and benefits, for blacks, the war was the last moment of formal exclusion from equal citizenship by the federal government. At this critical juncture, the social and political impossibility of integration precluded black gains on these terms. The opening of new opportunities for white ethnic religious minorities did not unsettle dominant social practices the way full black inclusion surely would have. As a result, though the military did offer African Americans tangible gains, these trailed the advantages presented to other outsiders by a dramatic margin. The effect, we now can see, was to produce a critical lag in the rate and conditions of black assimilation into the wider currents of American life.

Like all New Deal policies, the combination of military inclusion, segregation, and condescension offered black Americans more access than they had secured before, but far less than national policies offered to whites. Given conditions at the time, however, especially in the South where 77 percent of African Americans still lived, even such limited terms must have seemed attractive, at least at first, to many black recruits. Writing in 1942 as the highest-ranking black civilian concerned with the war effort, William Hastie took note of the "most spontaneous and most enthusiastic celebrations that have characterized black community send-offs. . . . The Negro soldier is the Negro youth of today. He believes in his ability. He believes in the ability of other Negroes. He expresses something deep inside of him when he says, 'Show them what we can do.'"[79] Despite recurring insults—including the racial segregation of blood contributed to the Red Cross,[80] military censorship of the black press,[81] movies that depicted servile black characters,[82] the forced shift to Jim Crow rail cars on southbound trains when they reached Washington, D.C.,[83] and the creation of separate black and white air raid shelters[84]—the opportunity to serve in large numbers was, in the circumstance, impossible for African Americans to refuse. Once again, the implicit promise of citizenship and social standing via even a partial inclusion in the armed services could not be resisted.[85]

Once the initial high barriers to entry at the start of the war were overcome by the sheer need for manpower, the black presence in the military grew rapidly, reaching much greater levels of participation than in the First World War. By the end of 1942, just over 10 percent of the total of 4,532,117 soldiers under arms were African American; within a year, their numbers had grown to 754,000, or 11 percent of the 6,778,000 mobilized troops. Their distribution was not comparable, however. Four in ten white troops were allocated to combat units, compared to half that rate for blacks, and many black combat units were used for heavy labor. By contrast, 35 percent of black soldiers served in service units, while only 14 percent of whites received such assignments.[86] The Navy, in particular, checked black horizons. By the end of December 1941, there were only some 5,000 sailors, or 2 percent of the total, all of whom served as stewards. Admiral Chester Nimitz explained that enlisted whites would not stand for the possibility of command by black officers at sea. Secretary Knox clarified the Navy's position, insisting that "we must be realists. If we put Negroes in the navy it would be like putting them in hell. The relationships on shipboard are such that white and colored just cannot be mixed."[87] Not until mid-1944, when James Forrestal took over as undersecretary, did the Navy authorize duties at sea for African Americans.[88]

Despite all these limitations reflecting a military version of white supremacy, the role of soldier remained very attractive to a great many young blacks. Compared to their day-to-day circumstances, particularly in the South, the military seemed to offer a host of otherwise unattainable opportunities, not least regular meals, fairly decent shelter, and health care. They were paid, most for the first time, on a par with whites doing comparable work. In 1939, the average black wage in the United States was $371; for the country as a whole, $964. In the military, cash wages and in-kind provisions were worth, the Army estimated, between $2,000 and $2,600 per year.[89]

Above all, military service made it possible for very poor individuals with little experience outside their home environments to enter a "modern" world. The opportunity to travel, witness diverse experiences and patterns of upbringing, meet fellow blacks from all parts of the country with varied class backgrounds, and experience a wide range of world views broadened their horizons. As one study of the impact of the war on the lives of black Americans has observed, "Military service thrust young men into markedly new work relationships. In keeping with modern organizational principles, the military was in theory governed by impersonal, public, rational rules aimed at task-specific efficiency."[90] This leap into modernity was remarkably profound for rural southerners who had lived in isolated, provincial rural environments.

Although the day-to-day experience of military life for black soldiers was deeply marked by the humiliations and limits of segregation, for many this form of institutional membership offered an almost revolutionary experience. To be sure, military segregation contradicted modern values and opportunities; but "service—more precisely training—exposed men at all levels to a universalistic ethos, to the demand for precise and predictable task performance, and to a view of an organization based largely on functionally specific roles rather than on particular persons."[91] Even second-class membership in the military wrenched blacks out of a tightly controlled racial order where access to learning and occupational skills was very meager. And it offered a route of escape from a system of agricultural compulsion that combined peonage and peasant standing. For blacks separated from their home communities, families, churches, social and economic relationships, and patterns of racial power, the Army now served as a powerful socializing "total institution," a gateway to modern America.[92]

For some blacks, moreover, the war proved to be a major opportunity for attaining new skills, enlarging contacts, and broadening their experience.[93] "Along with many of their white fellows," the leading student of segregation and desegregation in the armed forces has noted, "they acquired new skills and a new sophistication that prepared them for a different life of the postwar industrial world." During the war, Army training (as well as work in wartime industries) equipped formerly unskilled blacks to become semi-skilled workers, skilled craftsmen, and supervisors. Although their access to training was not nearly as abundant as that open to whites, the armed services did offer previously unskilled, largely agrarian black soldiers the chance to take courses in "psychology, postal service, water purification, chaplain's service, carpentry, painting, map reproduction, drafting, fuels and ignition, accounting and auditing . . . physical therapy, optical repair, cooking and baking, instrument repair, tire rebuilding, Diesel mechanics, watch repair, navigation, and a host of other subjects." Some of these gains came because units were segregated. Thus although, early in the war, out of each one thousand black recruits only three were carpenters, six auto mechanics, one a plumber, and almost none were machinists, welders, or draftsmen, the Engineer Corps to which many African Americans were assigned required these skills, and so "tens-of-thousands of Negroes learned a highly skilled trade in the Services . . . and still larger numbers of men mastered semi-skilled trades and labor discipline."[94] These fields, Robert Weaver observed near war's end, were "the very types of work from which Negroes have been consistently barred in the past."[95]

Arguably even more important, blacks realized that "their economic and political position could be changed."[96] The Army Air Force trained black pilots. Other occupational roles demanding a good deal of proficiency opened up to many for the first time. Some were sent to historically black colleges at Army expense to acquire particular skills. Over the course of the war, an increasing number of African Americans attended both officer training and special training schools on an integrated basis. As black medical facilities were created in Alabama and Arizona, opportunities emerged for black doctors and nurses.[97] Practice aside, the dominant articulated goals of the armed services and their war aim were universal in character. Many of the government's official statements about recruitment and life in the Army spoke of equal treatment as an ideal. Participation in this institution wrenched blacks out of a society of fixed and limited places into a world with a degree of mobility. While still enmeshed in Jim Crow, they lived far closer to its outer boundaries.

Perhaps most important, military service offered black soldiers the most basic and elementary requisite for an active participation in political, social, cultural, and economic life: literacy. As Stimson conceded, the substandard educational opportunities and achievements of blacks, especially southern blacks, had been deployed as an instrument to keep their numbers in uniform down. But, over the course of the war, this had proved an unsustainable policy. Faced with a major crisis in manpower yet coping with a pool of black recruits principally in the Fourth and Eighth Corps areas of the South who were a good deal less educated than whites, the Army was forced to turn to literacy training in combination with confined responsibilities. It could hardly reject something like half the black registrants. Since the military leaders put aside any notion of integrating combat units because of intense southern opposition and their own unwillingness to "experiment," only two possibilities remained: "make up for the deficiencies with which it [the Army] was presented" and restrict blacks mainly "to support functions and menial jobs in service commands."[98]

Estimates of the pool of illiterate recruits, defined as those who had not achieved a fourth-grade level of literacy, varied a good deal. A 1942 conference estimated there were some 430,000, of whom two in three were black. A Columbia University Teachers College consultant placed the overall number at the start of 1943 at 900,000, concluding that of these, 500,000 could be drafted. The decision to take and educate these individuals with marginal education was the result primarily of immense pressures from the field for more soldiers, but it also had another source. Across the South, white leaders, including some of its most vociferous racists like Mississippi's Senator Bilbo, were insisting that black men be removed from communities from which so many white men were absent but white women were still present. "In my state," he told a Senate committee in the fall 1942, "with a population one-half Negro and one half white . . . the system that you are using has resulted in taking all the whites to meet the quota and leaving the great majority of Negroes at home." In these circumstances, he advised the Department of War: "I [am] anxious that you develop the reservoir of the illiterate class . . . so that there would be an equal distribution."[99] Leading civil rights advocates promoted this view because they were keen to reverse the policy that had kept so many blacks who wished to serve out of the military.

The Army's response was to create a massive crash schooling program of Special Training Units. At the military reception centers, organized into segregated classrooms, two out of every three of their students were black. Once in place starting in June 1943, more than 300,000 inductees passed through this program. Half came from the Fourth Service Command that recruited in the deep South. A high proportion, 11 percent, of new white recruits were classified as illiterate, but fully 45 percent of the black newcomers lacked basic reading skills. Schooling lasted twelve weeks. "Specially prepared textbooks, such as *The Army Reader,* describing in simple words a day with Private Pete, were used. Bootie Mack, a sailor, enlivened the pages of *The Navy Reader.*"[100] The level of training was modest (the ability to write letters, read signs, use a clock, deploy basic arithmetic), but remarkably the great majority, some 250,000, were lifted out of illiteracy in this brief period.[101] Of the black members of these Special Training Units in the first six months of operation, fully 90 percent were assigned to regular units at the conclusion of their schooling, a higher proportion than the 85 percent of whites.

The response by blacks to this unexpected opportunity was quite profound. Many wrote to show appreciation for the chance to rectify the lack of education they had received back home. Fully seven in ten blacks in this program went on to receive further, more advanced training in the Army, and a remarkable 50 percent of the graduating cohort applied for educational assistance after the war under the GI Bill.[102] Arguably, this educational initiative later had the ironic effect—certainly unintended by Senator Bilbo and his fellow southern members of Congress—of creating a mass literate public for the postwar civil rights movement.

But if there were striking gains for the poorest and least educated blacks in the military as measured in their overrepresentation in this remedial education project, there were immense, almost impassible barriers in the way for better-equipped blacks who attempted to move ahead and secure advanced training. "The three branches which contained the bulk of Negro troops were traditionally those with many unskilled labor jobs to be performed, such as roadbuilding, stevedoring, laundering, and fumigation." Further, not much effort was made to assign blacks by taking their level of schooling into account. "Negroes who were high school graduates were assigned to about the same branches as Negroes with at most only grade school education." By war's end, some 11 percent of white men in the military were officers, but fewer than 1 percent of blacks, even though their aspirations for leadership were just as high. Whereas black units had both white and black officers, white units were only commanded by white leaders. An Army survey in March 1943 found that "58 per cent of the Negro troops reported that all of the lieutenants in their companies were white, 30 per cent said some white and some Negro, while only 12 per cent reported that all their company lieutenancies were held by Negroes."[103] Very few blacks, certainly far fewer than qualified by objective measures, were admitted to the Army Special Training Program, which placed individuals in civilian colleges to acquire a wide array of skills. The program reached its peak number—105,000—in December 1943; of these, fewer than 1 percent, just 789, were African American. In the great majority of segregated black units, no effort was made to identify qualified individuals. And even where they were singled out, segregation in higher education in the South where most were stationed starkly limited the number of available places although institutions of higher education had signed contracts with the Army that contained clauses proscribing discrimination. In these instances, state laws requiring separate facilities trumped such agreements.

As the leading military historian concerned with the deployment of black troops during the war reports, many units asked for clarification about the kind of skill training these soldiers could receive:

> Will there be a separate school for tire maintenance? the Civilian Aide's Office asked. Can Negro enlisted men be trained as guard patrolmen at Miami Beach? First Air Force wanted to know. May they be sent to the corps area horseshoeing school? Four Corps Area was asked. Are Negroes eligible for the General Mechanics Course at Motor Transport Schools the Replacement and School Command and the Antiaircraft

> Command inquired. Can Negroes be given observation aviation training? . . . Where can we send medical enlisted men for training? Second Army and the Flying Training Command inquired.[104]

Over and over again, the rigid separation of blacks and whites under Jim Crow rules hindered significant black advancement. With great regularity, the Army would announce training opportunities, only to hurriedly add a proviso that there were no appropriate facilities for Negro troops. At other times, when black trainees arrived at the relevant agency, they were transferred elsewhere without delay. Both Franz Kafka and Joseph Heller would have recognized a situation like this:

> The Air Force, desiring the Signal Corps to train Negro enlisted men for the 1000th Signal Company, 96th Service Group, learned that Signal Corps was training no Negroes in the required specialties. The Air Forces proceeded to make a search to obtain men from civilian life who had already had the required training and experience. Some six weeks later, it learned that Signal Corps was now training Negro soldiers in these specialties. Negro enlisted men arriving at the Parachute School in 1942 were immediately transferred on the grounds that the school had no facilities for training them and the Army had no units to which they could be assigned.[105]

Of course, the positions, instruction, and final placement that black soldiers did not enjoy were secured by whites, many of whom entered the military with limited experience, weak schooling, poor horizons, and provincial understanding. For them, military training offered a remarkable chance to break away from bounded prospects. Despite their second-class status, blacks too secured tangible gains from their time in the service. For some, there were radical changes in condition. But even in these cases, the limitations were almost immovable and the experience tinged with a regular and problematic imposition of racial borders. As with other New Deal policies, many blacks found and exploited openings that would not otherwise have been possible. But for most African American individuals, and certainly for the group as a whole, war service ended with a wider gap between whites and blacks, as white access to training and occupational advancement moved ahead at a much more vigorous rate.[106]

Not surprisingly, "the central point" found by a massive survey of black soldiers conducted in March 1943, at the same time as a large survey of white troops, was "the great extent to which Negro soldiers defined situations in 'racial' terms." Half wished to address President Roosevelt with questions about racism: "Will I as a Negro share this so-called democracy after the war?" "If the white and colored soldiers are fighting and dying for the same thing, why cant they train together?" "What are the chances of moving Negro troops from the South?" Where three in four white respondents thought they had been given a fair chance to win the war, only one in three blacks considered that they had. Whereas the replies of whites were consistent across educational levels, black dissatisfaction increased with greater schooling, irrespective of whether they lived in the North or South. "As the war ended," *The American Soldier* dryly commented, the black soldier was "less likely than others to think he had a square deal from the army."[107]

Even though many blacks gained advancement from their participation in the Second World War, the larger, overall effect created increasing racial disparity. The South held a tight grip on the racial policies of the armed services. Despite the valiant efforts demonstrated by black soldiers, the military, even if it had wanted to practice complete integration, would have found itself more unable to defeat Jim Crow than to decimate Germany and Japan's massive forces. Moreover, the lasting effects for ex-soldiers mirrored the experience of farmworkers and laborers, for postwar benefits created an affirmative action for white soldiers that contributed to a growing economic chasm between white and black veterans.

5

White Veterans Only

No other New Deal initiative had as great an impact on changing the country as the Selective Service Readjustment Act. Aimed at reintegrating 16 million veterans, it reached eight of ten men born during the 1920s.[1] Even today, this legislation, which quickly came to be called the GI Bill of Rights, qualifies as the most wide-ranging set of social benefits ever offered by the federal government in a single, comprehensive initiative. Between 1944 and 1971, federal spending for former soldiers in this "model welfare system" totaled over $95 billion.[2] By 1948, 15 percent of the federal budget was devoted to the GI Bill, and the Veterans Administration (VA) employed 17 percent of the federal workforce.

One by one, family by family, these expenditures transformed the United States by the way they eased the pathway of soldiers—the generation that was marrying and setting forth into adulthood—returning to civilian life. With the help of the GI Bill, millions bought homes, attended college, started business ventures, and found jobs commensurate with their skills. Through these opportunities, and by advancing the momentum toward suburban living, mass consumption, and the creation of wealth and economic security, this legislation created middle-class America.[3] No other instrument was nearly as important.

Fifty years after the death of Franklin Roosevelt, Bill Clinton affectionately recalled these accomplishments at a commemorative conference in Warm Springs, Georgia. FDR's "most enduring legacy," he contended, was not Social Security or any other landmark bill, but the "vision most clearly embodied in the G.I. Bill which passed Congress in June 1944, just a few days after D-Day," which "gave generations of veterans a chance to get an education, to build strong families and good lives, and to build the nation's strongest economy ever, to change the face of America. . . . The G.I. Bill helped to unleash a prosperity never before known."[4]

President Clinton reflected a widespread consensus. A year earlier, the editor of the journal of the American Council on Education prepared a special issue devoted to this omnibus program. He quickly discovered "the enthusiasm expressed by the friends, colleagues, and even total strangers with whom I had occasion to discuss my assignment."[5] As "the law that worked," one of his contributors observed, the GI Bill "enabled millions of working class Americans to go to college, buy their own homes, and become, in reality, members of the middle class." This landmark, he concluded, had produced "a true social revolution," one that "raised the entire nation to a plateau of social well-being never before experienced in U.S. history."[6]

The entire nation? This oft-repeated claim is remarkably misleading. To be sure, the GI Bill did create a more middle-class society, but almost exclusively for whites. Written under southern auspices, the law was deliberately designed to accommodate Jim Crow. Its administration widened the country's racial gap. The prevailing experience for blacks was starkly differential treatment.

At the time, some observers noticed. Two years after the passage of the GI Bill, Truman Gibson, Jr., Veterans Editor for the *Pittsburgh Courier*, documented "the sorry plight of Negro veterans, and particularly those living in the South" in a story headlined "Government Fails Negro Vets." He lamented how "the veterans' program had completely failed veterans of minority races."[7] The next year, *Our Negro Veterans*, a fact-filled report, drew attention to a "profound crisis" for black ex-soldiers. Summarizing studies conducted by the Bureau of the Census, the Southern Regional Council (an interracial group that promoted gradual change), the National Urban League, and the American Veterans Committee[8] (whose active membership included Franklin D. Roosevelt, Jr., and Ronald Reagan), it observed,

> There are two major sets of facts surrounding the life of Negro veterans in America today:
>
> (1) Over a million dark-skinned ex-service men are, by training, discipline, sacrifice, and determination, prepared for integration into the nation's life as first-class citizens. (2) The nation has almost universally failed to grasp the enormous opportunity which is presented through veterans' benefits for this minority group.[9]

It was, the document concluded, "as though the GI Bill had been earmarked 'For White Veterans Only.'"[10]

What had happened? How could a program so unparalleled and so inclusive be understood so quickly, and with good reason, as a policy "For White Veterans Only"?

I

IN THE MOVEMENT toward victory in Europe and in Asia, no one anticipated the profound ways in which GI Bill benefits and subsidies would help so many of the country's veterans. More than 200,000 used the bill's access to capital to acquire farms or start businesses. Veterans Administration mortgages paid for nearly 5 million new homes. Prior to the Second World War, banks often demanded that buyers pay half in cash and imposed short loan periods, effectively restricting purchases to members of the upper middle class and upper class. With GI Bill interest rates capped at modest rates, and down payments waived for loans up to thirty years, the potential clientele broadened dramatically. The balance decisively tilted away from renting toward purchasing. Between 1945 and 1954, the United States added 13 million new homes to its housing stock. In 1946 and 1947, VA mortgages alone accounted for more than 40 percent of the total,[11] a remarkable figure considering that young veterans were far less likely to have accumulated the substantial savings needed to buy property than those who had stayed home during the war. These loans were especially important in areas of high growth. In California, for example, the federal government only had insured 6 percent of home mortgages in 1936; by 1950, fully half.[12]

Residential ownership became the key foundation of economic security for the burgeoning and overwhelmingly white middle class. The social geography of the country altered dramatically.[13] The encouragement given to homeownership helped spawn the suburban sprawl that would characterize postwar growth. As Michael Bennett, author of the main history of the GI Bill, noted: "The GI Bill changed *where* and *how* Americans lived. Suburbs sprang up like mushrooms around every sizable city. . . . As surely as the Homestead Act of 1862 filled the prairies of the Far West, the GI Bill created and filled the suburbs."[14]

Accompanying this revolution in how and where Americans lived was the even more impressive expansion of education benefits. By 1950, the federal government had spent more on schooling for veterans than on expenditures for the Marshall Plan, which had successfully rebuilt Europe's devastated economic life after the war. On the eve of the Second World War, some 160,000 Americans were graduating from college each year. By the end of the decade, this number had tripled, to some 500,000. By 1955, about 2,250,000 veterans had participated in higher education. The country gained more than 400,000 engineers, 200,000 teachers, 90,000 scientists, 60,000 doctors, and 22,000 dentists. There is ample evidence that GI Bill students, who were older and likely to be more focused, performed at a higher academic level than their non-veteran peers after the war, and did better than any college age group in the prewar period.[15] Another 5,600,000 veterans enrolled in some 10,000 vocational institutions to study a wide array of trades from carpentry to refrigeration, plumbing to electricity, automobile and airplane repair to business training. For most returning soldiers, the full range of benefits—the entire cost of tuition plus a living stipend—was relatively easy to obtain, with access facilitated by a very large staff numbering some 225,000 by 1947, some serving in Washington but most in field offices.[16]

When he spoke at Warm Springs, President Clinton affirmed a long-standing agreement that the GI Bill's scope, influence, and democratic qualities had made it "the best deal ever made by Uncle Sam," the moment "when dreams came true."[17] From the start, the bill was enormously popular. It was passed by unanimous votes spanning the lines of party and region both in the Senate and the House of Representatives. Within eighteen months of the law's passage, Congress made its provisions even more generous.[18]

Celebrating "this remarkable bill" for making "massive tax-financed investments in young adults and families," Theda Skocpol, like many other commentators, has remarked on how the GI Bill "encompassed both more- and less-privileged Americans," and how "it joined benefits with service, citizenship rewards with citizenship responsibilities."[19] By democratizing access to education, diffusing skills, enhancing ownership, placing veterans in good jobs, and promoting geographic as well as occupational mobility, this federal set of policies created a world in the late 1940s in which "private life was aglow with possibilities."[20] The law enhanced the economic prospects of a huge proportion of young American families while producing social change "so sweeping and yet so much a part of everyday life that young people cannot imagine the world in which their grandparents lived."[21]

Aware of the possible benefits and advancements that lay ahead, black Americans also looked forward to the war's triumphant conclusion, hopeful that the GI Bill would improve their prospects. The back pages of *Opportunity*, the quarterly magazine of the National Urban League, began to fill with advertisements placed by black colleges. "Big post-war program is now laid for curriculum and building expansion," Maryland's Princess Anne College announced. "Prepare for post-war leadership," Kentucky State College exhorted. The larger, better established institutions simply listed their fields of study. Smaller, more vulnerable schools touted their distinct ambience ("home-like surroundings"; "gateway to Christian education"; "school of distinction and personality in the Sunny South").[22] Having endured a period of low wartime enrollment, these colleges sought to compete for the expected upsurge in demand once black veterans came home and took advantage of the higher education benefits in the Selective Service Readjustment Act of 1944. "It is agreed that never before in history has such an inclusive program been provided for national heroes of any war," Campbell Johnson, an African American colonel, wrote in the magazine's Winter 1945 issue. He stressed how this GI Bill of Rights promised each soldier, black as well as white, the status of an "unforgotten man."[23]

This did not seem a forlorn hope. The new law was more than the most comprehensive public policy to that moment in American history. It also was formally the most democratic. Unlike Social Security or legislation for minimum wages and maximum hours, no one was excluded who had served at least ninety days on active duty and had received other than a dishonorable discharge. Irrespective of region, class, ethnicity, and race, all veterans were equally recognized as entitled to the bounty of social rights. The GI Bill's remarkable array of advantages for American troops contained not "a single loophole for different treatment of white and black veterans."[24] It was, as Michael Bennett has put it, "America's first color-blind social legislation."[25]

The package of allowances and guidance—generous educational grants, subsidized mortgages and business loans, job training, and assistance to find work—thus summoned high expectations in black America. Though the armed forces remained segregated as the war drew to a close, each veteran, the law seemed to promise, would gain equal access to benefits that could not have been imagined just a few years earlier. Despite racial inequalities in the period's military, the legislation's unprecedented inclusiveness and financial comprehensiveness promised more than a million young black men and their families major improvements to their life circumstances.

Even with its Jim Crow structure, the Army had offered many, perhaps most, black soldiers an environment superior to their civilian situations. The Office of Education put the point in 1945, noting that military service "enabled Negroes to gain extensive and valuable occupational experience" in a wide variety of skilled and semi-skilled jobs. The level of black learning, moreover, had been raised by literacy education and officer training. "Many Negroes," this report observed, "will have gained some experience and knowledge in many . . . occupations, and with slight encouragement will seek further training. Here is offered an opportunity to lift a whole generation of Negroes onto another rung of the economic ladder."[26]

As they prepared to return to civilian life, demobilizing blacks thus seemed positioned to take advantage of the boost their status as veterans offered. By early 1945, the black press was crowded with stories reporting that "many GI's plan to study; go into business after war" and that "one third of soldiers plan more schooling; many taking interest in GI Bill."[27] Celebrating its official racial egalitarianism, these newspapers widely disseminated digests of the bill, summarizing eligibility for its various provisions.[28] All soldiers had access to publications like the brief "handy guide" prepared by the House Committee on World War Veterans' Legislation or the much longer *Veterans Handbook and Guide*, running some five hundred pages, published in 1946.[29] Opportunity beckoned.[30]

There is ample evidence that black soldiers expected the GI Bill to provide training and upward mobility, and indeed they applied for as many of its benefits as they could.[31] Testimony about the postwar plans of black and white veterans revealed far more similarities than differences. Surveys indicated that a large majority of all soldiers wished to take advantage of the bill. Hundreds of thousands, in fact, gained resources in many cases that were simply unavailable to non-GIs. To this day, many black veterans rightly credit these opportunities as turning points in their lives. There can be no doubt that given the paucity of other benefits and prospects, the GI Bill made a very big difference for these individuals.

"Imagine the excitement of men who could afford higher education under language that called it their right," the president of Spelman College, Johnnetta Cole, recalled in 1994, taking note of the impact of legislation not directly coded by color.[32] The law, as the political scientist Suzanne Mettler has argued, did extend "opportunity across the color line" and gave some, even many, black beneficiaries "boosts in educational attainment, income, and occupational status."[33]

Outside the South, some institutions that had discriminated against African Americans began to desist. In a study of the African American 92nd Infantry Division, Mettler found that some of its members had attended integrated institutions, including the University of Chicago, Purdue, Ohio State, Wayne State, and San Francisco State.[34] Within the South, enrollment at historically black colleges grew from 29,000 in 1940 to just over 73,000 in 1947, growth made possible, in part, by federal assistance.[35] Many famous African Americans, among them Massachusetts senator Edward Brooke and Federal District Court Judge Robert Carter, who gained the means to go to law school, and Harry Belafonte, who received support for training in the arts, were GI Bill graduates. Others, including Oliver Brown, the plaintiff in *Brown v. Board of Education*, used benefits from the bill to buy their homes.

It was this black section of middle-class America that provided President Johnson with most members of the audience he addressed at Howard University two decades after the end of the Second World War. "The GI bill was largely responsible," it is quite reasonable to conclude, "for developing a tiny group of professionals into the large, stable, and growing 'black bourgeoisie' that exists today, composed of doctors, lawyers, teachers, and mid-level civil servants"; and also that many political activists and civil rights organizers emerged from this group.[36] And it is reasonable to stress, if more cautiously, how GI Bill benefits "could take a marginalized population—African Americans—and boost many of its members into a productive middle class citizenry," or to emphasize how the bill "was creating a far larger black middle class than the past's cadre of preachers and teachers confined to the old Striver's Rows of segregated communities."[37]

When they could, blacks seized the chance. A systematic study conducted by the Research Division of the Veterans Administration in 1950 based on a survey of soldiers who had left the armed forces between September 1940 and August 1945 found that "the actual participation rates of the 14,571,000 white and 1,308,000 nonwhite veterans were almost identical: 73 and 75 per cent, respectively." Further, this study revealed that just over half, or 51 percent, of black veterans had participated in more than one GI Bill program, while only 44 percent of whites had done so.[38] Yet another study at the time found that the number of black participants was especially high among veterans who had taken part in the literacy program organized by the Army's Special Training Units.[39]

II

DESPITE THESE GAINS, Mettler's conclusion that the GI Bill "represented the most egalitarian and generous program black Americans had experienced, far more inclusive than New Deal social programs," is not so much wrong as misleading.[40] By amplifying the bill's achievements for returning black soldiers without sufficiently underscoring the high and often impassable barriers placed in their path, such an appraisal can be deceptive. When we take into account the legislative history of the statute and the way in which its various programs were administered, we come to see a rather different, more accurate picture. On balance, despite the assistance that black soldiers received, there was no greater instrument for widening an already huge racial gap in postwar America than the GI Bill. As southern black veterans attempted to gain from these new benefits, they encountered many well-established and some new restrictions. This combination of entrenched racism and willful exclusion either refused them entry or shunted them into second-class standing and conditions.

The playing field never was level. Indeed, one analyst maintains that "Race was contested terrain in the very inception of the GI Bill."[41]

When Walter White, executive secretary of the NAACP, wrote to President Roosevelt on October 5, 1944, four months after passage, to stress that "one of the most important instrumentalities toward assurance of equality of opportunity without regard to race, creed, color or national origin will be the Veterans Administration and the implementation by the Bureau of the . . . G.I. Bill of Rights Act," his words reflected a mixture of expectation and anxiety.[42] His hope lay in unimpeded access to material resources greater than any since Reconstruction, when citizen-soldiers similarly benefited. His disquiet was based on a deep familiarity with American racism and an understanding that the new law was vulnerable to Jim Crow.

It did not take long for reports of obstacles based on race to appear. "The discharged negro GI who returns to Lubbock [Texas] is having difficulty securing a home loan," one such story reported, in June 1945. Another from Los Angeles recounted how nineteen black Seabees who had been discharged without a hearing after complaining about "intolerable Jim Crow conditions at the Caribbean bases" had written to the secretary of the Navy "to ask for 'rights' under the G.I. Bill." A third from Atlanta described how a delegation "told the Veterans Administration on Friday that discharged Negro soldiers in the South are discouraged from enjoying the benefits of the 'GI Bill of Rights.' They are voicing the views of more than a million Negro servicemen and women, the majority of whom came out of the South."[43]

How could a program open to all veterans take this turn? The 1947 convention of the United Negro and Allied Veterans of America, a left-oriented group, tried its hand at an answer. It declared firmly that "racial prejudice" in the South "prevents the Negro veteran from securing full benefits under the GI bill."[44] But such a general explanation, true as it was, lacked one crucial political dimension. It missed how the conversion of bigoted values into racist practices had been built into the law's design and administration from the start.

The deep contradiction between color-blind benefits and profoundly biased allotments of resources invites closer examination. The GI Bill was crafted in the main by the Committee on World War

Legislation in the House of Representatives, which was chaired by John Rankin of Mississippi, one of the chamber's most unashamed racists (he was something of a thug, openly anti-black, anti-Jewish, and anti-Catholic). Guided by the model of administrative decentralization that the South had achieved in earlier New Deal laws, Rankin led the drafting of a law that left responsibility for implementation mainly to the states and localities, including, of course, those that practiced official racism without compromise.

The main forerunner to the GI Bill had been the unevenly organized benefits for health care, vocational rehabilitation, disability payments, and survivor's benefits provided for First World War veterans and their dependents between 1918 and 1928.[45] Three features of this legacy affected the shape of the new GI Bill. First, unhappiness among veterans with its often amateurish administration led to the creation of the House committee chaired by Rankin. Second, the direct federal welfare provisions that had been offered to families of soldiers during the war had unsettled many white southerners, who observed that with money in their pockets, black women often refused to take on menial household work and black youngsters stayed away from the fields. The supply of maids and farmworkers thus had diminished for a time. Rankin worked hard to avoid a repetition. Third, it gave rise both to the creation of a Veterans Bureau in Washington in 1921 (the Bureau became the Veterans Administration in 1930) and to a powerful American Legion, both of which sought to build support for munificent social provisions by appealing primarily to middle- and working-class whites in all parts of the country.

Moreover, officials at the Legion (which, like the Veterans of Foreign Wars, countenanced segregation and lacked any black leaders except in all-black posts) and the Veterans Administration (whose hospitals and housing were racially segregated) knew that legislation for veterans had to pass through southern hands and garner southern backing in Congress.[46] To cultivate this support, they made clear that they were disinclined to challenge the region's race relations and enforce equal treatment for all veterans. And they joined Rankin and his fellow southern representatives to oppose proposals put forward by the administration for a postwar program to be fully directed from Washington.

The suggestion by Roosevelt's National Resources Planning Board that postwar demobilization and benefits for veterans should be managed by "a strong central directive agency," with responsibility "for the integration of the administration of all Federal agencies engaged in the post-war readjustment of civilian and military personnel," was anathema to the South.[47] By contrast, as the commander of the Legion, Warren Atherton, put the point in April 1944, "We have endeavored to assure a measure of states rights in the legislation wherein control of many of the features of the bill will still rest with individual states." In writing to his deputy he further stressed that in the version he preferred, the one that passed into law, the VA would take care not to disturb arrangements within the South. Devolving administrative responsibilities to the state level would leave flexible discretion in the hands of white district officers to manage the law as they thought appropriate under local conditions.[48] The alliance of the Rankin-led South, the VA, and the Legion produced a bill combining generosity to veterans with provisions for the dispersion of administrative responsibilities that were designed to shield Jim Crow.

The most immediate precursor was Public Law 16. Providing for the rehabilitation of disabled veterans, it had passed Congress in March 1944, two months before the GI Bill. Rather than adopt the original proposal for a program to be administered centrally by the Federal Security Agency (the period's equivalent of today's Department of Health and Human Services), Congress placed day-to-day decisions about eligibility and policy in the hands of local district offices.[49] Three partners joined together to direct the legislation: Congress, dominated by southerners in key positions; the VA, happy to cooperate to keep competing bureaucracies at bay and to govern veterans' affairs one state at a time; and locally based agents who staffed and ran the programs in a manner consistent with their environment's racial laws and customs. The GI Bill extended and deepened this pattern.

President Roosevelt underscored the postwar economic benefits available to veterans, especially in the area of schooling, in a radio broadcast in July 1943, shortly after the draft age had been lowered to eighteen. The promise was politically appealing. It answered people's concern that depression conditions of mass unemployment might return, and it dealt with the social adjustment that soldiers, after their firsthand experience with violence and death, would soon be confronting. Almost immediately, members of Congress produced a surge of proposals, more than thirty, to reintegrate military veterans.[50] The American Legion sought to combine the most generous elements of these proposals into a wide-ranging program of loans, subsidies, and counseling. The organization's central strategy attempted to prevent the division of the bill into sections that would be directed to different congressional committees. Instead, the Legion successfully lobbied Congress to turn responsibility for the entire legislation to Rankin's committee, and a bargain was struck. The chairman now could guard the southern order and offer munificent treatment for veterans, advancing both goals at the same time.[51]

In the Senate, which played a secondary role, the legislative campaign was directed by Bennett Champ Clark of Missouri. His main task was to prevent Elbert Thomas of Utah, who chaired the Senate Education Committee, from taking charge of the education provisions of the bill, because Elbert preferred to place them in the Office of Education as a direct federal responsibility. With the South in control, a bill was fashioned in both houses that linked tight congressional oversight to locally compliant administrative decentralization. In this way, white privileges could be secured in the face of powerful impulses demanding equal treatment for all veterans.

The GI Bill's remarkable bounty thus could be directed to the country's poorest region while keeping its system of racial power intact. "Your bill," the director of a Mississippi business college astutely wrote to Rankin, "is particularly desirable for the Southern states."[52] He understood the importance of keeping the legislation's educational provisions out of the hands of the Office of Education, something of a wild card from the South's perspective. This agency, moreover, would have required 50 percent matching funds from the states on the model of the welfare provisions in the Social Security Act. By contrast, the approach Rankin took combined complete federal funding with state and local control under the auspices of the Veterans Administration. It also empowered private institutions, including banks and colleges, to offer services only to veterans they would choose to assist or admit.

Rankin fought assertively to make Jim Crow safe. He had reason to be anxious. The immense extension of federal largesse, he feared, could threaten segregation. He keenly grasped that black veterans would attempt to use their new status, based on service and sacrifice, along with a new body of federal funds, to shift the balance against segregation. Moreover, given the comparatively young age of the black population in the South, a significant proportion of African American men would be returning home after military service far more ready than before to assert their rights and claim their due.[53]

When the chairman's resolve wavered during the course of conducting his committee's nineteen executive sessions, the Legion mobilized the former governor of Alabama, Frank Dixon, and Stanley Rector, an expert on federalism whom Dixon trusted, to reassure Rankin that the racial status quo would be guarded zealously by the VA. Rector, Dixon informed Rankin, had been advising the Legion on how to prevent the bill "becoming an opening wedge for federalization." Rector then reported to Rankin just how clearly the approach to decentralization could be distinguished "from that of the social workers and planners in the Washington bureaus," who were utterly unreliable on racial questions.[54]

Throughout the process of writing the bill, Rankin was particularly worried about the educational provisions in Title II. With educators lobbying for a clause that would require the VA to consult the Office of Education and funnel funds only to institutions recognized on its approved list, Rankin insisted that the VA alone should administer this part of the legislation. The key paragraph stipulated the limits of federal power without any ambiguity. Rankin wrote that "No Department or Agency, or Offices of the United States in carrying out the provisions of this part, shall exercise any supervision or control whatsoever over any state educational agency." In explaining this provision, Rankin made clear to General Frank Hines, who led the agency, that "a definite line should be drawn in the schooling on the matter of race segregation." The minutes of the session, the historian Kathleen Frydl notes, "indicated Hines' assent, and the VA's record for sensitivity to local concerns spoke on his behalf."[55] Hines's successor, General Omar Bradley, recorded in his memoirs that "It was clear to all of us the best way to prepare the VA for the oncoming onrush of veterans was on a decentralized basis."[56]

The plan, in short, was designed from the start to mesh with the state and district levels of congressional representation and oversight in order to place vital powers in southern hands. Early in July 1944, one month after the GI Bill was signed into law, the Interstate Conference of Employment Security, a lobby group of state unemployment boards, insisted in a confidential memo to the Veterans Administration and the Bureau of the Budget that agencies of the states should "handle the interpretation" of the unemployment insurance section of the law, including "most of the disqualifying provisions." Decisions about who qualified should be kept in state hands. Some two weeks later, Hines affirmed to General Frank Yates, Acting Comptroller General of the United States, that the VA would not administer the legislation without the agreement of individual states. He took trouble to reassure not just the Interstate Conference but Congressman Rankin and other southern members that the VA's administration of unemployment insurance for black veterans would not undercut southern labor markets. Yates, in responding, avowed that "it is clear from the language [of the bill] . . . the administration of the VA should utilize, insofar as possible, existing facilities and services of . . . state departments and agencies under agreements executed with such departments and agencies."[57] As it turned out, local control strongly discouraged blacks from applying. Responding to an inquiry, the Mississippi Unemployment Compensation Committee assured

Rankin in July 1946, that after two years of eligibility for veterans, that some 2,600 blacks had submitted applications for unemployment payments, compared to 16,000 whites.[58]

To be sure, as a national program for all veterans, the GI Bill contained no clauses directly or indirectly excluding blacks or mandating racial discrimination. Even the NAACP's director of the Office of Veterans Affairs, Frank Dedmon, believed that "the VA administers the law as passed by Congress to both Negro and White alike."[59] But it was, as Frydl acutely observes, "a congressionally federalized program—one that was run through the states, supervised by Congress; one central policy making office and hundreds of district offices bounded, in a functional as well as political way, by state lines." Operating in this manner, she notes, the "exclusion of black veterans came through the mechanisms of administration," and this "flexibility that enabled discrimination against black veterans also worked to the advantage of many other veterans." In this aspect of affirmative action for whites, the path to job placement, loans, unemployment benefits, and schooling was tied to local VA centers, almost entirely staffed by white employees, or through local banks and both public and private educational institutions. By directing federal funding "in keeping with local favor," the veteran status that black soldiers had earned "was placed at the discretion of parochial intolerance."[60]

Sensitized by their experience of prior New Deal legislation, many African Americans understood the troubling implications of this key feature of the GI Bill. Shortly after he was hired by the Veterans Administration in 1946 as a Special Assistant for Negro Affairs, Joseph Albright quietly noted to General Bradley that equal treatment under the act was likely to be a myth. Though the law contained no racial distinctions, the assignment of powers to the states ensured discriminatory treatment for blacks. "The difficulties of the Negro veteran," he insisted, "are *not* the same as those of any other minority group of ex-servicemen, for the simple reason that all other minorities are considered as being white, and with but few isolated exceptions are treated as such."[61]

Similarly, in reflecting on the bill in 1947, W. A. Bender, an African

American minister from Mississippi, acutely analyzed the bind black veterans had been put in by this form of public administration. Writing to Ohio's conservative Republican senator Robert Taft, Bender identified "the first mistake" of the legislation as the choice "to bring different states into the set-up." Complaining that his own state's Department of Education had refused to approve many black vocational schools, he noted that "State committees appointed by Southern governors to control these schools start off with the determination that Negro soldiers shall not be trained under this bill, and they never let up."[62]

III

BLACKS ALSO FACED STRUCTURAL and demographic disadvantages—even if institutionalized racism had not been a key feature of the GI Bill, and even if it were the case, as the VA reported, that blacks in their twenties and thirties had been disproportionately underrepresented in the armed forces. A significantly lower portion had qualified for service based on the military's various tests for physical health, literacy, and aptitude. Throughout the Second World War, the rejection rate for blacks remained a good deal higher than that for whites. In all, only half of blacks in the relevant age group served in the military as compared to three out of every four whites.[63] Even in the period when manpower needs were most acute, black enlistments stayed at about 75–80 percent of the white proportion in the relevant pool from which soldiers were drawn.[64]

It is important to underscore, however, that this difference in eligibility was a good deal less significant in shaping the racial qualities of the GI Bill than the way in which its benefits were distributed by the nearly all-white decentralized apparatus charged with administration. Nowhere was this more true than in the realm of education. Even outside the South, black access to primarily white colleges and universities remained limited. De facto quotas and, in some cases, high selectivity closed these schools to the vast majority of blacks qualified for higher education. A Princeton poll conducted by a campus newspaper in 1942 discovered that nearly two in every three students opposed the admission of blacks, while those who favored a right of entry did so under the stipulation of limitations that "included such demands as a ban from Prospect Street, much higher standards than for white people, and definite quotas."[65] Of the nine thousand students at the University of Pennsylvania in 1946 (which, along with Columbia University, had the least restrictive policies in the Ivy League), only forty-six were black.[66] Writing about non-southern institutions, President Truman's Committee on Civil Rights found in 1948:

> It is clear there is much discrimination, based on prejudice, in admission of students to private colleges, vocational schools, and graduate schools. . . . Application blanks of many American colleges and universities include questions pertaining to the candidate's racial origin, religious preference, parents' birthplace, etc. In many of our northern educational institutions enrollment of Jewish students seems never to exceed certain fixed points and there is never more than a token enrollment of Negroes.[67]

In all, black enrollment in the North and West in higher education remained small, never exceeding five thousand during the late 1940s.[68] In principle, southern blacks could have taken their GI Bill vouchers to northern institutions, but this would have required overcoming persistent discrimination as well as discovering options about alternatives without access to adequate counseling.

So it was in the South, primarily in historically black colleges, where 95 percent of black veterans utilized their higher education benefits. As a lead editorial in the *Journal of Negro Education* underscored when the war was coming to an end, "The overwhelming majority of Negroes obtain their higher and professional education in segregated schools. . . . Thus, whether we like it or not, the problem of higher and professional education for Negroes is a problem of the Negro separate school with all of the disadvantages which that connotes."[69]

Still living in a world of segregation that had been sanctioned by the "separate but equal" doctrine the Supreme Court had applied in 1896 in *Plessy v. Ferguson* (upholding a Louisiana law that required separate railway cars for blacks and whites),[70] seventeen southern states stipulated separate schools at all levels. "White and colored persons shall not be taught in the same school," the Virginia Codes of 1928 and 1942 instructed. Tennessee law declared: "It shall be unlawful for any school, academy, college, or other place of learning to allow white and colored persons to attend the same school, academy, college or other place of learning." Mississippi's constitution was amended in 1942 and 1944 to specify which colleges were open to whites and which to blacks. For example, the state's code identified the purpose of the Mississippi State College for Women as "the moral and intellectual advancement of the white girls of the State"; in contrast, Alcorn Agricultural and Mechanical College existed "for the education of the colored youth of the state."[71]

The core of opportunity for African American veterans thus lay with black institutions. Seventeen of these colleges had been founded under the Second Morrill Act of 1890, which disallowed federal support to states if they did not create separate schools for blacks when other state colleges excluded them.[72] Of all the higher education enrollments in the United States, the region's historically black colleges accounted for less than 3 percent before and after the Second World War.[73] Both in absolute numbers and in proportion to their populations, white students had far more college places than blacks. Within the South, where blacks constituted a quarter of the population, white colleges in 1947 outnumbered black schools by more than five to one. In Mississippi, more than half the state's population was black, but just 7 of the 33 institutions; in Tennessee, 8 of 35; in all, 102 of 647.[74]

Throughout the country, colleges and universities struggled to keep up with the demand for higher education, but both quantitatively and qualitatively the problem was significantly more acute for black institutions, the poorest educational establishments in the country's most deprived region. During the war, as their enrollments decreased severely, their financial condition worsened significantly and their ability to maintain often inadequate facilities diminished.[75] It was to these places that the vast majority of the most talented and best qualified black soldiers had to turn. The GI Bill barely raised the ceiling on their ambitions. Before the war, many blacks aspiring to college were not able to go because they lacked the financial ability. Now that they had the means thanks to federal grants, the exclusion of so many and the substandard quality of the institutions, regardless of their teachers' best intentions, mocked the legislation's open-hearted promises.

Despite some federal assistance for black schools, the relative absence of support from the southern states left most black colleges unable to take in all the veterans who qualified. In 1947, some twenty thousand eligible black veterans could not find places even under incredibly crowded conditions.[76] As many as fifty thousand others might have sought admission had there been sufficient places.[77] Insufficient housing in segregated communities was a large part of the problem. "A survey of 21 of the southern black colleges," a recent analysis reports, "indicated that 55 per cent of all veteran applicants were turned away for lack of space, compared to about 28 per cent for all colleges and universities."[78] Alcorn State, the primary black college in Mississippi, only had room for four hundred.[79] Within the South's seventeen states in 1946, 51 percent of higher education students in white institutions were veterans, but just 30 percent in black colleges.[80] Without funds and facilities, there simply was insufficient room. By contrast, "flagship universities like the University of Wisconsin and the University of Michigan in the North and the University of Texas and the University of Alabama in the South were able to expand rapidly to meet the needs of returning veterans under the G.I. Bill."[81]

Though separate, black colleges hardly were equal. "Not a single one of these institutions offers work that is even *substantially* equal to that offered in the corresponding state institutions for whites," a 1945 assessment concluded, "and there is nothing to indicate that they will or can ever do so." At the start of the GI Bill, in Virginia, where Virginia State College was "one of the best of two or three of the Negro state colleges," the study found that "there is not a single library in any one of the nine white institutions—not even the teachers colleges—which is as small as Virginia State's. . . . It does not have the library resources, laboratory and other equipment, or personnel to maintain a first-class college," and the study concluded that "the State of Virginia does not intend to provide equal opportunities for higher education of Negroes in the near future; if at all."[82] Further, these tended to be intellectually and socially conservative institutions, with a "tendency to promote mechanical intelligence to the relative exclusion of both intellectual and social intelligences," as one 1944 appraisal discerned.[83]

Most black colleges were small; half enrolled fewer than 250 students and more than 90 percent taught fewer than 1,000 students. On average, the population at a black school was about half that of the average of 1,500 at exclusively or predominantly white institutions. Their budgets were stressed; their facilities often less than basic. Libraries were deficient; laboratories rudimentary. Given postwar pressures, these schools "admitted more students than even their increased plant facilities can reasonably accommodate."[84] Their faculties were understaffed and undertrained. Student-faculty ratios usually exceeded 20 to 1. Few, not more than 5 percent, were accredited by the Association of American Universities. Whereas at southern white colleges only two institutions offered training in trades, "29 fields of specialization were available in all institutions combined and all but 2 of these fields were listed by higher institutions for Negroes."[85] Similarly, there were immense disparities in the range of the liberal arts, and in graduate and professional training. No black college had a doctoral program or a certified engineering program. Only in the field of education was there something like parity across the racial divide, itself a reflection of the pressing need for black teachers in segregated primary and secondary schools.[86]

The pressure that veterans exerted on black institutions helped enlarge their curricula, which traditionally had been limited to education, theology, and various trades. Here the law's financial provisions did open doors where previously they had been closed. And those lucky enough to find a place had a much better chance at middle-class status than those who did not. Yet overall these gains were more limited, painfully modest, when set side by side with the vast extension of educational opportunity for returning white veterans.

The gap in educational attainment between blacks and whites widened rather than closed.[87] Of veterans born between 1923 and 1928, 28 per cent of whites but only 12 percent of blacks enrolled in college-level programs. Furthermore, blacks spent fewer months than whites in GI Bill schooling.[88] The most careful and sophisticated recent study of the impact of the bill's educational provisions demonstrated no difference in attendance or attainment that set apart southern from non-southern whites. All on average gained quite a lot. But for blacks, the analysis revealed a marked difference between the small minority in northern colleges and those students who attended educational institutions in the South. For the latter group, GI Bill higher education had little effect on their educational attainment or their life prospects.[89] White incomes tended to increase quite a bit more than black earnings as a result of gaining an advanced education.[90] As a result, the authors concluded, at the collegiate level, "the G.I. Bill exacerbated rather than narrowed the economic and educational differences between blacks and whites."[91]

IV

Of course, other schooling opportunities, including precollegiate vocational education and on-the-job training, beckoned. Such instruction formed a larger part of the GI Bill. In fact, over 700,000 veterans signed up for training on farms; 1.4 million for training on the job; and 3.5 million for vocational schools. Arguably, these subcollege programs, which cost the federal government $9 billion, were an especially significant means to economic advancement and stable middle-class jobs for the large majority of returning soldiers who lacked the level of schooling needed for higher education.[92]

Here, too, African Americans found themselves at a considerable disadvantage. Black access to agricultural training programs was limited both because such programs often offered wages higher than the prevailing levels and because southern administrators were reluctant to prepare blacks for farm ownership, one of the goals of the programs. They also worried that there would not be enough black farmers to work the land. A 1947 assessment of black veterans found that "On-the-farm training has usually been limited to owners and tenants, while most Negro veterans come from families who are either sharecroppers or laborers. The program is highly decentralized and the white land-holding interests who direct the training in many areas do not seem to be inclined to train Negroes to operate farms which they might some day own." These limitations proved severe. "Out of 28,000 veterans who have received on-the-farm training in the South, only 3,500, or approximately 11 per cent, are Negro veterans. Thus, only 1 per cent of the 350,000 Negro veterans who were drafted from farms received training for this vocation at government expense."[93]

On-the-job training, which paid veterans a subsistence allowance during their preparation for work in a skill or craft, proved a far more limited resource for blacks than whites. By early 1946, Georgia had approved 246 programs for job training; black veterans took part in six. Within the South overall, just 7,700 blacks out of a total of 102,000 veterans participated during the first two years of this program, reflecting the Southern Regional Council's estimate that only one in every 12 programs in the South was open to African Americans.[94] Before any veteran could enroll, he had to find an employer willing to take him on, a stipulation that effectively barred most blacks. White employers saw little reason to augment black skills. The much smaller number of black employers often feared potential competition.

The training usually was very meager. The 1947 report argued, moreover, that "a major obstacle" is "the attitude of state departments of education, who have to approve all programs. Many of these departments have followed tradition in conceiving of all training programs and schooling as being segregated, and have assumed that the on-the-job-training program is 'for whites only.' "[95] Often, these programs simply used the living wage provided by the GI Bill as a means to reduce or substitute for the wage paid by an employer. In some egregious instances, black workers were charged a fee by their bosses for the privilege of being trained.[96]

After he joined the VA as a special assistant, Joseph Albright twice toured its southern branch and regional offices. His first trip focused mainly on the woeful situation in black colleges. The second concentrated on employment. Again and again, he was told by federal officials on the spot that remedies for the problems of African Americans were beyond the scope of their agency. When Albright pressured the VA office in Port Jackson, South Carolina, to enhance black veterans' chances for job training, the area manager agreed that "all available opportunities for training Negro veterans" should be taken, but that "in doing so no action involving local customs should be taken which might reduce our already limited number of institutions offering training for Negro veterans." He went on to explain that such possibilities were severely limited "due to the fact that a small per centage of business establishments are owned and operated by members of the Negro race," while "white owners and operators of business establishments, due to long standing customs, will not accept Negro trainees, veteran or non-veteran, for training leading to objectives which are in the higher paying brackets."[97]

Since so many black veterans with high school educations were shut out of higher education, and since the average grade of education for black veterans was the fifth, most sought to enroll in vocational programs. These, too, required admission procedures that reflected a scarcity of slots. The act allowed each state to determine the number of public vocational schools. In the South, these segregated public sector institutions were limited in number, deficient in quality, and geared to send graduates on to "black jobs." An Urban League survey discovered that "Negro veterans attending trade schools have been particularly anxious to get training in radio and electrical work, machine shop and mechanics, business training, carpentry and woodwork, and commercial photography," only to be disappointed. "These trades have almost entirely been closed to Negroes."[98] Leading public black vocational schools often lacked facilities in such trades, by contrast to white institutions nearby, while offering classes instead in such fields as tailoring and dry cleaning.[99]

Side by side with these state-funded institutions were private vocational schools. Their expansion was astonishing. When the GI Bill passed, there were only thirty-five in the whole country. By 1950, the VA had certified 10,143.[100] Eager to move up the occupational ladder by acquiring new skills, African Americans were particularly vulnerable targets for all too many white and black scam artists who founded such "for profit" training schools funded entirely by tuition from GI Bill grants to individual veterans. Charging the top rates allowed by the law, many of these private schools were flimsy operations that provided little or no actual training.

A 1947 review by the Urban League of 314 private vocational schools for black students found most to be dreadful; worse overall than the inadequate schools blacks had attended before the close of the war.[101] Another report that year concluded: "Although these courses have, in every case, been approved by the Department of Education in the respective states, it is doubtful if many of them meet minimum standards for this type of training. In the absence of other opportunities, the Negro veteran may easily be exploited."[102]

Most state departments of education were too understaffed to impose minimum standards on these fledgling institutions. Oklahoma reported it had no ability to approve and supervise such schools operating for a profit. Louisiana and Mississippi lacked any process for approval. In the main, the problem of standards simply was disregarded. As a result, many for profit schools were fraudulent. Others offered training so rudimentary as to be useless. Because the GI Bill mandated state control, the VA could not supervise these schools directly or impose clear standards on the states.

Similar practices also shaped how job placement and access to capital for homes and businesses, the other key aspects of the bill, were administered. In these areas as well, the decentralization of authority from the federal government to states, localities, and private sector institutions vitiated any possibility that veterans of all backgrounds would be treated with at least a serious modicum of equality.

The United States Employment Service (USES) was mandated by the GI Bill to help veterans find jobs at their level of skill. Playing an active role in labor markets, it was the key agency for soldiers who sought information about employment upon their return.[103] With a staff of more than twenty thousand, it was well situated to help match workers with employers. The USES was radically decentralized in 1947. All of its responsibilities, still mainly funded by federal grants, were returned to the states. Before that date, in the early years of the GI Bill, responsibility lay with the War Manpower Commission and the Department of Labor.

Even then, the agency operated through local USES centers. When eligible African Americans applied for job assistance, their applications were processed by job counselors who were almost exclusively white and who tailored their advice to area conditions and practices. In the South, virtually no black veteran was given access to skilled employment by the USES, despite having had occupational training and work in the military. By channeling African American veterans into "black jobs" in the North as well as the South, the agency reinforced the existing division of labor by race.[104] By October 1946, 6,500 former soldiers had been placed in non-farm jobs by the USES in Mississippi; 86 percent of the skilled and semi-skilled positions were filled by whites, 92 percent of the unskilled by blacks.[105] Because unemployment insurance was made available only to those who could demonstrate a willingness to take a suitable job, and because suitability was defined by the USES, many blacks were compelled to take work far beneath their skill level. Carpenters became janitors; truck drivers dishwashers; communications repair experts porters.

A black field agent for the interracial Southern Regional Council summarized what the experience of seeking a job was like for many African American applicants:

> In trying to find a job he'd visit the local U.S. Employment Service Office. If he'll accept some laborer's job they'll readily place him—if he knows some of the old timey trades they can get him placed, but if he's qualified in some of the new skills that Negroes haven't traditionally been doing—or has some kind of professional training, then they just can't find a place for him and he'll be offered a job as a porter in a local hotel or the like.[106]

The case of Reuben Thompson of Rome, Georgia, who had entered the Army as a dishwasher but had been trained as a truck driver, illustrates how the process worked:

> I have been out of the Army for about five months. About a month ago I went to the U.S. Employment Service office to apply for a job of truck driving but I couldn't get one then they wanted to give me a job washing dishes but I didn't because café jobs here don't pay enough and I have a mother to support. They wanted to send me to a foundry I have not done anything like that and I am not able to. I put in for unemployment pay but I failed to get it. I am not asking them to give me anything if I could get the kind of job I am capable of doing. Most of the white boys get the unemployment with ease but very few colored get it.[107]

Blacks also were regularly denied access to the loans that the GI Bill promised. The federal government did not make loans of this or any other kind directly; rather, the Veterans Administration guaranteed them. In consequence, prospective borrowers had to convince banks to lend. And the vast majority of financial institutions refused to approve loans to African Americans. Black veterans were turned down because they lacked sufficient capital of their own, did not have established credit ratings, and lived in neighborhoods thought not to be locations for reliable investments.[108] They also were refused loans for nakedly racist reasons, targeted as being high-risk candidates. An irate black veteran in Corpus Christi, Texas, who had informed the NAACP that "financial backers of the GI Bill have so divided locations and placed restrictions on certain areas that as it is . . . NO NEGRO VETERAN is eligible for a loan," asked the GI Home Loan representative at the city's largest bank to explain why "a Negro veteran cannot obtain aid under this provision same as a white?" He reported the answer that came back as "It is almost impossible for a colored man to get a loan."[109] These impediments were not confined to the South. In New York and the northern New Jersey suburbs, fewer than 100 of the 67,000 mortgages insured by the GI Bill supported home purchases by non-whites.[110]

Applications for self-employment business assistance also were routinely denied to blacks, often on insubstantial grounds. Sharecroppers, for example, were told they were ineligible for small business loans because, having to share their profits with their landlords, they were not by definition self-employed. A survey of thirteen Mississippi cities by *Ebony* magazine found that of the 3,229 VA guaranteed home, business, and farm loans made in 1947, precisely two had gone to blacks.[111]

V

IT IS INDISPUTABLE THAT THE GI Bill offered eligible African Americans more benefits and more opportunities than they possibly could have imagined in the early 1940s.[112] Yet the way in which the law and its programs were organized and administered, and its ready accommodation to the larger discriminatory context within which it was embedded, produced practices that were more racially distinct and arguably more cruel than any other New Deal–era program. The performance of the GI Bill mocked the promise of fair treatment. The differential treatment meted out to African Americans sharply curtailed the statute's powerful egalitarian promise and significantly widened the country's large racial gap. Any celebration of postwar gains for veterans must reckon with these doleful practices and legacies.

6

Johnson's Ambitions, Powell's Principles: Thoughts on Renewing Affirmative Action

IMAGINE TWO COUNTRIES, one the richest in the world, the other amongst its most destitute. Then suppose that a global program of foreign aid transferred well over $100 billion, but to the rich nation, not the poor. This is exactly what happened in the United States as a result of the cumulative impact of the most important domestic policies of the 1930s and 1940s. Social Security began to pay old age pensions in 1939. By the end of the 1940s, its original provisions had been impressively improved. The GI Bill was the largest targeted fully national program of support in American history. The country passed new labor laws that promoted unions and protected people as they worked. The Army was a great engine of skill training and mobility during the Second World War. None of these was a marginal or secondary program. To the contrary, individually and collectively they organized a revolution in the role of government that remade the country's social structure in dramatic, positive ways.

But most blacks were left out. The damage to racial equity caused by each program was immense. Taken together, the effects of these public laws were devastating. Social Security, from which the majority of blacks were excluded until well into the 1950s, quickly became the country's most important social legislation. The labor laws of the New Deal and Fair Deal created a framework of protection for tens of millions of workers who secured minimum wages, maximum hours, and the right to join industrial as well as craft unions. African Americans who worked on the land or as domestics, the great majority, lacked these protections. When unions made inroads in the South, where most blacks lived, moreover, Congress changed the rules of the game to make organizing much more difficult. Perhaps most surprising and most important, the treatment of veterans after the war, despite the universal eligibility for the benefits offered by the GI Bill, perpetuated the blatant racism that had marked military affairs during the war itself. At no other time in American history have so much money and so many resources been put at the service of the generation completing education, entering the workforce, and forming families. Yet comparatively little of this largesse was available to black veterans. With these policies, the Gordian knot binding race to class tightened.

The most important feature of Lyndon Johnson's sweeping and assertive address at Howard University in June 1965 was his proposal to loosen this tie. He depicted policies that would not target the black middle-class audience he was addressing, but "the poor, the unemployed, the uprooted, and the dispossessed." At the time, he anticipated that the federal government would undertake a substantial effort to close massive gaps both between blacks and whites, and between more and less prosperous blacks. The past four decades have not been kind to this vision. Affirmative action has taken a different turn than the one envisioned in that speech. This concluding chapter offers a map to find the way back. It charts principles to retrieve Johnson's ambitious project. It connects those precepts to the history of racial bias that this book has chronicled. Finally, it sketches how affirmative action might return to the unrealized undertaking the president described as "the next and the more profound stage of the battle for civil rights."

I

WHEN THE PRESIDENT lingered to shake hands with the graduation audience, the civil rights movement, which had already begun to crest, was taken to a higher level. Though he doubtless understood that the vision of affirmative action he had just proposed would be controversial, he might well have thought the comprehensive program it envisaged could not prove any more difficult to achieve than the Civil Rights Act he had shepherded, the Great Society legislation he had sponsored, or the Voting Rights Act he was promoting.

Johnson's revolutionary brand of affirmative action, in fact, never happened. His desire to dramatically improve the lot of the least well off African Americans was never achieved. His sanguine goals were dashed by a number of events—by a radical transformation in race relations, the escalation of the Vietnam War, new divisions within the Democratic Party, and a Republican resurgence. After the bloodshed in Watts in August 1965, the intensification of racial violence in the summers that followed, and the spiraling use of aggressive racial language by enterprising white and black leaders, this plan became politically impossible. White public opinion, accurately reflected in the preferences of many members of Congress, revealed that a majority of whites were not willing to authorize a comprehensive racially oriented attack upon poverty and disadvantage. As a result, Johnson's vision came to seem like a mirage from a bygone time, and no social movement has since developed that could transform American society in this thoroughgoing way.[1]

But a first cousin, so to speak, a more limited race-conscious version of affirmative action, did soon develop. It was a momentous shift, nonetheless. As this book has demonstrated, affirmative action during the Democratic administrations of Franklin Roosevelt and Harry Truman had been exclusively white. Johnson's government turned this pattern on its head. After the Howard speech, a form of affirmative action emerged that opened access for blacks to jobs and places in higher education from which, in the main, they had been excluded.

Federal authority hastened the integration of many workplaces and universities and helped enlarge the black middle class.

As John F. Kennedy's vice president, Johnson already had had a hand in bringing forward the language of affirmative action. A year after the sit-in movement seized the country's consciousness in 1960, and just weeks before the Freedom Rides sent integrated buses to the South, President Kennedy issued an executive order in March 1961 to create a Presidential Committee on Equal Employment Opportunity. Two months earlier, Hobart Taylor, Jr., a young black lawyer from Houston, had been asked by Vice President Johnson to review a draft of this order. Taylor added language stating that it is the "policy of the United States to encourage by affirmative action the elimination of discrimination." Federal contractors, he further wrote, were obliged to engage in "affirmative action to ensure that applicants are employed and that employees are treated . . . without regard to their race, creed, color, or national origin."[2] Sitting back and waiting would not open the barriers facing African Americans.

As part of the quest for civil rights in the Kennedy years, affirmative action did not yet connote compensatory treatment or special preferences.[3] Rather, it simply implied positive deeds to combat racial discrimination. Yet even in the early 1960s the idiom of affirmation suggested more far-reaching possibilities. From the start of the decade, Johnson seemed to understand what he would later say aloud at Howard. Civil rights alone would not be sufficient. The growing gap between white and black Americans demanded more. When Johnson was designated in early 1961 to chair the Committee on Equal Employment Opportunity, he privately advised the president that the Eisenhower administration's non-discrimination clause for governmental contracts should "be revised to impose *not merely* the negative obligation of avoiding discrimination but the *affirmative duty* to employ applicants."[4]

In this early period of new, or explicit, affirmative action, it would have been difficult to foresee the form its programs might take. As Johnson's aspirations were dashed, an alternative model of affirmative action was developed by his administration; and it was secured, surprisingly, during the Nixon presidency, largely without the agreement of Congress and outside public view.[5] Federal agencies and federal courts soon required that employers and educators take race into account in order to rectify the second-class status of African Americans. An emphasis on specific, intentional acts of discrimination was supplanted by policies that gave advantages, even actual points, to membership in a specific racial group. Compensatory policies were adopted where black individuals could be chosen even if white applicants had more appropriate qualifications judged by customary measures like grades and test scores. Focusing on access to the top reaches of higher education and on highly desirable private and public sector jobs for people with considerable skills, these measures introduced a controversial new racial morality based on membership in a victimized category.

When called upon to interpret and enforce black rights, federal administrators in the Equal Employment Opportunity Commission (EEOC), which had been created by the Civil Rights Act, found themselves dealing with racial discrimination where individual prejudice and acts of bias alone did not account for the large differences in opportunity enjoyed by whites and blacks. Not without irony, it was Franklin D. Roosevelt, Jr., the president's son and the first chairman of the EEOC, who had to come to terms with these circumstances.[6] Lacking the staff or means quickly to process individual complaints, the agency moved away from one-person-at-a-time remedies.[7]

The EEOC dispatched racial reporting forms to all the employers and unions under its jurisdiction in March 1966.[8] Within months, the press was reporting that "the Johnson Administration soon will begin withholding federal business, at least in part, from contractors that fail to hire and promote Negroes and other minorities fast enough. . . . 'Affirmative Action' is the key."[9] By 1968, the agency had created a massive new source of data on racial patterns of employment in the United States. Now, it had a comprehensive collection of facts with which to choose targets of attention. Utilizing these statistics, the agency held public hearings, pressured companies and whole industries, and arranged conciliation agreements when the information the agency generated demonstrated disparities so large between white and black employment that "discriminatory intent might legally be inferred."[10] The burden of proof shifted from specific acts of discrimination to the justification of overall patterns of exclusion.

The Nixon administration, far from opposing these new measures, expanded the policy by further applying the doctrine of "disparate impact" (rather than "disparate treatment").[11] Seeking to embarrass organized labor, and enlarge a growing schism between the civil rights movement and white members of unions who might be persuaded to shift their votes to the Republican Party, Nixon enforced the Philadelphia Plan first drafted by Johnson's Department of Labor in 1967, which required that minority workers in the notoriously discriminatory construction trades be hired in rough proportion to their per centage in the local labor force. Soon, one or another form of the Philadelphia Plan—a plan Nixon called "that little extra start"—was adopted in fifty-five cities.[12] When the U.S. Comptroller General argued that this program violated Title VII of the Civil Rights Act, Attorney General John Mitchell rejoined that the "obligation of nondiscrimination" entails taking into account the racial implications of "outwardly neutral criteria" that might, nonetheless, produce deeply unequal outcomes by race.[13]

Advancing compensatory affirmative action of this type in the early 1970s, the Nixon administration applied a standard of "underutilization," identifying situations where there was a mismatch between the availability of minority workers and their presence in a particular type of job to more than 300,000 firms doing business with the federal government. In *Griggs v. Duke Power Company* in 1971, the Supreme Court authorized such programs. It found that the Civil Rights Act of 1964 applied not only to intentional acts of job discrimination but also to recruitment procedures, such as hiring tests, which were "fair in form but discriminatory in operation" because of their "adverse impact" on African Americans.[14] Company rules could count as discriminatory if they effectively excluded blacks or diminished their opportunity even if no such outcome was planned or anticipated.[15]

This decision marked a noteworthy constitutional turning point because it shifted the burden of proof.[16] No longer did individuals have to prove the discrimination they experienced was intentional. What counted, as Justice Warren Burger put it, was "the consequences of employment practices, not simply the motivation."[17] It now fell to employers to demonstrate that they were not discriminating against African Americans as a group. That year, the Civil Service Commission sanctioned the use of racial goals and timetables in federal government hiring. Comparable policies in higher education quickly followed.

Despite a long string of political and legal challenges, affirmative action has survived in this form first enacted in the late 1960s. In many respects, it has thrived. In sustaining and expanding a growing African American middle class that is better connected to the central institutions of American life than ever before, affirmative action has done more to advance fair treatment across racial lines than any other recent public policy. If affirmative action did not exist, the United States would be a vastly more segregated country. Without such efforts, most white Americans would have far less contact with their fellow black citizens. This post-1965 affirmative action has made our schools and our workplaces much more diverse. In the last three decades of the twentieth century, for example, some 15,000 black students graduated from the country's top 25 universities, some two thirds of whom had been admitted by affirmative action guidelines. Another 10,000 graduated from business school and more than 3,500 from medical school. In this era, the number of African American engineers and lawyers tripled; the number of black doctors doubled. In 1965, fewer than 5 percent of all college enrollments were African American, the same proportion as a decade earlier. By 1990, the per centage had increased to 12 percent, matching the share of African Americans in the population as a whole.[18] With this dramatic growth in skills, schooling, and certification, many African Americans—especially black women—have achieved quite dramatic occupational mobility.[19]

It is no longer conceivable to imagine American society without such gains to racial integration in our universities, firms, professions, and public bureaucracies promoted with the backing of judicial opinion and governmental regulation.[20] Even if Cornel West is right to call affirmative action a weak response to the historical plight of black Americans, it has been the most important tool that the federal government has endorsed and used since the heyday of the civil rights era to promote a more equitable society.[21]

And yet, affirmative action in this new century has reached something of an impasse. Its principles are insufficiently articulated, its legality is still in question, and its reach remains far more limited than Lyndon Johnson had hoped. Of course, we cannot return to June 1965 and start again. But we can envisage how affirmative action might be renewed and reinvigorated today in a form more in harmony with the objectives Johnson proclaimed in front of Frederick Douglass Hall.

II

AFFIRMATIVE ACTION PERFORMS acts of "corrective justice."[22] Public policy is used to compensate members of a deprived group for prior losses and for gains unfairly achieved by others that resulted from prior governmental action. Corrective justice, the legal philosopher Jules Coleman has noted, is different from a fair allocation of goods. Rather, it identifies interventions which remedy previously unjust decisions that made existing patterns of distribution even more unfair than they otherwise would have been.[23] When is such justice legitimate? How far can its remedies be extended, and on what basis? Can affirmative action as it presently exists, as well as a more inclusive affirmative action, rely on the same principles? How and when can they take race into account?

Strong opponents of affirmative action say never. It is important for supporters to meet the principled objections such opponents use when they call for an end to every kind of racially focused affirmative action with persuasive arguments pitched to the same level. If not, affirmative action will lack the reasoned thought explaining how past racial injustice should count that its legitimacy requires. Nor will its advocates be able to shape and guide the targets and measures of future policy "to end," as Johnson put it, "the one huge wrong of the American nation."

Though affirmative action's opponents have failed to eliminate race-conscious programs, they have succeeded in occupying the high ground of color-blind equality. Unfortunately, the arguments and rhetoric these adversaries have fashioned have not been countered by equally clear and defensible principles except for broad claims to compensation for the generalized history of slavery, segregation, and other forms of racism in American history. Defenders of affirmative action typically argue with a body of principled reasoning appreciably less developed than that of the opposition. "The theory under which affirmative action is justified is often not articulated," Jack Greenberg, the former director-counsel of the NAACP Legal Defense and Educational Fund, has remarked. Indeed, "advocates often do not define any supporting theory at all."[24] The respected journalist Nicholas Lemann has observed that while "the opponents of affirmative action have been honing their arguments for a good thirty years . . . arrayed against these compelling arguments is a very loud silence." Perhaps because proponents of affirmative action have been unable to persuade most white Americans that it is a good idea, they have mainly relied on decisions in executive agencies and the courts, usually skipping the effort to win broad support either in public opinion or in Congress. "So down through the decades," Lemann judged, "the muscles that liberals would have used to make a public case for affirmative action atrophied—and the conservatives' were becoming magnificently buffed and toned."[25]

Even the legal disputes that have reached the Supreme Court have been marked by this lopsidedness, with the honed principles of opponents confronting the more narrow and pragmatic stance of supporters. The structure of disagreement was present more than a quarter century ago when the Supreme Court decided in *United Steelworkers of*

America v. Weber to permit voluntary agreements that reserved half of all craft training positions until African American workers in a given plant came to match the per centage of blacks in the local labor force.[26] At issue in that case was whether Title VII of the Civil Rights Acts rules out the voluntary adoption of racial quotas to correct racial one-sidedness, and thus whether a compensatory program to remedy "manifest racial imbalance" is permissible when no proof of intentional wrongdoing or active discrimination has been demonstrated. Writing for the majority, Justice William Brennan reasoned in practical terms. He argued that prohibiting such hard targets in the name of the Civil Rights Act of 1964 would be excessively ironic. "A law triggered by a Nation's concern over centuries of racial injustice," he wrote, should not be used as the reason to prohibit "race conscious efforts to abolish traditional patterns of racial segregation and hierarchy." Dissenting, Justice William Rehnquist rejoined in a more principled way, stating there is "no irony in a law that prohibits *all* voluntary racial discrimination, even discrimination directed against whites in favor of blacks." He reasoned that as "the evil inherent in discrimination against Negroes" is its grounding in an "immutable characteristic, utterly irrelevant to employment decisions," discrimination is "no less evil" if it offers preferential treatment to blacks.[27]

A long line of Supreme Court decisions has navigated among these conflicting types of justification. It has not proved easy. Even within the same short period, as in the mid-1980s, the Court reached contrasting conclusions. In 1984, the Court ruled in *Firefighters v. Stotts* that senior white firefighters could not be laid off to make way for more junior blacks. Two years later, it ruled in *Wygant v. Jackson Board of Education* that minority employment was an insufficient reason to override the seniority white teachers had achieved. Yet it also upheld a judicially ordered racial quota in *Local 28, Sheet Metal Workers' International Association v. EEOC*, finding that the race-conscious remedy of numerical goals could be deployed to end the sharp underrepresentation of African Americans and Hispanics in Local 28, despite the fact that it did have some black members and that the International Union had repealed racial restrictions as long ago as 1946. Other decisions, including the 1987 cases of *United States v. Paradise* and *Johnson v. Transportation Agency of Santa Clara County*, further endorsed promotion quotas and voluntary plans motivated by the underrepresentation of minorities and women rather than direct personal experience of discrimination.[28] Tightly contested rulings and assessments have continued to characterize Court rulings on the subject ever since.[29]

The language of the justices has paralleled the uneven pattern dividing the types of arguments used by affirmative action's supporters and opponents in wider public and scholarly debates. Opponents have tended to argue that affirmative action is wrong as a matter of constitutional doctrine and principled tenets. "Every time the government places citizens on racial registers and makes race relevant to the provision of burdens or benefits, it demeans us all," Justice Clarence Thomas, only the second African American to sit on the Supreme Court, wrote in a stinging dissent in *Grutter v. Bollinger*, the June 2003 decision that upheld racial preferences in admissions at the University of Michigan Law School.[30] Arguing to the contrary for the one-vote majority, Justice Sandra Day O'Connor, the first woman justice, claimed that the compensatory steps offered by affirmative action in higher education fulfill a pressing social good, contending that "it is necessary that the path to leadership be visibly open to talented and qualified individuals of every race and ethnicity."[31]

In a long line of Court decisions, the opinion Justice Lewis Powell offered in 1978 in *Regents of the University of California v. Bakke* stands out because it both defended and circumscribed affirmative action on grounds that established clear, indeed principled, standards. Powell's guidelines can do more than certify the type of affirmative action that was created in the 1960s. As we will see, they also can guide a more extensive program closer to President Johnson's original intentions.

The Supreme Court had to consider whether the University of California, Davis, could reserve sixteen of its one hundred medical school places for minorities. Four justices (Warren Burger, William Rehnquist, John Paul Stevens, and Potter Stewart) found that this admissions process violated civil rights laws banning racial discrimination. To prefer on the basis of race, they argued, is wrong and illegal. Four other justices (Harry Blackmun, William Brennan, Thurgood Marshall, and Byron White) rejected the white student Allan Bakke's challenge. They reasoned that race-blind policies in a race-conscious society can make access by minorities too difficult. Justice Lewis Powell, the Court's swing voter, agreed that the constitutional requirement of equal protection had been violated by the quota system at Davis. Thus, by a 5–4 vote, Bakke was admitted to the medical school. Crucially, though, Powell also found that race could legitimately be used as a "plus" in making decisions on admission.[32]

In so ruling, he intervened in a debate far older than this case. After the Civil War, in the wake of the ratification of the Constitution's Fourteenth Amendment, Congress passed a series of race-conscious Reconstruction measures, most notably the 1866 Freedmen's Bureau Act, offering special remedial support to African Americans. Then, as later, supporters cited the need to rectify deep racial harms. Color-neutral policies, so soon after slavery, mocked the meaning of equality. Then, as later, opponents remonstrated against bills that specially benefited blacks, arguing that it is wrong to make "a distinction on account of color between the two races."[33] They often cited the amendment itself—stipulating that "No state shall make or enforce any law which shall abridge the privileges or immunities of citizens of the United States; nor shall any State deprive any person of life, liberty, or property, without due process of law; nor deny to any person within its jurisdiction the equal protection of the laws."

The Fourteenth Amendment's language about equal protection for all citizens has provided the bedrock argument for resistance to the way affirmative action has been conducted since 1965. It is not favored treatment as such that is in question. After all, any public policy, whether about taxes, welfare, or trade, confers advantages on some with costs paid by others. Legislation always sorts people into categories and ranks. Rather, it is preferential treatment for a group based on race. A central issue has been whether this mark of distinction ever can be taken into account legitimately in the public realm, and whether specific members of the disadvantaged racial group themselves have suffered harm as a result of membership in the group. Also in question is how collective racial categories can be squared with individual rights, and whether the costs imposed on whites to correct past harms to blacks are fair.

Powell rightly shared in the skepticism about the use of race in public life. Nevertheless, he authorized affirmative action within the scope of equal protection under quite demanding stipulations. Rejecting the claim "that would proscribe all considerations of race,"[34] he argued that modifications to color-blind policies could be undertaken to remedy race-based disadvantages when two conditions are met; otherwise, they are illegitimate. First, there must be a clear and tight link connecting affirmative action's remedies to specific historical harms based on race. This tie between past action and present policy has to be strong and precise; more general claims about racism in the country's past are not enough. And second, the goal to be pursued by affirmative action cannot be vague or only of moderate importance; it must be sufficiently valuable as a social good to justify suspending rules that ordinarily must be blind to race.[35] Further, if there is a non-racial way to pursue a given goal, that course should always be preferred. He insisted on these two principles—that racial injuries be specific and clear; and that a compelling public purpose must be identified when racial remedies are applied—because a color-blind society is desirable and color coding is inherently susceptible to misuse.

Powell's decision upset affirmative action's enemies. Writing in 1979 as a University of Chicago law professor, Antonin Scalia argued that Powell had been wrong to uphold affirmative action in any form. Restorative justice, he claimed, is inherently not right and not constitutional. "The affirmative action system now in place," he wrote, would produce perverse results that would "prefer the son of a prosperous and well-educated black doctor or lawyer—solely because of his race—to the son of a recent refugee from Eastern Europe who is working as a manual laborer to get his family ahead" because it "is based upon concepts of racial indebtedness and racial entitlement rather than individual worth and individual need; that is to say, because it is racist." This new form of "racial presumption" simply is wrong because it traduces color-blind standards. "From racist principles," he concluded, "flow racist results."[36]

Echoing the response to Reconstruction, affirmative action's challengers offer a rationale stressing that each individual should count as any other. Coding by color "is playing with fire."[37] Reverse racial discrimination can result in new kinds of discrimination. On this account, it damages the equality of individuals, undermines merit, and stigmatizes members of the group it advantages.[38] Racial categories are too blunt and inclusive to identify citizens who deserve special help. Individual rights always are threatened by racial counting. The price paid by whites is not just. So goes the argument.

As early as August 1965, the *Wall Street Journal* editorialized against "Negative Action," the label it gave to the dismissal of three white members of the CBS orchestra in Chicago in order to bring on three black musicians.[39] Soon, these themes were taken up by more scholarly authors. Writing in the mid-1970s, the sociologist Nathan Glazer remonstrated against "the new concept of 'affirmative action' that . . . assumes that everyone is guilty of discrimination; it then imposes on every employer the remedies which in the Civil Rights Act of 1964 could only be imposed of those guilty of discrimination." As a result, he argued, "the nation is by government action increasingly divided formally into racial and ethnic categories with differential rights," and he complained that the country now was partitioned between "groups that are entitled to statistical parity in certain key areas on the basis of race, color, and national origin, and those groups who are not."[40]

Such high-mindedness is too abstract and too removed from the country's historical record. "It is more than a little ironic," Justice Thurgood Marshall observed in 1978, in criticizing the admission of Allan Bakke to Davis, "that, after several hundred years of class-based discrimination against Negroes, the Court is unwilling to hold that a class-based remedy for that discrimination is permissible."[41] Powell disagreed with Marshall on the particular case but not on his broader view. Color-blind claims in the face of the racial dimensions of American history, he understood, furnish the misleading impression that color-conscious public policies supplanted long-standing and publicly legitimate color-blind practices only after the civil rights revolution and President Johnson's endorsement at Howard University of the standard calling for an equality of results. Glazer himself later took note of the moral authority of affirmative action in light of the history of black subordination. "The only possible comparison with Europe," he commented, "would be if the Saxons of England or the Gauls of France, had been held in a position of caste subservience for centuries." Further, as he acknowledged in a retraction of his former opposition to affirmative action, it was impossible to "ignore the remarkable and unique separation between blacks and others" that continues in American life.[42]

Blacks and whites have remained isolated from each other to a degree that would be even more pronounced if not for the limited type of affirmative action the country currently enjoys. In the half century since *Brown v. Board of Education*, the depth of racial segregation in most American schools, neighborhoods, and families has persisted. Of course, strict legal segregation has ended for schoolchildren, but, to date, racial integration, both in the North and the South, has not proceeded in the face of the pervasive residential separation of the races in suburbs as well as cities.[43] On virtually every social and economic dimension, blacks and whites are still a nation apart. The constellation of concentrated poverty, poor access to jobs, derisory housing conditions, high rates of incarceration, and challenges to traditional family formation continues to define issues of race and racism in the United States. "Negro poverty is not white poverty," Johnson declared, in seeking to understand these "deep, corrosive, obstinate differences." Now as then, the call for color-blindness implicitly scorns these social realities. At best, it is sightless. At worst, it is a soft version of bigotry.

Many supporters of affirmative action greeted Justice Powell's reasoning with dismay, but for rather different reasons. They were unhappy that he had held on more tightly to the principle of equal protection than the four liberal justices who found against Bakke. They also disapproved of his noticeable reluctance to grant African Americans as a group the same constitutional status as individuals who suffer discrimination. For this reason, Ronald Dworkin, the constitutional scholar, disputed Powell's insistence on quite tight standards and stringent inspection before affirmative action could be upheld. Powell, he argued, had failed to see that there is an important difference between the use of racial classification to inflict harm against the downtrodden and its utilization to correct or remedy these injustices.[44]

Two quite distinct lines of reasoning about affirmative action have dominated the arguments made by its supporters. Some submit a morally compelling petition demanding reparations for the great injuries of slavery and segregation. Speaking at the Riverside Church in 1969, James Foreman, one of the leaders of the Student Non-Violent Coordinating Committee (SNCC), read out "The Black Manifesto" demanding $500 million from the country's churches and synagogues for African Americans as recompense for brutality, murder, and exploitation. Since 1988, the National Coalition of Blacks for Reparations has been lobbying for payments to blacks descended from slaves. Its efforts have been endorsed by Michigan congressman John Conyers, Jr., a leading figure in the Black Caucus. Jesse Jackson has endorsed such a program of financial compensation following the 1999 UN World Conference Against Racism, and has made it a leading priority of Rainbow/PUSH. Two years later, a group of African American lawyers, including Johnnie Cochran, Jr., O. J. Simpson's attorney, readied a class action lawsuit seeking nearly a trillion dollars from the federal government.

In truth, the brutal harms inflicted by slavery and Jim Crow are far too substantial ever to be properly remedied. Epic historical crimes such as slavery, unremitting racial bigotry, and segregation are injuries that cannot be requited.[45] There is no adequate rejoinder to losses on this scale. In such situations, the request for large cash transfers places bravado ahead of substance, flirts with demagoguery, and risks political irrelevance. These calls also have practical problems. They suffer from slack precision and all-inclusive, grand dimensions. Who would qualify—only blacks descended from slaves or more recent African immigrants? What scale could cash transfers achieve? How could they ever be more than inadequate tokens? Whatever the abstract merits of such claims, this utopian politics seems entirely symbolic, not really serious.

Standing on lower ground, other supporters make more modest, pragmatic claims. Business firms defend affirmative action because it insulates them from anti-discrimination lawsuits. Universities appreciate diversity because it promotes intellectual pluralism. Various authorities argue that affirmative action helps secure racial peace and prevent "disorder and anarchy."[46] Some advocates, convinced that alternative routes to better social conditions for minorities are not available, promote affirmative action as the best available tool with which to achieve practical goals in employment and education.

Such utilitarian arguments tend to be shallow. Their ambitions are too small. They fail to make the case for corrective justice except on prudential or practical grounds. Rather than argue forthrightly that the purpose of affirmative action is to put a definitive end to the caste status of blacks in American life and thus also put an end to white privilege, or another such lofty goal, they identify aims that arguably could be attained by other means. Moreover, a pragmatic calculus, once offered, has to be considered in full. After all, it must be conceded, under some circumstances affirmative action can increase racial animosities, reduce standards in hiring and admissions, and damage the self-respect of its beneficiaries. To argue for affirmative action simply in pragmatic terms thus opens its various programs to cost-benefit calculations. Without a larger context of principles and priorities, it usually proves impossible to sort out when a system of preferences is compelling and when it is not.

In contrast to both sets of critics, I think Justice Powell's fine-grained assessment of affirmative action was just right. It would be callous to ignore the tremendous and devastating impact of racism on American life. In light of the particular harms inflicted on blacks in multiple institutional spheres, it has to be possible to override the understanding that equal protection ordinarily applies to individuals, not racial groups, in order "not only to end discrimination," Justice Ruth Bader Ginsburg has argued, "but also to counteract discrimination's lingering effects."[47] But such exceptions must be narrowly tailored. They must serve a sufficient public purpose to overcome a non-racial constitutional and moral presumption, and they must be conditional on the character and strength of the ties that connect specific past harms to present remedies. Every violation of color-blind norms, in short, must be justified with the goal of a just color-blind society in mind. Impartiality should be the predominant value. Wherever possible, race should not count for or against any given person. Not every injustice should be answered with preferential policies. When such corrective justice is utilized by the federal government, it must plausibly indicate the relationship between the victims of the given wrong and the recipients, some time later, of public benefits; and it has to show why a particular remedy is a good choice to compensate for wrongs committed in the past.

Building on Powell's principles has significant advantages. First, his demand for strict scrutiny appropriately sets the bar high, but not beyond reach.[48] It balances a widely shared desire to make color neutrality the dominant norm with the cheerless recognition that this goal cannot be achieved if the role race has played in American life is downplayed or, worse, ignored.

As such, this jurisprudence can appeal to the broad middle of the political spectrum. Properly explained and elaborated, it can widen the scope of support for affirmative action. As one example, Justice O'Connor, who, like Powell has often been the Court's pivotal voter, has endorsed this equilibrium. In an attempt to "dispel the notion that strict scrutiny is 'strict in theory but fatal in fact,'" she has written that even if ordinarily the government should not take race into account, "the unhappy persistence of both the practice and the effects of racial discrimination against minority groups in this country is an unfortunate reality, and government is not disqualified from acting in response to it."[49] Within the public at large, this approach offers the best chance to make it possible to win backing for what inevitably is a difficult set of policies to persuade non-beneficiaries to approve.

As settled law, Powell's deeply historical approach has been applied to the type of affirmative action developed during the Johnson and Nixon administrations, but it also can shape and motivate a considerably broader effort that might target affirmative action at those who are less well off. Affirmative action is constitutional, on his view, when the discrimination being remedied is specific, identifiable, and broadly institutional. Generalized racism or specific acts of individual prejudice or discrimination do not qualify for this kind of governmental response.

These distinctions place the onus of proof on the character of the historical evidence that is deployed to justify rectification. A focus on the policies that the southern wing of the Democratic Party successfully imposed during the New Deal and the Fair Deal is consistent with this requirement. They provide the content Justice Powell requires to justify acts of official rectification.

The *Bakke* decision, as we have seen, focused on higher education. In that context, Powell argued that affirmative action to achieve educational diversity was permissible because it addressed the specific situation created by the historical pattern of nearly all-white higher education. Considered in the context of the Roosevelt and Truman administrations, however, the harms inflicted on blacks by exclusion from national public policies invite a basic shift in focus and justification for affirmative action. Because such policies in the last-gasp era of Jim Crow constituted a massive transfer of privileges to white Americans, affirmative action can be redirected to this imbalance. The history of advantages offered to most whites and denied to many blacks in New Deal and Fair Deal policies is a particular story of targeted official institutional bias and great consequence. By understanding how the playing field fashioned by such fundamental public policies as Social Security, the Wagner Act, military segregation, and the GI Bill was racially skewed by design, and how their powerful negative effects have compounded in the past two generations, Lyndon Johnson's specific type of affirmative action can be advanced.

This history has been missing from public debate. Discussions about affirmative action usually begin with the 1960s, when its beneficiaries shifted from white to black. Such historical amnesia has weakened the case for affirmative action. The usual sole focus on present imbalances produces claims for racial rectification without offering enough historical justification to bring its benefits to most African Americans. Since all the major tools the federal government deployed during the New Deal and the Fair Deal created a powerful, if unstated, program of affirmative action for white Americans, the case for even more extensive affirmative action is more compelling than current arguments favoring such policies. Even today's proponents of affirmative action pay almost no heed to this recent record of profound and pervasive racial bias. Such a serious omission produces more than defective history. It limits the scope of public debate about affirmative action.

With hindsight, we can see that Justice Powell did more than turn a situational defeat into a strategic constitutional victory for affirmative action. The rules he designed to assess when the "plus" of race and affirmative action should be allowed to come into play can provide a framework to address affirmative action today. When this largely forgotten history is revealed and openly discussed, we can return to the goals set forth by Lyndon Johnson at Howard.

Retrospectively, we can also see how Johnson's graduation speech anticipated Powell's standards. The president's analysis of how the racial gap had widened, though deficient, sought to clarify the facts about the current status of blacks in American society. He provided a model of justification for affirmative action by summarizing the racial gap, arguing about causes, and spelling out why the divide distinguishing racial groups constituted a major public concern. By taking these steps, he fulfilled Justice Powell's second stipulation. He also sought to connect his remedies to the causes he had identified. In this approach, he followed Justice Powell's first requirement.

Combining Powell's principles and Johnson's ambition propels us back to the moment when key national policies advantaged whites. They also push us forward to a framework for public policies that can respond to the injuries inflicted by officially sanctioned racism. Though motivated by a desire to protect Jim Crow, many of the methods those programs used were adopted on a non-racial basis. A renewed, extended program of affirmative action could offer a reciprocal possibility. Affirmative action could be established in ways that at least partially transcend race, even while primarily rectifying racial injustice.

III

MUCH OF THIS BOOK has been an exercise in strict scrutiny. The application of this yardstick, the legal scholar Michael Perry indicates, has been "the Court's shrewd, practical way of ferreting out, indirectly or by proxy, what might otherwise be the hidden racist rationale for a law." For a given policy of exclusion to qualify as the basis that can justify affirmative action, such a practice need not have used race as an overt criterion through which to discriminate. Rather, Perry notes, the standards established by Justice Powell are complied with even when "the *real* reason for the law," its "actual basis," is "almost certainly racist."[50]

Not many statutes qualify. Usually, affirmative action has to be justified either as a response to unconcealed racism, such as segregated schools, racial covenants, or bans on racial intermarriage, or to established practices of exclusion not sanctioned by law, such as university admissions policies that often kept blacks out.[51] Of the subjects considered in earlier chapters, only military segregation possessed this nakedly racist character. By contrast, none of the legislation on social welfare, labor law, or veterans openly and unambiguously discriminated against African Americans. Nonetheless, the country's most subjugated, destitute, and politically marginal large group was given the wrong end of the federal stick over and over again. This history was the missing piece in

President Johnson's answers to the puzzle he posed about the growing disparities between black and white economic conditions.

Johnson's silence reflected popular memory and opinion, both then and now. Most Americans, including many African Americans, warmly remember New Deal and Fair Deal legislation. Social Security and the GI Bill are among the most affectionately recollected statutes over the past seven decades. This entire era, to tens of millions of Americans, summons up the image of a generous federal government that made a dramatic and tangible difference in the lives of the majority of its citizens.

Mostly for good reason, this high standing has become a routine theme in our public discussions. Freddie Mac, presently one of the two main pillars (alongside Fannie Mae) supporting housing mortgages, recently celebrated seventy years of national housing policy. Commemorating the New Deal, it placed advertisements headlined "The 30-Year Mortgage: A Unique System With Unique Benefits" in major American newspapers in June 2004. The one in the *Wall Street Journal* extolled the history of how, starting with the creation of the Federal Housing Authority in 1934 and the benefits in the 1940s, "federal support of long-term, fixed-rate and refinanceable mortgages has been continuous and indispensable." These loans, it noted, have been "the most democratic way Americans access capital to build wealth." It is through such means that most families "make their largest investment (their home)."[52]

This pronouncement omitted a key part of the story. During the foundational period of the 1930s and 1940s, these federally backed instruments, especially those created by the GI Bill for veterans, used redlining, local control, and overt discrimination to make it very difficult, often impossible, for blacks to qualify for mortgages. As in the other areas of public policy discussed in this book, the results that can be traced directly to public policy here were profound and long-lasting. Missed chances at homeownership obviously compound over time. Renters accumulate no equity, while homeowners almost always secure financial gains that exceed inflation.

The consequences proved profound. By 1984, when GI Bill mortgages had mainly matured, the median white household had a net worth of $39,135; the comparable figure for black households was only $3,397, or just 9 percent of white holdings. Most of this difference was accounted for by the absence of homeownership. Nearly seven in ten whites owned homes worth an average of $52,000. By comparison, only four in ten blacks were homeowners, and their houses had an average value of less than $30,000. African Americans who were not homeowners possessed virtually no wealth at all.[53]

Over time, it is much harder to make up gaps in wealth than in income. Slowly but measurably, the disparity between the races in income has diminished, in part as a result of affirmative action.[54] But the dramatic wealth gap has endured. At the end of the twentieth century, as a major study reported, "the net worth of the typical white family is $81,000 compared to $8,000 for black families . . . only 10 cents for every dollar of wealth held by white families." Having lost out in so dramatic a way when federal mortgages first came on line, African Americans have not begun to catch up. Today, "the most dramatic difference is the wealth effect of homeownership." The gains made by middle-class affirmative action helped increase black homeownership as a byproduct of more skills, better education, and improved access to good jobs. But whites, too, have moved ahead. The housing gap thus remains considerable, at more than 25 percent. It is especially stark at lower income levels.[55]

An array of economic studies of the period confirm the controlling importance of white affirmative action more broadly. Robert Margo, Thomas Maloney, and William Collins's detailed accounts of earnings have shown that black and white wages began to converge somewhat in the early 1940s, particularly outside the South. A number of factors were at work. The war created a tight labor market. Many blacks moved northward to seek war production work. The Fair Employment Practices Committee (FEPC), established in 1941, moderated racial discrimination. Strong unions began to include more black workers. The federal minimum wage rose from 25 to 40 cents an hour, raising the wages of all low-wage workers. But because blacks had begun from a lower base—the wages they had earned in unprotected occupations in the South—those who benefited from these trends found themselves improving their economic circumstances at a faster rate than most whites in comparable jobs.[56]

It was the reversal of this income convergence between whites and blacks that Lyndon Johnson underscored at Howard. With the war-era labor market no longer producing particularly favorable conditions for working-class African Americans, and with public policy now so powerfully and cumulatively shifting the balance of assistance offered by the federal government to favor whites, the black-white gap across a whole range of indicators actually began to widen.

Retrospectively, we can see what a basic branching moment this proved to be. If African Americans had been included on fair and equal terms in social welfare provisions, labor unions, work protection, the Army, and benefits for veterans, Lyndon Johnson might have offered a rather different speech in June 1965. He might have talked about a much larger black middle class, poised to take advantage of the chances the civil rights movement and legislation were opening up. He also might have explained how the national government had helped reduce racial inequalities during a period of mass prosperity to more manageable proportions, and how future policies entirely undertaken on a non-racial but class basis might close what remained of this gap.

By the time of Johnson's Howard address, the problems of black America, not only in the South but also in the growing urban settlements in the North, were growing worse after more than two decades of fiercely discriminatory public policy. Black migration northward and the beginning of desegregation in education eroded patterns of insulation that had protected the jobs of some members of the black middle class. There were lags in training, and a mismatch between the acquisition of skills by blacks and the characteristics of new middle-class jobs. Discrimination by employers, banks, landlords, and other purveyors of economic opportunity persisted. What is striking, however, is how the hallmark social policy innovations of the New Deal and the Fair Deal themselves operated more as brakes than as accelerators in incorporating African Americans into the country's rapidly expanding postwar middle class.

If Lyndon Johnson were speaking today, four decades later, he would still have to talk about black isolation. He would remark on large differences in income and wealth; oppressive levels of unemployment; high victimization, crime, and incarceration; much lower rates for school completion and marriage; and vast, often debilitating hardship for black children. Although the gap in education and earnings between whites and blacks has steadily closed for the top third of African Americans, the median income of the great majority of blacks lags behind that of whites by about one third; and the figures for family wealth are even more unequal, not only in homeownership but in other assets such as stock holdings, savings accounts, and retirement funds. This gap in net worth grew substantially in the 1990s with the run-up in the value of real estate and stocks. The old advantages and disadvantages have continued to compound.[57]

IV

THEN AT THE HELM OF THE Equal Employment Opportunity Commission, Clarence Thomas argued in 1987 that "The legal debate over affirmative action . . . is behind us." The same year, the eminent legal scholar Herman Schwartz estimated that "the affirmative action wars are over."[58] We now know, of course, they were both wrong. But the terms of reference and the repertoire of reasons that both sides in the argument have continued to deploy already were quite common at the time. Since, they have become fixed rituals pitting advocates of rectification against those who believe affirmative action perversely makes the disease of racism the cure.

All the while, the Supreme Court has sustained programs of racial rectification only by the thinnest possible margin, most recently in the decision about affirmative action at the University of Michigan,

Grutter v. Bollinger.[59] The shift of a single vote still could doom them. Some states, notably California and Washington, have amended their constitutions by referenda to prohibit any consideration of race in activities carried out by their governments.[60] In others, including Florida, Georgia, Mississippi, and Texas, governors and attorneys general have ended or severely restricted the operation of affirmative action. Politicians often mobilize voters by fighting racial preferences. At best, public opinion is conflicted. Most whites believe racial discrimination has declined so much that affirmative action's challenge to competition and mobility based on individual merit, effort, ambition, and color-blind equal opportunity is needed no longer. Others dislike it for uglier reasons.[61] Even if, on balance, affirmative action is likely to continue to move ahead in its now familiar groove, there are no grounds for complacency. In its present form, it is legally and politically insecure.

How can affirmative action be made both less vulnerable and less limited? Is it possible to move the debate beyond its familiar, by now unproductive inventory of positions? Can novel ways be found to talk about and advance the type of affirmative action that never was achieved?

These goals require coming to terms with the implications of the critical moment when affirmative action was white. Tracing its baneful influence is more than an exercise in revisionist history. It can help activate a broad application of Justice Powell's active standards in light of President Johnson's dormant aspirations. That history provides the necessary pivot joining constitutional backing to potential political support to broaden affirmative action from its primary focus on the black middle class.

In taking this turn, it will be important to distinguish when public policy should invoke racially specific remedies and when it should not. Of the various injuries inflicted by the national government for racial reasons reviewed in this book, only military segregation explicitly endorsed the practices, even the rationale, of Jim Crow. In this case, the relevant remedies have already been offered. Today, the armed forces in the United States provides excellent prospects for African Americans—better opportunities than those in any other institutional sphere in American life, perhaps with the exception of our most selective universities.

Curiously, a series of forgotten early experiments in affirmative action by the military just after the Second World War can help point the way. Affirmative action for blacks began well before the term existed. With millions of soldiers coming home but security needs still pressing, the Department of War conducted a sober assessment of the campaigns in Europe, North Africa, and Asia. The way race had been handled, it concluded, had diminished the fighting capability of the armed forces. Responding to the study, the military decided to raise the educational level of black troops to improve their readiness and create a deeper pool from which to recruit black officers. The Far East Command established such a program, aimed principally at blacks, to bring every soldier to a fifth-grade standard. Elsewhere, race was used more explicitly to define eligibility. At Georgia's Fort Benning, the Army initiated an educational program for members of the all-black 25th Combat Regiment who had secured less than an eighth-grade education. But the most far-reaching program took place in occupied Germany. Starting in 1947, thousands of black soldiers undergoing basic military training at the Grafenwohr Training Center received daily instruction for three months in academic subjects up to the level of the twelfth grade.

Soon, the training center moved to larger quarters at Mannheim Koafestal. By the close of the year, the results had been so positive that a larger, remarkably comprehensive program exclusively for black soldiers was launched at Germany's Kitzingen Air Base. All African American troops arriving from the United States passed through the program. Black units stationed in Europe were required to rotate through Kitzingen for refresher courses. Once this on-site instruction was completed, Army instructors traveled with the soldiers to continue their schooling in the field. The participants were required to stick with the course until they reached a high school equivalency level or demonstrated they could make no further gains. By 1950, two thirds of the 2,900 black soldiers in Europe were enrolled.

Military affirmative action worked. These men made striking advances in Army classification tests. That year, the European Command estimated that the program "was producing some of the finest trained black troops in the Army." Soon, the number of qualified black officers increased considerably.[62] Breaking with the masked white affirmative action of the 1930s and 1940s, race counted positively and explicitly to improve the circumstances of African Americans.

The use of federal power to advantage the country's most subjugated group promptly generated both the objections and the defenses recognizable to us today. With a shift in the racial target, many whites, then as still now, issued a call for color-blind policies. How could it be fair, they asked, that Kitzingen's schooling was reserved absolutely for blacks or that the courses offered to black soldiers were superior to the far more limited educational programs for literacy training then available to white troops? The military's response, based on the effects of historical patterns, was summarized by an official Army historian: "Command spokesmen quite openly justified the disparity on the grounds that Negroes on the whole had received fewer educational opportunities in the United States."[63] The military did not, directly, explicitly connect these programs to its own ugly history of segregation; but its responsible authorities did rightly distinguish the deployment of race to remedy injustice from the use of racial categories to create injustice.

These were programs without a name. They were soon forgotten.[64] But they established a positive mass-based model justified by principles much like those Justice Powell later elaborated. Because these policies fashioned by the Department of War were initiated without political consultation, they anticipated future aspects of affirmative action that were administered by regulatory bureaucracies rather than in an open political process. In this respect, they are not an appealing example. Any next steps must move through the democratic process on the basis of a broad and popular constituency.

Is this possible? I believe it is if the following conditions are complied with. Advocates of affirmative action must use the kind of rationale Johnson announced at Howard and the standards Powell certified in *Bakke.* These programs should neither be permanent nor typical of how government acts. They are called for to right particular past wrongs. In that, they are just. But they also are in the interest of all Americans. Properly tailored and bounded in time, they can help transcend, once and for all, not only the practice of racism but its enduring legacies. The best case for affirmative action is neither some very general reparation for massive harms nor the lighter and more limited, if desirable, objective of diversity. Rather, as the legal scholar Jack Greenberg has argued, the most compelling practical and moral goal should be that of "bettering the social conditions in which African-Americans live," conditions that "affect everyone in our society."[65]

Beneficiaries must be targeted with clarity and care. The colorblind critique argues that race, as a group category, is morally unacceptable even when it is used to counter discrimination. But this view misses an important distinction. African American individuals have been discriminated against because they were black, and for no other reason. Obviously, this violates basic norms of fairness. Under affirmative action, they are compensated not for being black but only because they were subject to unfair treatment at an earlier moment because they were black.[66] If, for others, the policies also were unjust, they, too, must be included in the remedies. When national policy kept out farmworkers and maids, the injury was not limited to African Americans.[67] Nor should the remedy be.

On this understanding it is important to identify recipients of affirmative compensation who have a direct relationship to the harm being remedied. This does not mean that they had to experience a specific act of discrimination directly. To qualify, however, it needs to be shown how discriminatory institutions, decisions, actions, and practices have negatively affected their circumstances. This approach does not limit remedies to individuals who have faced injustice directly, one at a time; neither does it justify remedies for African Americans as an exclusive group that has shared in a history of racism except when the harm, as in military segregation, was created with unambiguously racist categories.

Popular and political support, in short, as well as judicial legitimacy, will depend on the clarity and persuasiveness of the association between harms and remedies. One of two approaches is possible. In the first, a closely targeted program of corrective justice would search for identifiable individuals who have been harmed—even at the distance of one or two generations—by the pattern of exclusions and local administration this book has documented. This policy could yield both tangible and symbolic compensation. As examples:

- For the lag in entering the Social Security system, the excluded could be identified and they, or their heirs, could be offered one-time grants that would have to be paid into designated retirement funds.
- For the absence of access to the minimum wage, tax credits to an equivalence of the average loss could be tendered.
- For the lack of access to key programs under the GI Bill, programs of subsidized mortgages, small business loans, and educational grants could now be put in place.

These measures could be targeted toward those who stand in a direct line to people who were harmed; but both to keep the costs in check and to target spending on those most in need, they would also be available only up to a certain level before being taxed back.

Alternatively, a less administratively burdensome but still exacting approach could be crafted. Here, the broad target for assertive federal policies would be poor Americans who face conditions produced by the constellation of patterns of eligibility and administration the South placed inside the most important New Deal and Fair Deal programs. Although less exact at the individual and family level, this approach would authorize a major assault on inequality and poverty which would be justified by these historical patterns and remedied by interventions offering boosts into middle-class status. The major instruments would be the same as those the federal government utilized in the GI Bill: subsidized mortgages; generous grants for education and training; small business loans; and active job searching and placement. This line of attack also could deploy an expanded Earned Income Tax Credit, assure generous child care, and guarantee basic health insurance.

Either way, we have to identify not only the persons, or group of people, but the specific qualities of racial discrimination. There is something of a hierarchy. Individual private acts of prejudice and discrimination count for less than more pervasive institutional ones. Injuries dealt by government count for more than private patterns of institutional racism. When government is directly involved, claims for systemic compensation to match systemic harm become most compelling. Public policies, after all, have been the most decisive instruments dividing Americans into different racial groups with vastly different circumstances and possibilities.

Finally, it is worth remembering that more than material injuries remain to be addressed. For this reason, even when remedies are crafted in a way that moves the country toward a fully integrated, color-blind society, the racist motivations and primary targets of those who crafted affirmative action for whites must not be repressed. The programs discussed in this book did far more than cost people money or opportunity. They also projected humiliation, while stunting human imagination and possibility. Appropriate signs and deeds would represent a collective apology, and indicate a communal desire to transcend such insults, especially where they were based on racial, and racist, distinctions.[68]

After a review of affirmative action, President Bill Clinton famously proposed to mend, not end it. My appeal is different: Extend affirmative action in order to end it within one generation. If such a project were to succeed, the next assessment of affirmative action a president offers at Howard University could well be a celebration of success and culmination. Only then will affirmative action no longer be white or black.

APPENDIX: "TO FULFILL THESE RIGHTS"

President Lyndon B. Johnson's
Commencement Address at Howard University,
June 4, 1965

Dr. Nabrit, my fellow Americans:

I am delighted at the chance to speak at this important and this historic institution. Howard has long been an outstanding center for the education of Negro Americans. Its students are of every race and color and they come from many countries of the world. It is truly a working example of democratic excellence.

Our earth is the home of revolution. In every corner of every continent men charged with hope contend with ancient ways in the pursuit of justice. They reach for the newest of weapons to realize the oldest of dreams, that each may walk in freedom and pride, stretching his talents, enjoying the fruits of the earth.

Our enemies may occasionally seize the day of change, but it is the banner of our revolution they take. And our own future is linked to this process of swift and turbulent change in many lands in the world. But nothing in any country touches us more profoundly, and nothing is more freighted with meaning for our own destiny than the revolution of the Negro American.

In far too many ways American Negroes have been another nation: deprived of freedom, crippled by hatred, the doors of opportunity closed to hope.

In our time change has come to this Nation, too. The American Negro, acting with impressive restraint, has peacefully protested and marched, entered the courtrooms and the seats of government, demanding a justice that has long been denied. The voice of the Negro was the call to action. But it is a tribute to America that, once aroused, the courts and the Congress, the President and most of the people, have been the allies of progress.

Legal Protection for Human Rights

Thus we have seen the high court of the country declare that discrimination based on race was repugnant to the Constitution, and therefore void. We have seen in 1957, and 1960, and again in 1964, the first civil rights legislation in this Nation in almost an entire century.

As majority leader of the United States Senate, I helped to guide two of these bills through the Senate. And, as your President, I was proud to sign the third. And now very soon we will have the fourth—a new law guaranteeing every American the right to vote.

No act of my entire administration will give me greater satisfaction than the day when my signature makes this bill, too, the law of this land.

The voting rights bill will be the latest, and among the most important, in a long series of victories. But this victory—as Winston Churchill said of another triumph for freedom—"is not the end. It is not even the beginning of the end. But it is, perhaps, the end of the beginning."

That beginning is freedom; and the barriers to that freedom are tumbling down. Freedom is the right to share, share fully and equally, in American society—to vote, to hold a job, to enter a public place, to go to school. It is the right to be treated in every part of our national life as a person equal in dignity and promise to all others.

Freedom Is Not Enough

But freedom is not enough. You do not wipe away the scars of centuries by saying: Now you are free to go where you want, and do as you desire, and choose the leaders you please.

You do not take a person who, for years, has been hobbled by chains and liberate him, bring him up to the starting line of a race and then say, "you are free to compete with all the others," and still justly believe that you have been completely fair.

Thus it is not enough just to open the gates of opportunity. All our citizens must have the ability to walk through those gates.

This is the next and the more profound stage of the battle for civil rights. We seek not just freedom but opportunity. We seek not just legal equity but human ability, not just equality as a right and a theory but equality as a fact and equality as a result.

For the task is to give 20 million Negroes the same chance as every other American to learn and grow, to work and share in society, to develop their abilities—physical, mental and spiritual, and to pursue their individual happiness.

To this end equal opportunity is essential, but not enough, not enough. Men and women of all races are born with the same range of abilities. But ability is not just the product of birth. Ability is stretched or stunted by the family that you live with, and the neighborhood you live in—by the school you go to and the poverty or the richness of your surroundings. It is the product of a hundred unseen forces playing upon the little infant, the child, and finally the man.

Progress for Some

This graduating class at Howard University is witness to the indomitable determination of the Negro American to win his way in American life.

The number of Negroes in schools of higher learning has almost doubled in 15 years. The number of nonwhite professional workers has more than doubled in 10 years. The median income of Negro college women tonight exceeds that of white college women. And there are also the enormous accomplishments of distinguished individual Negroes—many of them graduates of this institution, and one of them the first lady ambassador in the history of the United States.

These are proud and impressive achievements. But they tell only the story of a growing middle class minority, steadily narrowing the gap between them and their white counterparts.

A Widening Gulf

But for the great majority of Negro Americans—the poor, the unemployed, the uprooted, and the dispossessed—there is a much grimmer story. They still, as we meet here tonight, are another nation. Despite the court orders and the laws, despite the legislative victories and the speeches, for them the walls are rising and the gulf is widening.

Here are some of the facts of this American failure.

Thirty-five years ago the rate of unemployment for Negroes and whites was about the same. Tonight the Negro rate is twice as high.

In 1948 the 8 percent unemployment rate for Negro teenage boys was actually less than that of whites. By last year that rate had grown to 23 percent, as against 13 percent for whites unemployed.

Between 1949 and 1959, the income of Negro men relative to white men declined in every section of this country. From 1952 to 1963 the median income of Negro families compared to white actually dropped from 57 percent to 53 percent.

In the years 1955 through 1957, 22 percent of experienced Negro workers were out of work at some time during the year. In 1961 through 1963 that proportion had soared to 29 percent.

Since 1947 the number of white families living in poverty has decreased 27 percent while the number of poorer nonwhite families decreased only 3 percent.

The infant mortality of nonwhites in 1940 was 70 percent greater than whites. Twenty-two years later it was 90 percent greater.

Moreover, the isolation of Negro from white communities is increasing, rather than decreasing as Negroes crowd into the central cities and become a city within a city.

Of course Negro Americans as well as white Americans have shared in our rising national abundance. But the harsh fact of the matter is that in the battle for true equality too many—far too many—are losing ground every day.

The Causes of Inequality

We are not completely sure why this is. We know the causes are complex and subtle. But we do know the two broad basic reasons. And we do know that we have to act.

First, Negroes are trapped—as many whites are trapped—in inherited, gateless poverty. They lack training and skills. They are shut in, in slums, without decent medical care. Private and public poverty combine to cripple their capacities.

We are trying to attack these evils through our poverty program, through our education program, through our medical care and our other health programs, and a dozen more of the Great Society programs that are aimed at the root causes of this poverty.

We will increase, and we will accelerate, and we will broaden this attack in years to come until this most enduring of foes finally yields to our unyielding will.

But there is a second cause—much more difficult to explain, more deeply grounded, more desperate in its force. It is the devastating heritage of long years of slavery; and a century of oppression, hatred, and injustice.

Special Nature of Negro Poverty

For Negro poverty is not white poverty. Many of its causes and many of its cures are the same. But there are differences—deep, corrosive, obstinate differences—radiating painful roots into the community, and into the family, and the nature of the individual.

These differences are not racial differences. They are solely and simply the consequence of ancient brutality, past injustice, and present prejudice. They are anguishing to observe. For the Negro they are a constant reminder of oppression. For the white they are a constant reminder of guilt. But they must be faced and they must be dealt with and they must be overcome, if we are ever to reach the time when the only difference between Negroes and whites is the color of their skin.

Nor can we find a complete answer in the experience of other American minorities. They made a valiant and a largely successful effort to emerge from poverty and prejudice.

The Negro, like these others, will have to rely mostly upon his own efforts. But he just cannot do it alone. For they did not have the heritage of centuries to overcome, and they did not have a cultural tradition which had been twisted and battered by endless years of hatred and hopelessness, nor were they excluded—these others—because of race or color—a feeling whose dark intensity is matched by no other prejudice in our society.

Nor can these differences be understood as isolated infirmities. They are a seamless web. They cause each other. They result from each other. They reinforce each other.

Much of the Negro community is buried under a blanket of history and circumstance. It is not a lasting solution to lift just one corner of that blanket. We must stand on all sides and we must raise the entire cover if we are to liberate our fellow citizens.

The Roots of Injustice

One of the differences is the increased concentration of Negroes in our cities. More than 73 percent of all Negroes live in urban areas compared with less than 70 percent of the whites. Most of these Negroes live in slums. Most of these Negroes live together—a separated people.

Men are shaped by their world. When it is a world of decay, ringed by an invisible wall, when escape is arduous and uncertain, and the saving pressures of a more hopeful society are unknown, it can cripple the youth and it can desolate the men.

There is also the burden that a dark skin can add to the search for a productive place in our society. Unemployment strikes most swiftly and broadly at the Negro, and this burden erodes hope. Blighted hope breeds despair. Despair brings indifferences to the learning which offers a way out. And despair, coupled with indifferences, is often the source of destructive rebellion against the fabric of society.

There is also the lacerating hurt of early collision with white hatred or prejudice, distaste or condescension. Other groups have felt similar intolerance. But success and achievement could wipe it away. They do not change the color of a man's skin. I have seen this uncomprehending pain in the eyes of the little, young Mexican-American schoolchildren that I taught many years ago. But it can be overcome. But, for many, the wounds are always open.

Family Breakdown

Perhaps most important—its influence radiating to every part of life—is the breakdown of the Negro family structure. For this, most of all, white America must accept responsibility. It flows from centuries of oppression and persecution of the Negro man. It flows from the long years of degradation and discrimination, which have attacked his dignity and assaulted his ability to produce for his family.

This, too, is not pleasant to look upon. But it must be faced by those whose serious intent is to improve the life of all Americans.

Only a minority—less than half—of all Negro children reach the age of 18 having lived all their lives with both of their parents. At this moment, tonight, little less than two-thirds are at home with both of their parents. Probably a majority of all Negro children receive federally-aided public assistance sometime during their childhood.

The family is the cornerstone of our society. More than any other force it shapes the attitude, the hopes, the ambitions, and the values of the child. And when the family collapses it is the children that are usually damaged. When it happens on a massive scale the community itself is crippled.

So, unless we work to strengthen the family, to create conditions under which most parents will stay together—all the rest: schools, and playgrounds, and public assistance, and private concern, will never be enough to cut completely the circle of despair and deprivation.

To Fulfill These Rights

There is no single easy answer to all of these problems.

Jobs are part of the answer. They bring the income which permits a man to provide for his family.

Decent homes in decent surroundings and a chance to learn—an equal chance to learn—are part of the answer.

Welfare and social programs better designed to hold families together are part of the answer.

Care for the sick is part of the answer.

An understanding heart by all Americans is another big part of the answer.

And to all of these fronts—and a dozen more—I will dedicate the expanding efforts of the Johnson administration.

But there are other answers that are still to be found. Nor do we fully understand even all of the problems. Therefore, I want to announce tonight that this fall I intend to call a White House conference of scholars, and experts, and outstanding Negro leaders—men of both races—and officials of Government at every level.

This White House conference's theme and title will be "To Fulfill These Rights."

Its object will be to help the American Negro fulfill the rights which, after the long time of injustice, he is finally about to secure.

To move beyond opportunity to achievement.

To shatter forever not only the barriers of law and public practice, but the walls which bound the condition of many by the color of his skin.

To dissolve, as best we can, the antique enmities of the heart which diminish the holder, divide the great democracy, and do wrong—great wrong—to the children of God.

And I pledge you tonight that this will be a chief goal of my administration, and of my program next year, and in the years to come. And I hope, and I pray, and I believe, it will be a part of the program of all America.

What Is Justice?

For what is justice?

It is to fulfill the fair expectations of man.

Thus, American justice is a very special thing. For, from the first, this has been a land of towering expectations. It was to be a nation where each man could be ruled by the common consent of all—enshrined in law, given life by institutions, guided by men themselves subject to its rule. And all—all of every station and origin—would be touched equally in obligation and in liberty.

Beyond the law lay the land. It was a rich land, glowing with more abundant promise than man had ever seen. Here, unlike any place yet known, all were to share the harvest.

And beyond this was the dignity of man. Each could become whatever his qualities of mind and spirit would permit—to strive, to seek, and, if he could, to find his happiness.

This is American justice. We have pursued it faithfully to the edge of our imperfections, and we have failed to find it for the American Negro.

So, it is the glorious opportunity of this generation to end the one huge wrong of the American Nation and, in so doing, to find America for ourselves, with the same immense thrill of discovery which gripped those who first began to realize that here, at last, was a home for freedom.

All it will take is for all of us to understand what this country is and what this country must become.

The Scripture promises: "I shall light a candle of understanding in thine heart, which shall not be put out."

Together, and with millions more, we can light that candle of understanding in the heart of all America.

And, once lit, it will never again go out.

Notes

Preface

1. W. E. B. Du Bois, "A Negro Nation Within the Nation," *Current History*, 4 (June 1935), in Eric J. Sundquist, *The Oxford W. E. B. Du Bois Reader* (New York: Oxford University Press, 1996), p. 431.
2. Ibid.
3. I have only found one reference to this phrase in the literature, in this instance concerning alumni legacy undergraduate admissions at colleges and universities: "Naked Hypocrisy: The Nationwide System of Affirmative Action for Whites," *Journal of Blacks in Higher Education*, 18 (Winter 1997–98).
4. Randall Kennedy, "Persuasion and Distrust: A Comment on the Affirmative Action Debate," *Harvard Law Review*, 99 (1986), p. 1327.
5. Robert Bartley, "'Affirmative Action': Devil in the Details," *Wall Street Journal*, February 10, 2003, p. A15.
6. Jill Quadagno, *The Transformation of Old Age Security: Class and Politics in the American Welfare State* (Chicago: University of Chicago Press, 1988), and *The Color of Welfare* (New York: Oxford University Press, 1994); Michael K. Brown, *Race, Money, and the American Welfare State* (Ithaca: Cornell University Press, 1999); Suzanne Mettler, *Dividing Citizens: Gender and Federalism in New Deal Public Policy* (Ithaca: Cornell University Press, 1998); Neil Foley, *The White Scourge: Mexicans, Blacks, and Poor Whites in Texas Cotton Culture* (Berkeley: University of California Press, 1997); Lizabeth Cohen, *A Consumer's Republic: The Politics of Mass Consumption in Postwar America* (New York: Knopf, 2003); Daniel Kryder, *Divided Arsenal: Race and the American State During World War Two* (New York: Cambridge University Press, 2000); Desmond King, *Separate and Unequal: Black Americans and the US Federal Government* (Oxford: Clarendon Press, 1995); Nancy J. Weiss, *Farewell to the Party of Lincoln: Black Politics in the Age of FDR* (Princeton: Princeton University Press, 1983); and William Julius Wilson, *The*

Declining Significance of Race: Blacks and Changing American Institutions (Chicago: University of Chicago Press, 1978).

Chapter 1

1. "To Fulfill These Rights," *Public Papers of the Presidents of the United States: Lyndon B. Johnson, 1965*. Vol. II (Washington, DC: Government Printing Office, 1966), pp. 635–40. The opening reference was to Dr. James M. Nabrit, Jr., Howard University's president, who, as a professor of law, had joined Thurgood Marshall and George E. C. Hayes to argue against segregation in schools before the Supreme Court when it considered *Brown v. Board of Education* in 1954. The full text of the speech, written by two young aides, Richard Goodwin and Daniel Patrick Moynihan, and heavily edited by the president, can be found in the appendix.
2. Roy Reed, "Alabama Police Use Gas and Clubs to Rout Negroes," *New York Times*, March 8, 1965, in Claybourne Carson, David Garrow, Bill Kovach, and Carol Polsgrove, eds., *Reporting Civil Rights, Part Two: American Journalism 1963–1973* (New York: Library of America, 2003), p. 322.
3. Cited in ibid., p. 327. John Lewis, now a member of Congress from Georgia, had just been admitted to Good Samaritan Hospital in Selma with a probable skull fracture.
4. Andrew Kopkind, "Selma: 'Ain't Gonna Let Nobody Turn Me 'Round,'" *New Republic*, March 20, 1965, in Carson, et al., eds., *Reporting Civil Rights, Part Two*, pp. 342–43. Later in the month, King successfully led a march from Selma to Montgomery. It began on March 21 at Browns Chapel in Selma with just over 3,000 people and ended outside the state capitol four days later with some 25,000 demonstrators at hand. That night, a civil rights workers from Detroit, Viola Liuzzo, was killed in Lowndes County, Alabama, by members of the Ku Klux Klan.
5. The term "Jim Crow" dates to the caricature of a black by that name first used in 1828 in a minstrel show for white audiences.
6. My inclusion of all seventeen states that practiced legal segregation inside the South is atypical. Most of the time the count is limited either to the eleven states of the Confederacy, or these plus Oklahoma and Kentucky. I see no justification for these alternatives when defining the region. As the South's key hallmark was the distinctiveness of its racial order, and all that followed from its premises, the larger tally seems compelling. Further, this total includes the fifteen states that practiced legally sanctioned slavery on the eve of the Civil War, plus Oklahoma and West Virginia, which only later joined the union as distinct states. This reckoning was more common in African American sources. Examples can be found in Ambrose Caliver, "Some Problems in the Education and Placement of Negro Teachers," *Journal of Negro Education*, 4 (January 1935), p. 99, which refers to "reports sent to the Office of Education from 17 Southern states and the District of Columbia" (also a bastion of segregation); and in Charles H. Thompson, "Editorial Comment: Some Critical Aspects of the Problem of the Higher and Professional Education for Negroes," *Journal of*

Negro Education, 14 (Autumn 1945), p. 507, who writes of "the 17 Southern states and the District of Columbia which require by law separation of the races for purposes of education." Similarly, the crucial American Council on Education Study of the 1940s distinguishes the thirty-one states which did not segregate their schools from the seventeen that did. See John K. North and Eugene Lawler, *An Inventory of Public School Expenditures in the United States: A Report of the Cooperative Study of Public School Expenditure.* Vol. II (Washington, DC: American Council on Education, 1944), chapter 8.

7. For key works on the theme of "whiteness," see Alexander Saxton, *The Rise and Fall of the White Republic: Class Politics and Mass Culture in Nineteenth Century America* (London: Verso Books, 1990); David Roediger, *The Wages of Whiteness: Race and the Making of the American Working Class* (London: Verso Books, 1991); Matthew Frye Jacobson, *Whiteness of a Different Color: European Immigrants and the Alchemy of Race* (Cambridge: Harvard University Press, 1998); and Grace Elizabeth Hale, *Making Whiteness: The Culture of Segregation in the South, 1890–1940* (New York: Vintage Books, 1999).
8. *Congressional Record*, 79th Cong., 1st sess. (1945), pp. 6336–37.
9. Gary M. Pomerantz, *Where Peachtree Meets Sweet Auburn: A Saga of Race and Family* (New York: Penguin Books, 1966), pp. 134–35.
10. A useful contemporaneous overview of the uneven history of the Supreme Court in protecting and advancing black rights is Raymond Pace Alexander, "The Upgrading of the Negro's Status by Supreme Court Decisions," *Journal of Negro History*, 30 (April 1945).
11. President Harry Truman's Committee on Civil Rights had described the situation of African Americans in Washington, DC, this way just after the Second World War ended:

> For Negro Americans, Washington is not just the nation's capital. It is the point at which all public transportation into the South becomes "Jim Crow." If he stops in Washington, a Negro may dine like other men in the Union Station, but as soon as he steps out into the capital, he leaves such democratic practices behind. With very few exceptions, he is refused service at downtown restaurants, he may not attend a downtown movie or play, and he has to go into the poorer section of the city to find a night's lodging. The Negro who decides to settle in the District must often find a home in an overcrowded area. He must often take a job below the level of his ability. He must send his children to the inferior schools set aside for Negroes and entrust his family's health to medical agencies which give inferior service. In addition, he must endure the countless daily humiliations that the system of segregation imposes upon the one-third of Washington that is Negro.
>
> —President's Committee on Civil Rights, *To Secure These Rights* (New York: Simon & Schuster, 1947), p. 89.

12. On lynching, see E. M. Beck and Stewart Tolnay, *A Festival of Violence: An Analysis of Southern Lynchings, 1882–1930* (Urbana: University of Illinois Press, 1995); W. Fitzhugh Brundage, *Lynching in the New South: Georgia and Virginia, 1880–1930* (Urbana, University of Illinois Press, 1993); Philip Dray, *At the Hands of Persons Unknown: The Lynching of Black America* (New York: Random House, 2002); Ralph Ginzberg, *100 Years of Lynching* (New York: Lancer Books, 1962); Robert Zangrando, *The NAACP Crusade Against Lynching, 1909–1950* (Philadelphia: Temple University Press, 1980); and the classic studies by Ida Wells, *Southern Horrors: Lynch Law in All Its Phases* (New York: New York Age Printing, 1929); Walter White, *Rope and Faggot: A Biography of Judge Lynch* (New York: Alfred A. Knopf, 1929); and Arthur Raper, *The Tragedy of Lynching* (Chapel Hill: University of North Carolina Press, 1933).
13. *To Secure These Rights*, pp. 79, 82. An even more hard-hitting overview of "The Condition of Our Rights" was issued in 1948 by the Southern Regional Council, an interracial organization with headquarters in Atlanta founded in 1944 (as the successor to the Commission on Interracial Cooperation, begun in 1919) and dedicated to attaining "through research and action the ideals and practices of equal opportunity for all peoples of the region." The most impressive feature of this 39-page document is its unremitting emphasis on the South's pervasive climate of violence, not just in the dramatic instances of lynching (the number had declined to just one in 1947, but thirty-one attempted lynchings had been averted at the last moment by police, private citizens, or circumstances allowing the target to escape), but in the brutal police misconduct, the parole system as a form of involuntary servitude, Klan rallies, intimidation of potential black voters, assaults on labor organizers, and the widespread circulation of nakedly racist hate sheets, in addition to the paucity of hospital beds for African Americans, deeply unequal schooling, and job ceilings. The Council's first president was Howard Odum, a white sociologist at the University of North Carolina, Chapel Hill, and the first chair of its executive committee was Charles Johnson, the black sociologist, then president of Fisk University.
14. *To Secure These Rights*, p. 166.
15. *Congressional Record*, 81st. Cong., 1st sess. (1949), pp. 2042–49.
16. A discussion of how Johnson sought to cull favor with Richard Russell, the South's most influential senator, by delivering this speech can be found in Robert A. Caro, *The Years of Lyndon Johnson: Master of the Senate* (New York: Knopf, 2002), chapter 8. By the time Russell died in 1971, not one member of the Senate or House who offered tribute spoke even one word about his long-standing battles against civil rights.
17. Robert Mann, *The Walls of Jericho: Lyndon Johnson, Hubert Humphrey, Richard Russell, and the Struggle for Civil Rights* (New York: Harcourt Brace & Company, 1996), pp. 48, 65, 86.
18. Cited in Caro, *Master of the Senate*, p. 215; Mann, *Walls of Jericho*, p. 84. Johnson continued to do battle with civil rights initiatives in the Democratic Party at least until the middle 1950s. In the 82nd Congress, for example, when he moved

into the leadership as the majority whip, he was "opposed to FEPC and to any major liberalization of Rule Twenty-two" requiring two thirds of the entire Senate to vote to close debate rather than the resolution that did pass the Rules Committee to the effect that cloture should require only two thirds of those present and voting—William C. Berman, *The Politics of Civil Rights in the Truman Administration* (Columbus: Ohio State University Press, 1970), pp. 184, 195. Later in the decade, as his presidential ambitions grew, he played a leading role as majority leader to pass a moderate and primarily symbolic civil rights law in 1957.

19. Kenneth B. Clark, *Dark Ghetto: Dilemmas of Social Power* (New York: Harper & Row, 1965), p. 11.
20. Hugh Davis Graham, *Collision Course: The Strange Convergence of Affirmative Action and Immigration Policy* (New York: Oxford University Press, 2002), p. 77 (italics in the original).
21. Thomas Sugrue, "The Tangled Roots of Affirmative Action," *American Behavioral Scientist*, 41 (April 1998), pp. 895–96; a revised and extended version appears in John David Skrentny, ed., *Color Lines: Affirmative Action, Immigration, and Civil Rights Options for America* (Chicago: University of Chicago Press, 2001).
22. Haynes Johnson, "Selma Revisited: 4 Months After Their 'Finest Hour' Rights Forces Are in Disarray," *Washington Star*, July 26, 1965, in Carson, et al., eds., *Reporting Civil Rights, Part Two*, p. 411.
23. Emblematic statements include Stokely Carmichael and Charles V. Hamilton, *Black Power: The Politics of Liberation in America* (New York: Random House, 1967); and Eldridge Cleaver, *Soul on Ice* (New York: Dell Publishing, 1968).
24. This is a subject I treat in *Black Men, White Cities: Race, Politics and Migration in the United States, 1900–30 and West Indian Migration to Britain, 1948–68* (New York: Oxford University Press, 1973).
25. There had been one main exception to this rule: the programs of public works and employment created by the "alphabet agencies" of the New Deal, including the CCC and the WPA. Although often restrictive and racist in their administration, they produced jobs where otherwise there were none, some of which were skilled and supervisory. To be sure, on balance, blacks were treated more poorly than white participants in these New Deal programs; yet the advances they offered, together with other forms of cash relief, persuaded most African American voters (where they could vote, mainly outside the South) to shift their allegiance from the Republican Party, the party of Lincoln and Reconstruction, to Franklin Roosevelt's Democratic Party, despite the presence of a southern segregationist wing at its core.
26. U.S. Department of Labor, Office of Policy Planning and Research, *The Negro Family: The Case for National Action* (Washington, DC: Government Printing Office, March 1965), pp. 5, 29, 47. Similar language about "social pathology in the Negro community" was first used by E. Franklin Frazier, *Negro Youth at the Crossways: Their Personality Development in the Middle States* (New York:

American Council on Education, 1940), especially in the appendix. A sharp critique of this position, arguing that it had confused consequences and causes, is Andrew Billingsley's, *Black Families in White America* (Englewood Cliffs, NJ: Prentice-Hall, 1968).

27. William Julius Wilson, *The Declining Significance of Race: Blacks and Changing American Institutions* (Chicago: University of Chicago Press, 1978). For an earlier consideration of the bases and character of the black middle class, see E. Franklin Frazier, *Black Bourgeoisie: The Rise of a New Middle Class in the United States* (Glencoe, IL: Free Press, 1957). Three excellent sources for assessing both the absolute and relative condition of African Americans in the 1940s are Richard Sterner, *The Negro's Share: A Study of Income, Consumption, Housing, and Public Assistance* (New York: Harper & Brothers, 1943); Gunnar Myrdal, *An American Dilemma: The Negro Problem and American Democracy*, Vols. 1 and 2 (New York: Harper & Brothers, 1944); and Maurice R. Davie, *Negroes in American Society* (New York: McGraw-Hill, 1949). Still useful for an earlier period is Clarence Heer, *Income and Wages in the South* (Chapel Hill: University of North Carolina Press, 1930). The best study of the sources and character of southern outmigration remains Neil Fligstein, *Going North: Migration of Blacks and Whites from the South, 1900–1950* (New York: Academic Press, 1981). An admirable, data-rich summary of postwar trends can be found in Reynolds Farley and Walter R. Allen, *The Color Line and the Quality of Life in America* (New York: Russell Sage Foundation for the National Committee for Research on the 1980 Census, 1987).
28. For a discussion, see Melvin L. Oliver and Thomas M. Shapiro, *Black Wealth/White Wealth: A New Perspective on Racial Inequality* (New York: Routledge, 1997). A successor volume is Thomas M. Shapiro, *The Hidden Cost of Being African American: How Wealth Perpetuates Inequality* (New York: Oxford University Press, 2004). The methodological challenges concerning how to assess the relative gains of blacks and whites are considerable. They are discussed, along with empirical findings for the 1970s and early 1980s, but also with useful data for the earlier postwar period, in Reynolds Farley, *Blacks and Whites: Narrowing the Gap?* (Cambridge: Harvard University Press, 1984).
29. Caro, *The Years of Lyndon Johnson: Master of the Senate.*
30. V. O. Key, Jr., *Southern Politics in State and Nation* (New York: Knopf, 1949), pp. 8, 9. Key still provides the most impressive assessment of how the heterogeneity of the faction-ridden politics in the southern states was transformed into regional solidarity in the halls of Congress. See also Alexander Heard, *A Two-Party South?* (Chapel Hill: University of North Carolina Press, 1952); and the concise overview in Dewey Grantham, *The Democratic South* (Athens: University of Georgia Press, 1963).
31. Even when the Democratic Party controlled Congress with unprecedented majorities, as it did after the landslides of 1932, 1934, and 1936, non-southern Democrats never composed a majority of the House or Senate.
32. Key, *Southern Politics*, chapters 16, 17.

33. See David Sarashohn, *The Party of Reform: Democrats in the Progressive Era* (Jackson: University Press of Mississippi, 1989), and David Burner, *The Politics of Provincialism: The Democratic Party in Transition, 1918–1932* (Cambridge: Harvard University Press, 1986).
34. Writing in the 1950s, Denis Brogan, the famous Scottish historian of the United States, wrote: "Here the Liberal conscience is most deeply touched and his political behaviour seems (to the unfriendly outsider) most schizophrenic. The representative Liberal is a Democrat, or an ally of the Democrats, but in the ranks of 'the Democracy' are most of the most violent enemies of the integration of the Negro into the American community. This is no doubt accidental; it arises from the localization of the most acute form of the colour problem in the region where the Democratic party is traditionally strongest. The necessity of holding the national party together makes for strange bedfellows and strange deals"—D. W. Brogan, "American Liberalism Today," in H. C. Allen and C. P. Hill, eds., *British Essays in American History* (New York: St. Martin's Press, 1957), p. 326. By the mid-1940s, it was clear this relationship was charged with tension. Four years before a positive vote on a civil rights plank induced a walkout by many southern delegates at the 1948 party's convention, followed by the States' Rights Party challenge led by Strom Thurmond, a demand by Philip Murray, the president of the CIO, urging the adoption of a strong anti-discrimination plank "so aroused delegates from the Southern States" that it "stiffened their resistance to even a mild anti-discrimination plank"—Charles E. Egan, "Race Issue Snarls the Platform: Southerners Halt Compromise," *New York Times*, July 19, 1944, p. 1.
35. *Congressional Record*, House of Representatives, January 10, 1940, p. 248.
36. This letter of July 29, 1948, is cited in Caro, *Master of the Senate*, p. 202.
37. Robert C. Lieberman, *Shifting the Color Line: Race and the American Welfare State* (Cambridge: Harvard University Press, 1998), p. 7.
38. For an analysis of the centrality of the revivalist tradition in both black and white Protestant denominations in the South to the civil rights movement, see David L. Chappell, *A Stone of Hope: Prophetic Religion and the Death of Jim Crow* (Chapel Hill: University of North Carolina Press, 2004).

Chapter 2

1. A fine overview showing why, despite the reinforcement of discrimination, the New Deal was the best short-term offer for black America is Raymond Wolters, "The New Deal and the Negro," in John Braeman, Robert H. Bremner, and David Brody, eds., *The New Deal: The National Level* (Columbus: Ohio State University Press, 1975). By contrast, as "the nemesis of reform," the Republican Party, while often rhetorically opposing Jim Crow but not having taken steps in power to attack it, now found itself both out of power and regularly contesting just those programs that funneled much-needed help to African Americans. On the Republican Party, see Ralph J. Bunche, *The Political Status of the Negro in the Age of FDR* (Chicago: University of Chicago Press, 1973), esp. chapter 16, "Some

Notes on Republican Politics in the South"; and Clyde P. Weed, *The Nemesis of Reform: The Republican Party During the New Deal* (New York: Columbia University Press, 1994).

2. W. E. B. Du Bois, "Du Bois States His Reasons for Backing President Roosevelt," *People's Voice*, October 21, 1944.
3. W. E. B. Du Bois, "The Winds of Time," *Chicago Defender*, February 1, 1947.
4. Excellent discussions of the black press of the 1930s and early 1940s can be found in Gunnar Myrdal, *An American Dilemma: The Negro Problem and Modern Democracy*, Vol. 2 (New York: Harper & Brothers, 1944), pp. 908–24; Maurice R. Davie, *Negroes in American Society* (New York: McGraw-Hill, 1949), pp. 197–205; and John H. Burma, "An Analysis of the Present Negro Press," *Social Forces*, 26 (December 1947), pp. 172–80. These authors underscore the robust growth of the black press, its penchant for protest, its middle-class status, and its significance in shaping black opinion, especially elite opinion.
5. "We Disapprove," *Pittsburgh Courier*, April 20, 1939.
6. "Some Things the Democratic Party Must Do," *Kansas City Plain Dealer*, October 27, 1939.
7. "Roosevelt or Willkie?" *Baltimore Afro American*, October 19, 1940. Similarly, the Republican *New York Age*'s pro-Willkie editorial stressed how "under the Social Security Law the masses of Negroes who are in domestic service and casual unskilled labor and farm groups are deprived of its benefits"—November 2, 1940.
8. Bishop R. R. Wright, Jr., "The Final Word: Elect Roosevelt," *Chicago Bee*, November 3, 1940.
9. "Why the Negro Should Support the New Deal: Don't Bite the Hand That Feeds You," *Oklahoma City Black Dispatch*, November 2, 1940.
10. "Why Are Negroes Supporting President Roosevelt?" *Kansas City Plain Dealer*, October 27, 1944.
11. "Negroes Get Recognition Under New Deal," *Chicago Bee*, November 1, 1942; "The Democratic Convention," *Oklahoma City Black Dispatch*, July 27, 1940.
12. *The Secret Diary of Harold L. Ickes*. Vol. 2 (New York: Simon & Schuster, 1954), p. 115, cited in David L. Chappell, *A Stone of Hope: Prophetic Religion and the Death of Jim Crow* (Chapel Hill: University of North Carolina Press, 2004), p. 10. Chappell observes that even in this diary by the New Deal's leading civil rights figure, Eleanor Roosevelt aside, who had headed the Chicago branch of the NAACP, black rights issues appear very infrequently. Ickes "assumed the futility of any attack on segregation" and "took it for granted that public association of New Deal officials with desegregation would be 'prejudicial'—would injure Roosevelt's standing with his key constituency, the enfranchised white South" (pp. 197, 10).
13. Myrdal, *An American Dilemma*, Vol. 1, p. 205.
14. Bureau of the Census, U.S. Department of Commerce, Fifteenth Census of the United States: 1930 (1933); Bureau of the Census, U.S. Department of Commerce, Sixteenth Census of the United States: 1940 (1943).

15. Richard Sterner, *The Negro's Share: A Study of Income, Consumption, Housing, and Public Assistance* (New York: Harper & Brothers, 1943), p. 14.
16. Violence took both legal and extralegal form. There is a subtle treatment of this theme in Nancy MacLean, *Behind the Mask of Chivalry: The Making of the Second Ku Klux Klan* (New York: Oxford University Press, 1994).
17. Allison Davis, *Deep South: A Social Anthropological Study of Caste and Class* (Chicago: University of Chicago Press, 1941), pp. 379, 381.
18. Gordon S. Watkins and Paul A. Dodd, *Labor Problems* (New York: Thomas Y. Crowell, 1940), p. 477. A useful discussion of black labor can be found on pp. 507–21. Gunnar Myrdal reported that the average tenant family in 1937 had a net cash income of $300—Myrdal, *An American Dilemma*, Vol. 1, p. 257.
19. Clarence Heer, *Income and Wages in the South* (Chapel Hill: University of North Carolina Press, 1930), pp. 12–22.
20. Calvin B. Hoover and B. U. Ratchford, *Economic Resources and Policies in the South* (New York: Macmillan, 1951), p. 103; Myrdal, *An American Dilemma*, Vol. 1, p. 245.
21. Davie, *Negroes in American Society*, p. 111; Myrdal, *An American Dilemma*, Vol. 2, pp. 1082–87; Sterner, *Negro's Share*, p. 23; Gwendolyn Mink, *The Lady and the Tramp: Race, Gender, and the Origins of the American Welfare State* (Madison: University of Wisconsin Press, 1990).
22. James R. McGovern, *And a Time for Hope: Americans in the Great Depression* (Westport, CT: Praeger, 2000), p. 119.
23. Sterner, *Negro's Share*, p. 60. If anything, he points out, "the race differentials were probably greater. . . . Several significant low income groups were excluded from the southern rural sample . . . and it is likely that as a result the rural income figures are too high. This is of more importance for Negroes than whites" (p. 61).
24. Ibid., pp. 71, 72, 85, 86.
25. Ibid., pp. 166–209.
26. Davie, *Negroes in American Society*, pp. 234–37; Southern Regional Council, "The Condition of Our Rights," Atlanta, 1948, p. 31; H. A. Callis, "The Need and Training of Negro Physicians," *Journal of Negro Education*, 4 (January 1935), p. 34.
27. John K. North and Eugene Lawler, *An Inventory of Public School Expenditures in the United States: A Report of the Cooperative Study of Public School Expenditure.* Vol. II (Washington, DC: American Council on Education, 1944), chapter 8.
28. Davie, *Negroes in American Society*, p. 150.
29. North and Lawler, *Inventory*, chapter 7; Davie, *Negroes in American Society*, p. 111.
30. An excellent overview can be found in Myrdal, *American Dilemma*, Vol. 1, chapter 15.
31. Ibid., pp. 399–400.
32. Michael Brown, *Race, Money, and the American Welfare State* (Ithaca: Cornell University Press, 1999), pp. 77–78.
33. Ibid., p. 42.
34. Sterner, *Negro's Share*, pp. 220, 221, 223, 225.
35. Ibid., p. 234. The report he cited is A. R. Magnes, *Changing Aspects of Rural Relief*,

Research Monograph XIV (Washington, DC: Works Progress Administration, 1938).

36. Myrdal observes that another factor was in play. Because of the depths of black poverty, this part of the population had paid relatively little in taxes. "The observer is frequently told by white Southerners that . . . whatever they get is a charitable gift for which they should be grateful. There can be no sense in talking about discrimination, it is held, as Negroes have no right to anything, but get something out of the white's benevolence"—Myrdal, *American Dilemma*, Vol. 1, pp. 335–36.
37. William R. Brock, *Welfare, Democracy, and the New Deal* (Cambridge: Cambridge University Press, 1988), p. 6.
38. George B. Tindall, *The Emergence of the New South, 1913–1945* (Baton Rouge: Louisiana State University Press, 1967), p. 272.
39. This data from the *Statistical Abstract of the United States, 1935* is summarized in Brock, *Welfare*, p. 249.
40. Tindall, *New South*, p. 482.
41. Ibid., p. 476.
42. For a discussion of the tension between low regional wages and the possibility of more uniform national standards in the case of the NRA, see Bruce J. Schulman, *From Cotton Belt to Sunbelt: Federal Policy, Economic Development, and the Transformation of the South, 1938–1980* (Durham: Duke University Press, 1994), p. 21. Black workers tended to lose either way. Where local standards prevailed, they were paid less than whites, often a good deal less. Where national standards were imposed, they were at a high risk of being laid off because their wages would now exceed southern norms.
43. Quoted in *Congressional Record*, 74th Cong., 2nd sess. (1936), 3938, cited in Tindall, *Welfare*, p. 491.
44. Brock, *Welfare*, p. 204.
45. Ibid., p. 224.
46. Cited in Ronald L. Heinmann, *Depression and the New Deal in Virginia* (Charlottesville: University of Virginia Press, 1983), p. 80.
47. Michael S. Holmes, *The New Deal in Georgia: An Administrative History* (Westport, CT: Greenwood Press, 1975), p. 22. Talmadge's administration was marked by a patronage and personal control, to the point of signing relief checks personally. Harry Hopkins removed his relief commissioner, installing instead Gay Shepperson, who was effectively prevented from carrying out her job by the governor—Roger Biles, *The South and the New Deal* (Lexington: University of Kentucky Press, 1994), pp. 64–65.
48. Cited in Douglas L. Smith, *The New Deal in the Urban South* (Baton Rouge: Louisiana State University Press, 1988), p. 233.
49. Myrdal, *American Dilemma*, Vol. 1, p. 354.
50. Cited in Schulman, *Cotton Belt*, p. 46.
51. Myrdal, *An American Dilemma*, Vol. 1, p. 299.
52. Federal Security Agency, Social Security Board, *Old-Age and Survivors' Insurance*

Statistics: Employment and Wages of Covered Workers: 1938 (Washington, DC: Government Printing Office, 1940), pp. 16–18. In this respect, the United States was more racially inclusive than Australia, New Zealand, and South Africa, all of which limited their old age assistance programs to people of European stock.

53. Sterner, *Negro's Share*, p. 215.
54. U.S. Committee on Economic Security, *Report to the President* (Washington, DC: Government Printing Office, 1935), pp. 18, 49, cited in Robert Lieberman, *Shifting the Color Line: Race and the American Welfare State* (Cambridge: Harvard University Press, 1998), p. 31.
55. Sterner, *Negro's Share*, p. 214.
56. The leading argument along these lines is Gareth Davies and Martha Derthick, "Race and Social Welfare Policy: The Social Security Act of 1935," *Political Science Quarterly*, 112 (Summer 1997). Both Jill Quadagno and Michael Brown, who equally place race at the center of their stories, have stressed either the way the southern rural economy and especially the planter class helped created occupational exclusions with a racial bias or how fiscal imperatives help direct this result. See Jill Quadagno, *The Color of Welfare: How Racism Undermined the War on Poverty* (New York: Oxford University Press, 1994), and Brown, *Race, Money, and the American Welfare State.* Brown also stresses that the northern white working class, a key source of support for the New Deal, had little incentive to oppose occupational exclusions. These, of course, are not mutually exclusive explanations.
57. Lieberman, *Shifting the Color Line*, pp. 5, 7. More than any other scholar, Lieberman has underscored how occupational exclusions shaped the welfare state created by the Social Security Act of 1935, arguing that they were inserted at southern insistence. Davies and Derthick have criticized this inference, arguing, as noted, that there are other reasons why farmworkers and maids might have been excluded. The fact that a common pattern was instituted, as we soon will see, across the entire relevant range of key New Deal legislation strongly supports Lieberman's historical reading.
58. Cited in Dona Cooper Hamilton and Charles V. Hamilton, *The Dual Agenda* (New York: Columbia University Press, 1997), p. 29.
59. Lieberman, *Shifting the Color Line*, p. 38.
60. The key discussion in Lieberman can be found on pp. 39–48.
61. ADC is considered in ibid., pp. 48–56.
62. Sterner, *Negro's Share*, p. 283.
63. Ibid., pp. 282–84.
64. Social Security Board, *Fourth Annual Report of the Social Security Board for the Fiscal Year Ended June 30, 1939* (Washington, DC: Government Printing Office, 1940), p. 92, cited in Sterner, *Negro's Share*, p. 274.
65. Sterner, *Negro's Share*, pp. 275–77. A revealing feature of the administration of old age assistance is the age gap between whites and blacks. African American recipients were older. "It appears likely that welfare agencies are more inclined

to consider Negroes under 70 years of age able to support themselves by odd jobs than whites of corresponding age and also that the agencies have greater difficulties in ascertaining the ages of Negroes than whites, which may cause delays in accepting the former in the program. Since the definitions of need in the various state plays are not precise, they make such differential treatment possible" (p. 274).

66. Edwin Amenta, *Bold Relief: Institutional Politics and the Origins of Modern American Social Policy* (Princeton: Princeton University Press, 1998).
67. For discussions, see Brown, *Race, Money*, pp. 48–51, and Lieberman, *Shifting the Color Line*, pp. 56–64.
68. Cited in Hamilton and Hamilton, *Dual Agenda*, pp. 30, 31. The citations are to Charles Houston of the NAACP and T. Arnold Hill of the National Urban League.
69. Brown, *Race, Money*, p. 132.
70. Cited in Allan H. Ryskind, *Hubert: An Unauthorized Biography of the Vice President* (New York: Basic Books, 1995), p. 173.
71. Carl Solberg, *Hubert Humphrey: A Biography* (New York: W. W. Norton, 1984), p. 169. When Humphrey wrote the southern editors, he warmly referred to his years as a graduate student in political science at Louisiana State University, where he had earned a master of arts degree in 1939. His thesis, published in 1970, had offered a stalwart defense of the New Deal, but had been entirely silent about race and the South—Hubert Humphrey, *The Political Philosophy of the New Deal* (Baton Rouge: Louisiana State University Press, 1970).
72. Judith N. Shklar, *American Citizenship: The Quest for Inclusion* (Cambridge: Harvard University Press, 1991), p. 23.

Chapter 3

1. This chapter draws heavily on "The Southern Imposition: Congress and Labor in the New Deal and Fair Deal," a paper I co-authored with Sean Farhang for the American Political Science Meeting in Boston, August 29, 2001.
2. J. David Greenstone, *Labor in American Politics* (New York: Knopf, 1969), p. 71.
3. National Labor Relations Act of 1935, §§7, 8(a), reprinted in *Legislative History of the National Labor Relations Act, 1935*, comp. National Labor Relations Board (Government Printing Office, Washington, DC: 1959). Further references to the NLRA are from this source. The standard history is James A. Gross, *The Making of the National Labor Relations Board: A Study in Economics, Politics, and Law.* Vol. I: *1933–1937* (Albany: State University of New York Press, 1974). Gross discusses implementation in his *The Reshaping of the National Labor Relations Board: National Labor Policy in Transition, 1937–1947* (Albany: State University of New York Press, 1981). See also Murray Edelman, "New Deal Sensitivity to Labor Interests," in Milton Derber and Edwin Young, eds., *Labor and the New Deal* (Madison: University of Wisconsin Press, 1961); David Plotke, "The Wagner Act, Again: Politics and Labor, 1935–1937," *Studies in American Political Development*, 3 (1989); Michael Goldfield, "Worker Insurgency, Radical

Organization, and New Deal Labor Legislation," *American Political Science Review*, 83 (December 1989); and Mark Barenberg, "The Political Economy of the Wagner Act: Power, Symbol, and Workplace Cooperation," *Harvard Law Review*, 106 (May 1993).

4. See Frank W. McCulloch and Tim Bornstein, *The National Labor Relations Board* (New York: Frederick Praeger, 1974). Gross, *Reshaping of the National Labor Relations Board*, pp. 132–36, discusses the relatively greater power and independence of the NLRB under the NLRA compared to previous labor boards.
5. Despite their focus on the relationship of price changes and union growth, Ashenfelter and Pencavel acknowledge the importance of what they rather blandly refer to as "a favorable political environment"—Orley Ashenfelter and John H. Pencavel, "American Trade Union Growth: 1900–1960," *Quarterly Journal of Economics*, 83 (August 1969), p. 446.
6. Leo Wolman, "Concentration of Union Membership," *Proceedings of Fifth Annual Meeting of the Industrial Relations Research Association* (1952), cited in Milton Derber, "Growth and Expansion," in Derber and Young, eds., *Labor and the New Deal*, p. 17.
7. Irving Bernstein, "The Growth of American Unions," *American Economic Review*, 44 (June 1954), pp. 303–04.
8. Fair Labor Standards Act of 1938, §2, 6–7, in Irving J. Sloan, ed., *American Landmark Legislation: The Fair Labor Standards Act of 1938* (Dobbs Ferry, NY: Oceana, 1984). Further references to the FLSA are from this source. Rather than actually setting maximum permissible work hours, these "maximum" hours provisions established a threshold above which overtime wages (time and one half) had to be paid.
9. Since maids did not constitute an "industry," their exclusion usually was tacit; what they did was not named as eligible. By contrast, agricultural workers were excluded explicitly. To be sure, southerners were not alone in seeking to circumscribe labor legislation so as to keep agricultural labor unregulated by the central state. In what has been called the "marriage of corn and cotton," during the New Deal period "[t]he impact of the southern bloc in Congress was augmented considerably by the implementation of a strategic voting alliance with midwesterners"—Edward L. Schapsmeier and Frederick H. Schapsmeier, "Farm Policy from FDR to Eisenhower: Southern Democrats and the Politics of Agriculture," *Agricultural History*, 53 (January 1979), pp. 352, 355.
10. The text of the act is reprinted in Leverett S. Lyon, *The National Recovery Administration: An Analysis and Appraisal* (Washington, DC: Brookings Institution, 1935).
11. Milton Derber, "Growth and Expansion," in Derber and Young, eds., *Labor and the New Deal*, pp. 38–39.
12. *Congressional Record*, 73rd Cong., 1st sess. (1933), 77: 5241.
13. Marc Linder, "Farm Workers and the Fair Labor Standards Act: Racial Discrimination in the New Deal," *Texas Law Review*, 65 (June 1987), p. 1356.
14. S. 2926, 73rd Cong., 2nd sess., introduced in the Senate on February 28 (calen-

dar day, March 1), and referred to the Committee on Education and Labor—*Congressional Record*, 73rd Cong., 2nd sess. (1934), 78: 3444.

15. James R. Wason, "Legislative History of the Exclusion of Agricultural Employees from the National Labor Relations Act, 1935 and the Fair Labor Standards Act of 1938," Congressional Research Service, Library of Congress, p. 3.
16. The three men were Richard Murphy of Iowa, Elbert Duncan Thomas of Utah, and John Erickson of Montana.
17. See Senate Report 2926, 73rd Cong., 2nd sess., reported on May 10 (calendar day, May 26), 1934, by Senator Walsh—*Congressional Record*, 73rd Cong., 2nd sess. (1934), 78: 9607; and Senate Report 1184, 73rd Cong., 2nd sess. (May 10 [calendar day May 26], 1934). Almost seven decades later, agriculture and domestic laborers remain outside the ambit of NLRA protection. For a discussion of efforts to organize southern agricultural workers during the New Deal, see F. Ray Marshall, *Labor in the South* (Cambridge: Harvard University Press, 1967), chapter 6.
18. For a useful overview, see Phyllis Palmer, "Outside the Law: Agricultural and Domestic Workers Under the Fair Labor Standards Act," *Journal of Policy History*, 7 (#4, 1995).
19. Paul H. Douglas and Joseph Hackman, "The Fair Labor Standards Act of 1938 I," *Political Science Quarterly*, 53 (December 1938), p. 493.
20. Wason, "Legislative History of the Exclusion of Agricultural Employees," p. 499.
21. Suzanne Mettler, *Dividing Citizens: Gender and Federalism in New Deal Public Policy* (Ithaca: Cornell University Press, 1998), pp. 185, 204, 209.
22. Quoted in Wason, "Legislative History of Exclusion," p. 11.
23. Douglas and Hackman, "Fair Labor Standards Act," pp. 503–05.
24. Fair Labor Standards Act of 1938, §3(f). For a treatment of the FSLA as a law balancing between labor demands and southern hesitations, see Ronnie Steinberg, *Wages and Hours: Labor and Reform in Twentieth-Century America* (New Brunswick: Rutgers University Press, 1982).
25. Linder, "Farm Workers," p. 1347.
26. *Congressional Record*, 75th Cong., 2nd sess. (1937), 82: 1404. Ibid., 82: 1387–88, cited in Patterson, *Congressional Conservatism*, p. 195. *Congressional Record*, 75th Cong., 2nd sess. (1937), 82: 442 (appendix).
27. Senator Smith (D-NC), *Congressional Record*, 75th Cong., 1st sess. (1937), 81: 7881–82. Representative Dies (D-TX), *Congressional Record*, 75th Cong., 2nd sess. (1937), 82: 1388.
28. Later, southern concern about growing federal administrative authority over the employment relationship during the Second World War was an important cause of its defection from the New Deal coalition on labor. However, during the construction of the early New Deal labor regime most southerners did not appear to regard this as a threat. Though a few southern legislators expressed apprehension over the growing central bureaucracy during debates over the NIRA (*Congressional Record*, 73rd Cong., 1st sess. [1933], 77: 4222, 4225–26, 5175,

5178), no significant efforts were made by southerners to weaken or shape the broad administrative authority over the employment relationship and labor-management relations created in either the NIRA or the NLRA. In the case of the FLSA, the original bill included an administrative apparatus with an independent board given substantial discretion to set wages and hours that was analogous to the NLRB. The principal southern response during the legislative process was not so much to seek to undercut the board's power as to advance southern interests by ensuring strong southern representation among board members, and requiring the board to consider regional economic conditions when setting minimum wages.

29. Orme W. Phelps, "Public Policy in Labor Disputes: The Crisis of 1946," *Journal of Political Economy*, 55 (June 1947). See also Arthur F. McClure, *The Truman Administration and the Problems of Postwar Labor, 1945–1948* (Rutherford, NJ: Fairleigh Dickinson University Press, 1969).
30. Richard Bensel, *Sectionalism and American Political Development, 1880 to 1980* (Madison: University of Wisconsin Press, 1982), pp. 381–85.
31. Labor Management Relations Act of 1947, §14(b), in *Legislative History of the Labor Management Relations Act, 1947*, comp. National Labor Relations Board (Government Printing Office, Washington, DC: 1948). Further references to the LBRA are from this source. Southern states moved rapidly and disproportionately to adopt right-to-work laws. Of seven states to pass right-to-work laws in the year Taft-Hartley passed, five were southern: Georgia, North Carolina, Tennessee, Texas, and Virginia (Arkansas and Florida had pioneered by passing the first right-to-work laws by public referenda in 1944, and Louisiana had adopted such a statute in 1946). See Gilbert J. Gall, *The Politics of Right to Work: The Labor Federations as Special Interests, 1943–1979* (New York: Greenwood Press, 1988); Keith Lumsden and Craig Peterson, "The Impact of Right-to-Work Laws on Unionization in the United States," *Journal of Political Economy*, 83 (December 1975); and David T. Ellwood and Glenn Fine, "The Impact of Right-to-Work Laws on Union Organizing," *Journal of Political Economy*, 95 (April 1987).
32. Mancur Olson famously devoted a chapter to this question in his *The Logic of Collective Action* (Cambridge: Harvard University Press, 1971).
33. House Report 245, 80th Cong., 1st sess., 68–69 (April 11, 1947); Senate Report 105, 80th Cong., 1st sess., 19 (April 17, 1947); William B. Gould, *A Primer on American Labor Law* (Cambridge: MIT Press, 1993), p. 30.
34. This restructuring of NLRB authority was taken from amendments earlier proposed unsuccessfully by the Smith Committee (led by Representative Howard Smith, the Virginia Democrat who was a vociferous opponent of the board) after its investigation of the NLRB in 1940—Gross, *Reshaping of the National Labor Relations Board*, pp. 253–54, 264.
35. See Gould, *American Labor Law*, p. 41.
36. Over time the ranks of the "supervisor" (which has a very low threshold) have swelled, making increasingly large numbers of workers ineligible to organize—

Lichtenstein, *State of the Union.* The number of independent contractors also has grown dramatically over time, now comprising roughly 8.6 million workers, or 6.4 percent of total employment—Bureau of Labor Statistics, February 2001 (http://www.bls.gov/opub/working/page15b.htm).

37. House Report 245, 80th Cong., 1st sess., 68–69 (April 11, 1947). Senate Report 105, 80th Cong., 1st sess., 19 (April 17, 1947). House Conference Report 510, 80th Cong., 1st sess., 33 (June 3, 1947). House Minority Report 245, 80th Cong., 1st sess. (April 11, 1947); Senate Minority Report 105, pt. 2, 80th Cong., 1st sess. (April 22, 1947).
38. *Congressional Record*, 80th Cong., 1st sess. (1947), 93: 1489; Senate Report 48, 80th Congress, 1st sess. (1947).
39. Marc Linder, *"Moments are the Elements of Profit": Overtime and the Deregulation of Working Hours Under the Fair Labor Standards Act* (Iowa City: Fanpìhuà Press, 2000), pp. 280–85.
40. *Congressional Record*, 80th Cong., 1st sess. (1947), 93: 1489; Senate Report 48, 80th Congress, 1st sess. (1947).
41. *Congressional Record*, 80th Cong., 1st sess. (1947), 93: 2376; Senate Report 48, 80th Congress, 1st sess. (1947); House Conference Report 326, 80th Congress, 1st sess. (1947).
42. *Congressional Record*. 80th Cong., 1st sess. (1947), 93: 1503, 1509. House Conference Report 326, 80th Cong., 1st sess. (1947); Senate Report 48, 80th Congress, 1st sess. (1947). *Congressional Record*, 80th Cong., 1st sess. (1947), 93: 1521, 1557–59. The two-year period enacted as the federal standard approximated to what already prevailed in southern states, which had the shortest limitations period for wage and hour claims—*Congressional Record*, 80th Cong., 1st sess. (1947), 93: 1495, 1500. House Conference Report 326, 80th Congress, 1st sess. (1947). Speaking against the House version of this last amendment, Representative Emmanuel Celler, a Brooklyn Democrat, asked: "[I]f we pass this act as it is worded now we practically take away the so-called liquidated damages, which is the incentive for an employer to abide by the law. If a man violates a law, all he will be responsible for, despite his violation, is the amount of wages he would have had to pay in the first instance. What kind of penalty do you have then? What kind of incentive is there in the act so that the law will be obeyed?"—*Congressional Record*, 80th Cong., 1st sess. (1947), 93: 1495.
43. House Conference Report 326, 80th Cong., 1st sess., 13–15 (1947).
44. Derber, "Growth and Expansion," p. 28.
45. There is a good compact discussion of this in George Brown Tindall, *The Emergence of the New South: 1913–1945* (Baton Rouge: Louisiana State University Press, 1967), chapter 10 ("When Southern Labor Stirred").
46. For an overview of these changes, see Numan Bartley, *The New South: 1945–1980* (Baton Rouge: Louisiana State University Press, 1995), pp. 1–12.
47. Frank Traver De Vyver, "The Present Status of Labor Unions in the South," *Southern Economic Journal*, 5 (April 1939); Frank T. De Vyver, "The Present Status of Labor Unions in the South—1948," *Southern Economic Journal*, 16 (July 1949);

and Leo Troy, "The Growth of Union Membership in the South, 1939–1953," *Southern Economic Journal*, 24 (April 1958). See also Derber, "Growth and Expansion," p. 34.

48. H. M. Douty, "Development of Trade-Unionism in the South," *Monthly Labor Review*, 63 (October 1946), p. 581. There is a very large literature debating the character and extent of union multiracialism in the South, but measured against practices at the time, the labor movement—and especially the CIO, despite lingering racist mechanisms—clearly constituted the most widespread and effective popular force across racial lines in the 1940s.
49. For a discussion, see Myrdal, *An American Dilemma*, Vol. 1, pp. 401–08.
50. Douty, "Development," pp. 576–79.
51. Cited in Robert H. Zieger, *The CIO, 1939–1955* (Chapel Hill: University of North Carolina Press, 1995), p. 230.
52. Marshall, *Labor in the South*, p. 246.
53. Bartley, *New South*, p. 47. In 1946 the national convention of the AFL voted against supporting continuation of the Fair Employment Practices Committee.
54. "Congressional enactment of the Taft-Hartley Labor Management Relations Act in June, 1947, was a blow to the southern campaigns of the CIO and AFL alike," Numan Bartley concluded, ". . . and one of its immediate purposes was to impede unionization in the South"—Bartley, *New South*, p. 49. The CIO's Operation Dixie did not formally end until 1953.
55. *Congressional Record*, 76th Cong., 1st sess. (1939), 84: 9582, 9591.
56. It did so by separating the prosecutorial and judicial functions of the NLRB while increasing judicial review of board decisions and requiring that it apply rules of evidence applicable in federal courts—*Congressional Record*, 76th Cong., 3rd sess. (1940), 86: 7712–12, 7772–75.
57. See, e.g., *Congressional Record*, 78th Cong., 1st sess. (1943), 89: 5225, 5229, 5243, 5309, 5311–12.
58. Bureau of National Affairs, "The Taft-Hartley Act . . . After One Year" (1948), p. 1.
59. Editors, "Developments in the Law: The Taft-Hartley Act," *Harvard Law Review*, 64 (March 1951), p. 781; Emily Clark Brown, *National Labor Policy: Taft-Hartley After Three Years, and the Next Steps*, Public Affairs Institute (1950), p. 22. See also Edwin Witte, "An Appraisal of the Taft-Hartley Act," *American Economic Review*, 38 (May 1948).
60. Research Department, United Textile Workers of America, "Danger! Watch Out! What You Should Know about the Taft-Hartley Law" (July 1947), inside cover.
61. International Association of Machinists, "The Truth About the Taft-Hartley Law and its Consequences to the Labor Movement" (April 1948).
62. International Typographical Union, *The Taft Hartley Law IS a Slave Labor Law*, pamphlet, February 10, 1949, pp. 1, 5–15. The ITU, it should be noted, refused to sign Taft-Hartley's non-Communist affidavit as a matter of principle—Zieger, *CIO*, p. 279. Similar reasoning can be found in the American Federation of Labor, "What's Wrong with the Taft-Hartley Law?" 1948.
63. Bell, "Interest and Ideology," p. 203.

64. Industrial Union Department, AFL-CIO, *Taft-Hartley, A Case Study: What Has Happened to the American Federation of Hosiery Workers*" (1947), p. 8; Industrial Union Department, *Unfair: Industrial Unions and Taft-Hartley* (1947), p. 9.
65. Brown, "National Labor Policy," pp. 33–34. For a discussion of how political pressures had already induced the National Labor Relations Board to "soften up" and "unmistakably move to the 'right'" in the 1940s before Taft-Hartley in its interpretations and enforcement of the Wagner Act, see Julius Cohen and Lillian Cohen, "The National Labor Relations Board in Retrospect," *Industrial and Labor Relations Review*, 1 (July 1948).
66. Paul H. Douglas, *In the Fullness of Time* (New York: Harcourt Brace Jovanovich, 1972), p. 373. The result was a "situation operated as a restraining force upon both unionism and Northern wage scales."
67. Administrative Office of the U.S. Courts, *Judicial Business of the United States Courts*, Table C-4 (multiple years).
68. Virginia G. Cook, "State Cooperation in Enforcement of the Federal Wage-Hour Law," *American Political Science Review*, 48 (September 1954).
69. They also began an attempt that first bore fruit in a UAW-Ford agreement in 1955, to have employers provide supplemental unemployment insurance. For discussions, see H. M. Douty, "Post-War Wage Bargaining in the United States," in Walter Galenson and Seymour Martin Lipset, eds., *Labor and Trade Unionism: An Interdisciplinary Reader* (New York: Wiley, 1960, pp. 192–202; Neil W. Chamberlain, *Labor* (New York: McGraw-Hill, 1958), esp. chapters 1–3; Joel Seidman, Jack London, Bernard Karsh, and Daisy L. Tagliacozzo, *The Worker Views His Union* (Chicago: University of Chicago Press, 1958); Beth Stevens, "Labor Unions, Employee Benefits, and the Privatization of the American Welfare State," *Journal of Policy History*, 2 (#3, 1990); Frank Dobbins, "The Origins of Private Social Insurance: Public Policy and Fringe Benefits in America, 1920–1950," *American Journal of Sociology*, 97 (March 1992); and Marie Gottschalk, *The Shadow Welfare State: Labor, Business, and the Politics of Health-Care in the United States* (Ithaca: ILR Press, 2000). Stevens rightly concludes that the decision taken by labor leaders to "negotiate with corporations for employee benefits rather than engage in political mobilization to force the government to expand the welfare state" was not the result of their abandonment of social welfare goals or bureaucratic conservatism, but because, after Taft-Hartley, "they were encouraged by political and economic forces to turn their attention elsewhere" (p. 254).
70. This despite the first preference of black leaders to refuse such a choice. See Dona C. Hamilton and Charles V. Hamilton, *The Dual Agenda: Race and Social Welfare Policies of Civil Rights Organizations* (New York: Columbia University Press, 1997).

Chapter 4

1. Tom Brokaw, *The Greatest Generation* (New York: Random House, 1998); Studs Terkel, *The Good War: An Oral History of World War Two* (New York: Pantheon Books, 1984).

2. John Hope Franklin, "Their War and Mine," *Journal of American History*, 77 (September 1990), pp. 576–77. Franklin is best known for his pioneering survey, *From Slavery to Freedom: A History of American Negroes* (New York: Knopf, 1947). The book has had many subsequent editions.
3. Franklin, "Their War," p. 578. This inference was confirmed, he observed, by the "treatment given my older brother, a college graduate and high school principal, who was abused by his white, uneducated staff sergeant, consigned to the kitchen brigade, and driven to an early grave, two years after the close of the war, by the insensitive, barbaric treatment of those who draped themselves in the flag and sang the national anthem even as they destroyed the nation's ideals and its people."
4. Cited in Gail Buckley, *American Patriots: The Story of Blacks in the Military from the Revolution to Desert Storm* (New York: Random House, 2001), p. 323.
5. Morris J. MacGregor, Jr., *Integration of the Armed Forces, 1940–1965* (Washington, DC: Center of Military History, U.S. Army, 1981), p. 312. For a useful history, see also Sherie Mershon and Steven Schlossman, *Foxholes & Color Lines: Desegregating the U.S. Armed Forces* (Baltimore: Johns Hopkins University Press, 1998). Congressional debates on the subject made it clear that a southern veto would stifle any effort at military desegregation, thus offering the president no choice but to take the route of an executive order. As late as 1950, the Eighth Army in Japan still was segregated. Integrated Army training began in August 1950.
6. The last remnants of Jim Crow were eliminated from the military in 1956, three years after the end of the Korean War—Charles C. Moskos, Jr., "Racial Integration in the Armed Forces," *American Journal of Sociology*, 72 (September 1966), p. 135.
7. "Close Ranks," *The Crisis*, 16 (July 1918), p. 111 (italics in the original).
8. Mark Ellis, *Race, War, and Surveillance: African Americans and the United States Government During World War I* (Bloomington: Indiana University Press, 2001).
9. Editorials, "Our Special Grievances" and "The Reward," *The Crisis*, 16 (September 1918), p. 217.
10. Cited in Gunnar Myrdal, *An American Dilemma: The Negro Problem and American Democracy.* Vol. 1 (New York: Harper & Brothers, 1944), p. 420.
11. Emmett J. Scott, *The American Negro in the World War* (Chicago: Homewood Press, 1919), pp. 59, 64. In 1933, Scott, then secretary of Howard University, addressed a gathering of black veterans from the 92nd and 93rd divisions of the Expeditionary Forces of the First World War: "I confess, personally, a deep sense of disappointment, of poignant pain, that a great country in time of need should promise so much and afterward perform so little"—"Howard University Official Pleads for New Deal," *Chicago Defender*, October 7, 1933.
12. For overviews of the black experience in the First World War, see Jack D. Foner, *Blacks and the Military in American History: A New Perspective.* (New York: Praeger, 1974), pp. 109–32; and Gerald Astor, *The Right to Fight: A History of African Americans in the Military* (Novato, CA: Presidio, 1998), pp. 108–24.

13. Ulysses Lee, *The Employment of Negro Troops* (Washington, DC: U.S. Army, 1994), pp. 5, 6–20. This book appeared in the Army's Center of Military History series, *United States Army in World War II.*
14. Maj. Gen. Robert L. Bullard, *Personalities and Reminiscences of the War* (New York: Doubleday Page, 1925), p. 298.
15. Cited in Thomas Borstelmann, *The Cold War and the Color Line: American Race Relations in the Global Arena* (Cambridge: Harvard University Press, 2001), pp. 23–25.
16. In 1923, Houston had been the first black member of the editorial group at the *Harvard Law Review.* He became dean at Howard Law School in 1932, and in 1933 joined the NAACP to coordinate its litigation campaign against segregation. A warm intellectual and biographical salute to Houston can be found in Charles J. Ogletree, Jr., *All Deliberate Speed: Reflections of the First Half-Century of* Brown v. Board of Education (New York: W. W. Norton, 2004), pp. 111–23.
17. "Houston Has Polite Way of Calling U.S. Army Chief of Staff a Liar," *Baltimore Afro-American*, September 15, 1934. Ironically, it was MacArthur who first placed a black unit—albeit a small one, a quartermaster railhead company, under black command in the Southwest Pacific—"M'Arthur Sets Precedent, All Black Unit," *Boston Guardian*, May 23, 1943.
18. Cited in Carol Anderson, *Eyes Off the Prize: The United Nations and the American Struggle for Human Rights, 1944–1955* (Cambridge: Cambridge University Press, 2003), pp. 8, 9.
19. The campaign was initiated by the *Pittsburgh Courier.* See John Morton Blum, *V Was for Victory: Politics and American Culture During World War II* (New York: Harcourt Brace Jovanovich, 1976), p. 208.
20. W. E. B. Du Bois, "As the Crow Flies," *Amsterdam News*, March 14, 1942, cited in David Levering Lewis, *W. E. B. Dubois: The Fight for Equality and the American Century, 1919–1963* (New York: Henry Holt, 2000), p. 470. Many African Americans were more enthusiastic supporters of the war. Horace Mann Bond, for example, president of the historically black Fort Valley State College in Georgia and a specialist in black education, wrote in 1942 that "every American wishes desperately that the United States of America will win this war and such other wars as may engage the national and individual destinies of Americans. So feels, indeed, that quintessential American, the Negro in the United States"—Horace Mann Bond, "Should the Negro Care Who Wins the War?" in J. P. Shalloo and Donald Young, eds., "Minority Peoples in a Nation at War," *The Annals*, 223 (September 1942), p. 80.
21. W. E. B. Du Bois, "As the Crow Flies," *Amsterdam News*, December 23, 1939, cited in Lewis, *W. E. B. Dubois,* p. 463.
22. The Gold Coast became Ghana after decolonization.
23. Lewis, *W. E. B. Dubois*, pp. 469–70.
24. Anderson, *Eyes Off*, p. 9.
25. *The Crisis*, 47 (July 1940), p. 209 (italics in the original).
26. "Now is Not the Time to be Silent," *The Crisis*, 49 (January 1942), p. 7. The iso-

lationist press used this issue to argue against American participation in the war. For a discussion, see Lee, *Negro Troops*, pp. 65–66.

27. Roi Ottley, "Negro Morale," *New Republic*, November 10, 1941, in Clayborne Carson, David Garrow, Bill Kovach, and Carol Polsgrove, eds., *Reporting Civil Rights: Part One, American Journalism 1941–1963* (New York: The Library of America, 2003), p. 5.
28. Cited in Blum, *Victory*, p. 195.
29. Cited in Alan M. Osur, *Blacks in the Army Air Forces During World War II: The Problem of Race Relations* (Washington, DC: Office of Air Force History, 1977), p. 79.
30. Nonetheless, many southern whites reacted sharply to its publication. Congressman John Rankin of Mississippi denounced it as a "Communistic pamphlet"—Osur, *Army Air Forces*, p. 79. The Office of War Information also commissioned Frank Capra to produce and direct a film, *The Negro Soldier*, that stressed the role African Americans had played in the military as a means to enhance their pride and solidarity with the war and to educate whites.
31. Cited in Lewis, *W. E. B. Dubois*, pp. 465, 466; Neil A. Wynn, *The Afro-Americans and the Second World War* (New York: Holmes & Meier, 1975), p. 22; Osur, *Army Air Forces*, pp. 10–20.
32. Cited in Ottley, "Negro Morale," p. 9.
33. Cited in Lee, *Negro Troops*, pp. 158–59, 705.
34. Lucille Miller, "Jim Crow in the Army," *New Republic*, March 13, 1944, in Carson, et al., eds., *Reporting Civil Rights*, p. 53. For a useful overview of blacks and military affairs during the Second World War, see Desmond King, *Separate and Unequal: Black Americans and the US Federal Government* (Oxford: Clarendon Press, 1995), pp. 111–41. As in the First World War, no black was awarded a Medal of Honor in the Second. When Dorie Miller, a Navy messman, proved a hero at Pearl Harbor, he was awarded the Navy Cross after Secretary of the Navy Knox opposed granting the Medal of Honor on the grounds that such an award "carries with it for life the privilege of the floor of the House of Representatives"—"Navy Cross Awarded to Dorie Miller," *Baltimore Afro-American*, July 16, 1942.
35. Phillip McGuire, ed., *Taps for a Jim Crow Army: Letters from Black Soldiers in World War II* (Lexington: University of Kentucky Press, 1983), p. 135.
36. Ibid., pp. 19, 63, 50, 198, 191, 218. Complementing such letters, but also to be used with care because the principles of selection are unclear, is the oral history compiled and edited by Mary Penick Motley, *The Invisible Soldier: The Experience of the Black Soldier, World War II* (Detroit: Wayne State University Press, 1975). See also Maggi M. Morehouse, *Fighting in the Jim Crow Army: Black Men and Women Remember World War II* (Lanham, MD: Rowman & Littlefield, 2000).
37. MacGregor, *Integration*, pp. 46–49.
38. The original proposal had been for blacks to be integrated as individuals as the demand for troops at the front accelerated, but this plan was rejected by Dwight Eisenhower and replaced by a plan to integrate black platoons within

white companies—ibid., p. 52. This development is not mentioned in Eisenhower's memoir of the war. In a book of some 550 pages, the president speaks of black soldiers only once, when discussing "minor difficulties between Negro troops and other soldiers, or civilians" at his first press conference in Britain: "These incidents frequently involved social contacts between our Negro soldiers and British girls. The British population, except in large cities and among wealthy classes, lacks the racial consciousness which is so strong in the United States. The small-town British girl would go to a movie or a dance with a Negro quite as readily as she would with anyone else, a practice that our white soldiers could not understand. Brawls often resulted and our white soldiers were further bewildered when they found out that the British press took a firm stand on the side of the Negro"—Dwight D. Eisenhower, *Crusade in Europe* (New York: Doubleday & Company, 1948), pp. 58–59.

39. Cited in Osur, *Army Air Forces*, pp. 76–77. For a discussion of the 1943 shifts in the management of race in the military, see Daniel Kryder, *Divided Arsenal: Race and the American State During World War II* (New York: Cambridge University Press, 2000), p. 153.
40. Cited in Osur, *Army Air Forces*, p. 78.
41. Cited in Lee, *Negro Troops*, p. 223.
42. Cited in Blum, *Victory*, p. 211.
43. Kryder, *Divided Arsenal*, pp. 261, 140–41. A wave of racial violence involving larger numbers erupted later, in the spring of 1943. "By early summer, the harvest of racial antagonism was beginning to assume bumper proportions. Serious disorders occurred at Camp Van Dorn, Mississippi; Camp Stewart, Georgia; Lake Charles, Louisiana; March Field and Camp San Luis Obispo, California; Camp Bliss, Texas; Camp Phillips, Kansas; Camp Breckenridge, Kentucky; and Camp Shenango, Pennsylvania. Other camps had lesser disorders and rumors of unrest"—Lee, *Negro Troops*, p. 366.
44. Foner, *Blacks and the Military*, p. 154.
45. Cited in MacGregor, *Integration*, p. 23. For an incisive account of the depths of racism in the first decades of the twentieth century, see Claudia Roth Pierpont, "The Measure of America: The Anthropologist Who Fought Racism," *The New Yorker*, March 8, 2004, pp. 48–63.
46. Cited in MacGregor, *Integration*, pp. 21–22, 20. For a summary of the first lady's position that "The nation cannot expect colored people to feel that the United States is worth defending if the Negro continues to be treated as he is being treated now," see "'U.S. Can't Expect Loyalty of Negro Under Present Conditions': Mrs. FDR," *Chicago Defender*, January 17, 1942.
47. Samuel A. Stouffer, et al., *The American Soldier: Adjustment During Army Life*. Vol. 1 (Princeton: Princeton University Press, 1949), pp. 486–87.
48. Lee, *Negro Troops*, p. 76.
49. Ibid., p. 77.
50. Less than a fortnight earlier, President Roosevelt had met, at his wife's urging, with a black delegation to discuss the armed forces. It included Walter White,

A. Philip Randolph, and T. Arnold Hill, who requested the administration institute a policy that would place black soldiers exclusively on the basis of their ability and training. They viewed the October 9 policy as a betrayal. The president's main response was to appoint Judge William Hastie, then dean of Howard University Law School, as his civilian aide on Negro Affairs, who later resigned (1943) to protest his ineffectual position and the meager opportunities offered black soldiers, and to promote Benjamin O. Davis, the senior black officer in the Army, to the rank of brigadier general. Davis's son was a leading general during the Vietnam War.

51. MacGregor, *Integration*, p. 56.
52. "Negro Soldiers Only 2.5 P.C. of U.S. Army," *Baltimore Afro-American*, February 20, 1932.
53. "Don't Forget the Negro Soldiers," *Pittsburgh Courier*, July 21, 1934; "A Bigger Army and the Negro Soldier," *Pittsburgh Courier*, June 2, 1934.
54. "255,700 Men in U.S. Army; Only 2954 Are Colored," *Baltimore Afro-American*, December 15, 1934; "G.O.P Changed Regular Army Units into Stable Boys," *Baltimore Afro-American*, October 3, 1936.
55. "Courier Campaigns for Army, Navy Recognition; Race Demands Fighting Chance on Land, Sea, In Air," *Pittsburgh Courier*, February 19, 1938.
56. "Because! Ten Cardinal Points In Courier's Campaign for Army and Navy Equality," *Pittsburgh Courier*, March 26, 1938.
57. Cited in Richard M. Dalfiume, *Desegregation of the U.S. Armed Forces: Fighting on Two Fronts, 1939–1953* (Columbia: University of Missouri Press, 1969), p. 38.
58. "Southern Americanism," *Pittsburgh Courier*, November 23, 1940.
59. Ruth Danenhower Wilson, *Jim Crow Joins Up: A Study of Negroes in the Armed Forces of the United States* (New York: William J. Clark, 1944), p. 7.
60. An unpublished provision called for black units to be led by 50 per cent more officers than white units because blacks were thought to need closer supervision.
61. Lee, *Negro Troops*, pp. 30–32, 37–44; Dalfiume, *Desegregation*, pp. 22–23.
62. Lee, *Negro Troops*, p. 45.
63. "Southern Americanism," *Pittsburgh Courier*, November 29, 1940.
64. George Q. Flynn, "Selective Service and American Blacks During World War II," *Journal of Negro History*, 69 (Winter 1984), pp. 15, 16, 17, 19, 20. See also Paul T. Murray, "Blacks and the Draft: A History of Institutional Racism," *Journal of Black Studies*, 2 (September 1971), p. 66; and Harry A. Marmion, "Historical Background of Selective Service in the United States," in Roger W. Little, ed., *Selective Service and American Society* (New York: Russell Sage Foundation, 1969), pp. 40–42.
65. For a discussion, see Joseph Schiffman, "The Education of Negro Soldiers in World War II," *Journal of Negro Education*, 18 (Winter 1949).
66. Stouffer, *American Soldier*, p. 490.
67. Phillip McGuire, "Desegregation of the Armed Forces: Black Leadership, Protest, and World War II," *Journal of Negro History*, 68 (Spring 1983), p. 148.

68. Cited in McGuire, "Desegregation," p. 148.
69. Cited in ibid., p. 155.
70. Flynn, "Selective Service," p. 21.
71. Beth S. Wenger, *New York Jews and the Great Depression: Uncertain Promise* (New Haven: Yale University Press, 1996), p. 2.
72. See Harold S. Wechsler, *The Qualified Student: A History of Selective College Admissions in America* (New York: John Wiley, 1977); Susanne Klingenstein, *Jews in the American Academy, 1900–1940: The Dynamics of Cultural Assimilation* (New Haven: Yale University Press, 1991); and Marcia Graham Scott, *The Half-Opened Door: Discrimination and Admissions at Harvard, Yale, and Princeton, 1900–1970* (Westport, CT: Greenwood Press, 1979).
73. For a useful overview, see Edward S. Shapiro, "World War II and American Jewish Identity," *Modern Judaism*, 10 (February 1990). Shapiro cites estimates that in the early 1940s, nearly one in three job categories in the United States were restricted to Christians. Other discussions of the period's anti-Semitic upsurge include Donald Strong, *Organized Anti-Semitism in America: The Rise of Group Prejudice During the Decade 1930–1940* (Washington, DC: American Council on Public Affairs, 1941); Alan Brinkley, *Voices of Protest: Huey Long, Father Coughlin and the Great Depression* (New York: Knopf, 1982); and Ronald H. Bayor, *Neighbors in Conflict: The Irish, Germans, Jews, and Italians of New York City, 1929–1941* (Baltimore: Johns Hopkins University Press, 1978).
74. The men questioning the decision were Henry Morgenthau, Jr., and Arthur Hayes Sulzberger; the judge was Felix Frankfurter. For a discussion, see Leonard Dinnerstein, *Anti-Semitism in America* (New York: Oxford University Press, 1994), p. 125.
75. Marshall Sklare, ed., *The Jews: Social Patterns of an American Group* (Glencoe, IL: Free Press, 1957).
76. For an overview, see Edward S. Shapiro, *A Time for Healing: American Jewry Since World War II* (Baltimore: Johns Hopkins University Press, 1992).
77. For an example, see Geroid Tanquary Robinson, "Racial Minorities," in Harold E. Stearns, ed., *Civilization in the United States: An Enquiry by Thirty Americans* (London: Jonathan Cape, 1922).
78. For discussions, see Karen Brodkin, *How Jews Became White Folks and What That Says About Race in America* (New Brunswick: Rutgers University Press, 1998); and Gary Gerstle, *Working-class Americanism: The Politics of Labor in a Textile City, 1914–1960* (New York: Cambridge University Press, 1989), and *American Crucible: Race and Nation in the Twentieth Century* (Princeton: Princeton University Press, 2001).
79. William H. Hastie, "The Negro in the Army Today," in Shalloo and Young, eds., "Minority Peoples," p. 59.
80. Buckley, *American Patriots*, p. 273; MacGregor, *Integration*, p. 36.
81. Morehouse, *Fighting in the Jim Crow Army*, pp. 112–14.
82. Buckley, *American Patriots*, p. 282.
83. Lee, *Negro Troops*, p. 316.

84. "Jim Crow Air Raid Shelters?" *The Crisis*, 49 (January 1941), p. 7.
85. Years later, African Americans often celebrated their pride in their war, which retrospectively has come to be understood as the birth time of civil rights. For an example, see the coffee table book filled with photographs of heroic soldiers and hagiographic prose by Robert Ewell Greene, *Black Defenders of America, 1775–1973* (Chicago: Johnson Publishing Co., 1974), pp. 185–210.
86. Lee, *Negro Troops*, p. 406.
87. "Admiral Says Negroes Too Intelligent: Would Dominate Navy Service If Enlisted," *Oklahoma City Black Dispatch*, February 1, 1941. The Navy's instructions to its black sailors were tailored to fit the limited category they could occupy. In a directive of "Information and Instructions for Messmen Branch (For Negroes Only)," the Navy listed sixteen rules. They included, "1. Bathe daily and keep clean at all times . . . 5. Do no loud talking in or about pantry or mess room . . . 8. If the bell rings when both watch boy and relief boy are absent from pantry, any boy there should answer the bell and will be expected to do so at once . . . 9. All mess attendants . . . will help set tables and clear tables for each meal." Cited in "Here Is the Type of Work Our Boys Do as Messmen in the U.S. Navy," *Pittsburgh Courier*, December 3, 1941.
88. MacGregor, *Integration*, pp. 58, 84.
89. Schiffman, "Education of Negro Soldiers," p. 25.
90. John Modell, Marc Goulden, and Sigurdur Magnusson, "World War II in the Lives of Black Americans: Some Findings and an Interpretation," *Journal of American History*, 76 (December 1989), p. 838.
91. Ibid., p. 839.
92. For a discussion of total institutions, see Erving Goffman, *Asylums: Essays on the Social Situation of Mental Patients and Other Inmates* (Chicago: Aldine Publishing, 1961).
93. Charles C. Moskos, Jr., "The Military," *Annual Review of Sociology*, 2 (1976), pp. 55–77; Richard H. Kohn, "The Social History of the American Soldier," *American Historical Review*, 86 (June 1981), pp. 553–67; *The United States Army in World War II: The Organization of Ground Combat Troops* (Washington, DC: Government Printing Office, 1947); Pete Daniel, "Going Among Strangers: Southern Reactions to World War II," *Journal of American History*, 77 (December 1990).
94. Schiffman, "Education of Negro Soldiers," p. 23.
95. Robert C. Weaver, "The Negro Veteran," in Paul Webbink, ed., "Postwar Jobs for Veterans," *The Annals*, 238 (March 1945), p. 129.
96. MacGregor, *Integration*, p. 125.
97. McGuire, "Desegregation," p. 155.
98. Paula Fass, *Outside In: Minorities and the Transformation of American Education* (New York: Oxford University Press, 1989), p. 142. There were wide disparities in schooling; 41 percent of whites in the Army had graduated from high school but just 17 percent of blacks; in all, 70 percent of whites had experienced some formal education after grade school, but just 43 percent of blacks (ibid.).

99. Cited in ibid., p. 144.
100. Schiffman, "Education of Negro Troops," p. 22.
101. For discussions, see Lee, *Negro Troops*, pp. 257–70; Fass, *Outside In*, pp. 139–51.
102. Fass, *Outside In*, pp. 148–49; Eli Ginzberg and Douglas W. Bray, *The Uneducated* (New York: Columbia University Press, 1953), pp. 125, 131.
103. Stouffer, *American Soldier*, pp. 495–96, 499, 501, 502, 583.
104. Lee, *Negro Troops*, p. 271.
105. Ibid., p. 272.
106. The military situation in some key respects thus resembled the earlier Civilian Conservation Corps (CCC) experience. Because New Deal relief programs did not last beyond the onset of the war, the military, in effect, replaced those programs as a source of training and funds. On a larger and more authoritative scale, the situation of those blacks who were taken by the armed services resembled the condition of African Americans in the CCC program. There, too, about 10 percent of the participants had been black men. There, too, residential programs had been coupled with basic literacy and skills training. There, too, the camps, basically under white supervision, were segregated by race. For a discussion of the educational features of the program, see John A. Salmond, *The Civilian Conservation Corps, 1933–1942: A New Deal Case Study* (Durham: Duke University Press, 1967), pp. 47–54.
107. Stouffer, *American Soldier*, pp. 502, 504–06, 535.

Chapter 5

1. Robert D. Putnam, *Bowling Alone: The Collapse and Revival of American Community* (New York: Simon & Schuster, 2000), p. 268.
2. Sar A. Levitan and Karen A. Cleary, *Old Wars Remain Unfinished: The Veterans Benefits System* (Baltimore: Johns Hopkins University Press, 1973), pp. 27, 3.
3. "Everything was new: new homes, new cars, new appliances, new markets, new foods, new friends, new ways of entertaining . . . new schools, even new churches. . . . Rarely in the history of the world had more people enjoyed so many new things so quickly. At the same time, those people were making themselves into a new people in a social culture defined, above all, by home ownership in the suburbs"—Michael J. Bennett, *When Dreams Came True: The GI Bill and the Making of Modern America* (McLean, VA: Brassey's Publishing, 1996), p. 279.
4. Office of the Press Secretary, The White House, "Remarks by the President at 'Remembering Franklin D. Roosevelt,' 50th Anniversary Commemorative Services," The Little White House, Warm Springs, Georgia, April 12, 1995, cited in Theda Skocpol, "The G.I. Bill and U.S. Social Policy, Past and Future," *Social Philosophy and Policy*, 14 (Summer 1997), pp. 95–96. Allied forces invaded Normandy on June 6; President Roosevelt signed the GI Bill into law on June 22.
5. Milton Greenburg, "The GI Bill," *Educational Record*, 75 (Fall 1994), pp. 56–57.
6. Michael Bennett, "The Law That Worked," *Educational Record*, 75 (Fall 1994), pp. 6, 12.

7. Truman K. Gibson, Jr., "Government Fails Negro Vets: Systematic Denial of Rights Under GI Bill Scored at Conference; New Technique Needed to Get Results Under Government Program," *Pittsburgh Courier*, April 13, 1946.
8. As a kind of "popular front" organization that included Communists, the American Veterans Committee (AVC) was the most left-wing veterans' organization. It also was the only one that was racially integrated. By contrast, American Legion and Veterans of Foreign Wars posts in the South were segregated, though blacks were permitted to form their own posts.
9. Charles G. Bolte and Louis Harris, *Our Negro Veterans* (New York: Public Affairs Committee, Pamphlet #128, 1947), p. 28. Bolte was chairman of the American Veterans Committee.
10. Ibid., p. 20.
11. There were 1,015,200 housing starts in 1946, and 412,000 VA mortgages; for 1947, the comparable numbers were 1,265,100 and 542,000—Bennett, *When Dreams*, p. 287.
12. Ronald Tobey, Charles Wetherell, and Jay Brigham, "Moving Out and Settling In: Residential Mobility, Home Owning, and the Public Enframing of Citizenship, 1921–1950," *American Historical Review*, 95 (December 1990), p. 1414.
13. For an excellent overview, see Kenneth T. Jackson, *Crabgrass Frontier: The Suburbanization of the United States* (New York: Oxford University Press, 1985).
14. Bennett, *When Dreams*, p. 24 (italics in the original).
15. Helen Lefkowitz Horowitz, *Campus Life: Undergraduate Culture from the End of the Eighteenth Century to the Present* (Chicago: University of Chicago Press, 1987), pp. 185–86.
16. Keith W. Olson, *The G.I. Bill, the Veterans, and the Colleges* (Lexington: University of Kentucky Press, 1974), pp. 59, 44.
17. Edwin Kiester, Jr., "The G.I. Bill May Be the Best Deal Ever Made by Uncle Sam," *Smithsonian*, 25 (November 1994), pp. 129–39; Bennett, *When Dreams.* This hagiographic treatment is the norm. It certainly marks not only these works but the first major book on the subject: David R. B. Ross, *Preparing for Ulysses: The Federal Government and Non-Disabled World War Two Veterans, 1940–1946* (New York: Columbia University Press, 1967). "This time, for the first time," Michael Bennett argued, "the federal government, having carefully selected and trained its most intelligent and vigorous young people to kill in war, would give them the tools to make new lives in peacetime. The result was a revolution of changing expectations, which swiftly became rising ones. For the first time in history, a social revolution was being made, not by storming barricades, but by leaping over them. People were doing it on their own, as individuals, not as members of a class or race or ethnic group or political party" (p. 7).
18. Veterans no longer had to demonstrate their schooling had been interrupted by the war, and the size of grants for those in school was raised. Loan guarantees were enhanced, and interest capped at 4 percent—"Liberalization of GI Bill of Rights," *Monthly Labor Review*, 62 (April 1946), p. 595.

19. Skocpol, "G.I. Bill," pp. 114–15. Her overview mentions only two shortcomings: the way the legislation retarded the entry of women into colleges and universities because of the advantages it gave men, who represented some 98 per cent of veterans, and the country's inadequate system of vocational education. As in the vast majority of writing on the GI Bill, race is not mentioned at all as a distinct subject or problem. To be sure, Skocpol has written an excellent overview of "African Americans in U.S. Social Policy" in Paul E. Peterson, ed., *Classifying by Race* (Princeton: Princeton University Press, 1996). This text discusses New Deal social policy thoughtfully, if briefly, and rightly concludes that "in many ways African Americans were as much excluded and marginalized—and perhaps, over time, more symbolically stigmatized—by the major social policies of the New Deal era as they were by the major policies of the Civil War and Maternalist eras." But it only considers the bill in favorable terms, without assessing the way in which it, too, classified by race. In addition to Social Security, Skocpol notes, the "only other truly generous and comprehensive part of national social provision was the GI Bill of 1944, which featured employment assistance and educational and housing loans for military veterans" (pp. 144, 133). See also the discussion in Skocpol, "Delivering for Young Families: The Resonance of the GI Bill," *American Prospect*, 28 (September–October 1996), pp. 66–72.
20. Frederick F. Siegel, *Troubled Journey: From Pearl Harbor to Ronald Reagan* (New York: Hill & Wang, 1984), p. 95.
21. Bennett, *When Dreams*, p. 7.
22. *Opportunity*, 23 (Winter 1945), pp. 51–56.
23. Colonel Campbell C. Johnson, "The Unforgotten Man," *Opportunity*, 23 (Winter 1945), p. 20.
24. Charles Hurd, "Democracy Challenged," *Opportunity*, 23 (Spring 1945), p. 63.
25. Bennett, *When Dreams*, p. 26.
26. Ambrose Caliver, *Postwar Education of Negroes: Educational Implications of Army Data and Experiences of Negro Veterans and War Workers* (Washington, DC: Federal Security Agency, U.S. Office of Education, 1945), pp. 11, 8, 39. Caliver was titled Senior Specialist in the Education of Negroes.
27. *Baltimore Afro-American*, January 6, 1945; *Atlanta World*, January 11, 1945.
28. As examples: "Vets Get $1,000 Year for Schooling; Others Who Want to Buy Homes, Farms, Enter Business Can Get $2,000 Loans," *Baltimore Afro-American*, August 5, 1944; "G.I. Bill of Rights and What It Means," *New Orleans Weekly*, September 16, 1944; "The G.I. Bill of Rights," *Philadelphia Tribune*, January 20, 1945.
29. *Servicemen's Rights and Benefits: A Handy Guide for Veterans of the Armed Forces and Their Dependents* (Washington, DC: Government Printing Office, 1944); Tracy Goodwin, *Veterans Handbook and Guide* (Cincinnati: Goodwin Publications, 1946).
30. "Postwar Plans of Negro and White Veterans," *The Southern Frontier*, 6 (June 1945), p. 1.

31. John Modell, Marc Goulden, and Sigurdur Magnusson, "World War II in the Lives of Black Americans: Some Findings and an Interpretation," *Journal of American History*, 76 (December 1989), p. 842.
32. Cited in Greenburg, "GI Bill," p. 63.
33. Suzanne Mettler, "'The Only Good Thing Was the G.I. Bill': Racial Incorporation and the Educational Provisions of the G.I. Bill Among World War II Veterans," paper prepared for the Annual Meeting of the American Political Science Association, Boston, August 29–September 1, 2002, p. 14. Mettler reached these conclusions based on black participation rates and the feedback she received in a survey she conducted with Second World War veterans between 1998 and 2001 as well as interviews with grateful black veterans who had fought with the 92nd Infantry Division. This, it might be noted, was not a typical African American unit. It was the only completely black force deployed in European combat, losing 25 percent of its men between August 1944 and April 1945. The gains black veterans made, despite discrimination, provide a major theme in Mettler's forthcoming book, *Civic Generation: The G.I. Bill in the Lives of World War II Veterans* (New York: Oxford University Press, n.d.).
34. Mettler, "Only Good Thing," p. 19.
35. James A. Atkins, "Negro Educational Institutions and the Veterans Educational Facilities Program," *Journal of Negro Education*, 27 (Spring 1948), pp. 144–46. The 1945 amendments to the Lanham Act of 1940 and the Veterans Educational Facilities Program created in 1946 were the sources of federal aid to historically black colleges—Mettler, "Only Good Thing," p. 22.
36. Bennett, *When Dreams*, p. 27; see also John Dittmer, *Local People: The Struggle for Civil Rights in Mississippi* (Urbana: University of Illinois Press, 1994). This trend in which veterans took the lead was clear as early as late 1945. "Several hundred veterans held a spirited mass meeting last week at Morehouse College" in Atlanta, the *Louisiana Weekly* reported, "and pledged themselves to follow a program of action designed to bring a 'full share of the democracy they fought for in the war'"—"Georgia Veterans Pledge to Seek Democracy in Ga.," *Louisiana Weekly*, December 15, 1945.
37. Robert A. Eubanks, "GI Bill Expands Access for African Americans," *The Educational Record*, 75 (Fall 1994), pp. 32, 40; Bennett, *When Dreams*, p. 26. For a brief summary of the "unexpected benefits for Blacks" and for how the bill "provided for much of today's Black middle class and the education of a generation of African Americans who helped spear the civil rights movement," see Ronald Roach, "From Combat to Campus: GI Bill Gave a Generation of African Americans an Opportunity to Pursue the American Dream," *Black Issues in Higher Education*, 14 (August 1997), p. 26.
38. Research Division, Coordination Service, Veterans Administration, "Benefits and Services Received by World War II Veterans Under the Major Veterans Administration Programs: Report of a Special Study," RG 5, ser. 39.20a, Box 9, National Archives, pp. 12, 13, 20. The report is undated but is attributed as

August 1950 in Michael G. Brown, *Race, Money, and the American Welfare State* (Ithaca: Cornell University Press, 1999), p. 190. I am keenly indebted to Michael Brown for providing me with a photocopy of the report, which he unearthed in the National Archives. This document's data has to be read with extreme caution. That the sample size is small is not itself a problem; the margin of error is within a range of just 1 percent. But the document does not report on the demographic characteristics of the approximately fifteen thousand veterans who did respond, including the racial distribution of respondents. Further, given the upward tilt of most respondents, there is good reason to believe that the African Americans who were surveyed were disproportionately northern, better off, and more likely to have used the GI Bill.

39. Eli Ginzburg and Douglas W. Bray, *The Uneducated* (New York: Columbia University Press, 1953), p. 126. See also Samuel Goldberg, *Army Training of Illiterates in World War II* (New York: Columbia University Press, 1951).
40. Mettler, "Only Good Thing," p. 36.
41. Hilary Herbold, "Never a Level Playing Field: Blacks and the GI Bill," *Journal of Blacks in Higher Education*, 6 (Winter 1994–95), p. 104. I was first directed to the line of analysis in the discussion that follows by this brief, suggestive article, which offered a perspective I had not seen before. Then I heard David Onkst speak in October 1995 at the Hagley Museum and Library. The paper he presented drew on his master's thesis for the Department of History, University of Georgia, 1990; it was later published as David H. Onkst, "'First a Negro . . . Incidentally a Veteran': Black World War Two Veterans and the G.I. Bill of Rights in the Deep South, 1944–1948," *Journal of Social History*, 31 (Spring 1998), pp. 517–43. The most thorough consideration of the bill from this critical perspective is the excellent Ph.D. dissertation by Kathleen Hill Frydl, "The GI Bill," Department of History, University of Chicago, 2000. The GI Bill also strengthened traditional gender relationships. By offering benefits only to veterans, 98 percent of whom were men, the legislation reinforced the position of men as head of household. Women did benefit, but indirectly, as members of a given family. For a discussion of how "it was mostly male veterans who found their transition back to civilian life eased by government largesse," see Lizabeth Cohen, *A Consumers' Republic: The Politics of Mass Consumption in Postwar America* (New York: Knopf, 2003), pp. 137–43.
42. White to Roosevelt, October 5, 1944, "Colored Matters (Negroes)," October–December 1944, Box 6, OF 93, Franklin D. Roosevelt Library, Hyde Park, New York, cited in Mettler, "Only Good Thing," pp. 16–17.
43. *Lubbock Avalanche*, June 6, 1945; *Los Angeles Tribune*, September 11, 1944; *Atlanta Daily World*, October 25, 1945.
44. *New York Times*, June 2, 1944, p. 16.
45. For an overview of the way in which the First World War helped fashion an early, if still rather primitive American welfare state, see Karl Hickel's Ph.D. dissertation "Entitling Citizen: World War I, Progressivism, and the Origins of the American Welfare State, 1917–1928," Department of History, Columbia

University, 1999. See also his treatment of the payment of allotments to wives of servicemen and the impact on both white and black women in the South in K. Walter Hickel, "War, Region, and Social Welfare: Federal Aid to Servicemen's Dependents in the South," *Journal of American History*, 87 (March 2001).

46. Skocpol correctly emphasizes the key role of the Legion in crafting and passing the GI Bill, stressing the role of voluntary civic organizations in American politics. But she does not point to the organization's accommodation to racism. This oversight tends to recur in the literature on civic participation, especially when it celebrates the 1940s as the baseline from which to lament subsequent declines. See Putnam, *Bowling Alone.*
47. Bureau of the Budget Memorandum, September 2, 1943; cited in Frydl, "GI Bill," p. 132.
48. Cited in ibid., p. 182.
49. Ibid., p. 76.
50. For a discussion of postwar economic fears, see Alan Brinkley, *The End of Reform: New Deal Liberalism in Recession and War* (New York: Knopf, 1995), pp. 227–64. For social adjustment and psychological well-being issues, I have profited from reading Christopher P. Loss, "Between Citizens and the State: World War II, Education, and the G.I. Bill of Rights," University of Virginia Miller Center of Public Affairs, 20th Century Colloquium, December 5, 2003.
51. In contentious debates in his committee about Title V, on unemployment, it became clear that Rankin's commitment to segregation was the stronger of the two preferences.
52. William Wheeler, director of Wheeler Business College, to Rankin, January 28, 1943, cited in Frydl, "GI Bill," p. 175.
53. "Black enlistments for southern states in per centage of total black population: Alabama: 24%; Arkansas: 16.3%; DC: 26.2%; Florida: 22.7%; Georgia: 21.5%; Louisiana: 27.6%; Mississippi: 38.5%; North Carolina: 19.6%; South Carolina: 28.1%; Virginia: 19.6%. On average, a state could expect to receive one fifth of its black population back from service"—Frydl, "GI Bill," p. 296.
54. Cited in ibid., pp. 183, 184.
55. Cited in ibid., pp. 185, 186.
56. Omar N. Bradley (with Clay Blair), *A General's Life: An Autobiography by the General of the Army, Omar N, Bradley* (New York: Simon & Schuster, 1983), p. 450.
57. Cited in Frydl, "GI Bill," pp. 310, 309.
58. Ibid., p. 311.
59. March 25, 1946, cited in ibid., p. 312.
60. Ibid., pp. 224, 295, 224. Frydl reports that, in 1951, the Veterans Administration destroyed copies of agreements it signed with individual states. "However, Representative John Rankin made certain to obtain a copy of Mississippi's contract for himself. This contract, signed the day after the GI Bill became effective, survives in House records. Along with sending the contract, the Mississippi Unemployment Compensation Commission sent a letter assuring

the Congressman that they felt confident 'in administering Title V of the Servicemen's Readjustment Act of 1944,' that it would 'demonstrate, as indeed [it had] in administering the Unemployment Compensation Law, that it can do a better job than could be done under Federal administration'" (p. 310).

61. Joseph Albright to Omar Bradley, October 25, 1946, cited in ibid., p. 328. Albright, a Second World War veteran, had been working at the Associated Negro Press.
62. Cited in ibid., pp. 321, 333.
63. U.S. Selective Service System, *Selective Service and Victory: The 4th Report of the Director of Selective Service* (Washington, DC: Government Printing Office, 1948), pp. 187–96; Ulysses Lee, *The Employment of Negro Troops* (Washington, DC: U.S. Army, 1994), pp. 239–99; Modell, Goulden, and Magnusson, "World War II," p. 841; Mettler, "Only Good Thing," p. 6.
64. Levitan and Cleary, *Old Wars*, pp. 4–5.
65. *Nassau Sovereign*, October 1942, cited in Herbold, "Never a Level Playing Field," p. 107.
66. Herbold, "Never a Level Playing Field," p. 107.
67. President's Committee on Civil Rights, *To Secure These Rights: The Report of the President's Committee on Civil Rights* (New York: Simon & Schuster, 1947), p. 66. The report also noted prejudice against Catholic applicants. For discussions of how the GI Bill reshaped the educational opportunities of Jews and Catholics, see Deborah Dash Moore, *GI Jews: How World War II Changed a Generation* (Cambridge: Harvard University Press, 2004), esp. chapter 8, "Coming Home"; and Elizabeth A. Edmonson, "Without Comment or Controversy: The G.I. Bill and Catholic Colleges," *Church History*, 71 (December 2002).
68. Charles H. Thompson, "The Critical Situation in Negro Higher and Professional Education," *Journal of Negro Education*, 25 (Fall 1946), p. 590.
69. Charles H. Thompson, "Editorial Comment: Some Critical Aspects of the Problem of the Higher and Professional Education for Negroes," *Journal of Negro Education*, 14 (Autumn 1945), p. 509.
70. In 1892, Homer Adolph Plessy, who was seven-eighths Caucasian, had taken a seat in a "whites only" car of a Louisiana train. He was arrested when he refused to move to the car reserved for blacks. The Court found that the equal protection requirements of the Fourteenth Amendment, "in the nature of things . . . could not have been intended to abolish distinctions based upon color, or to enforce social, as distinguished from political equality, or a commingling of the two races unsatisfactory to either"—*Plessy v. Ferguson*, 163 U.S. 537 (1896).
71. Pauli Murray, ed., *States' Laws on Race and Color* (New York: Women's Division of Christian Service, 1950), pp. 463, 429, 239, 240. This remarkable compilation (over 700 pp) was published by a division of the Methodist Church to provide guidance to "state laws that have in some measure determined racial patterns and practices throughout the nation."
72. The first, in 1862, had provided federal funds for land-grant colleges.
73. President's Commission on Higher Education, *Higher Education for American*

Democracy: A Report of the President's Commission on Higher Education. Vol. VI: *Resource Data* (New York: Harper & Brothers, 1948), p. 21.

74. Atkins, "Negro Educational Institutions," p. 146; Martin D. Jenkins, "The Availability of Higher Education for Negroes in the Southern States," *Journal of Negro Education*, 16 (Summer 1947), p. 460.
75. Caliver, *Postwar Education*, p. 35.
76. Olson, *G.I. Bill*, p. 74. "The overcrowding encountered by the 1,800,000 veterans who have applied for schools has been particularly serious for Negro veterans. Most white colleges have strict quotas for Negroes, and Negro colleges are small and few in number"—Bolte and Harris, *Negro Veterans*, p. 10.
77. Cohen, *Consumer's Republic*, p. 169.
78. Sarah Turner and John Bound, *Closing the Gap or Widening the Divide: The Effects of the G.I. Bill and World War II on the Educational Outcomes of Black Americans* (Washington, DC: National Bureau of Economic Research, Working Paper 9044, 2002), p. 8.
79. Martin D. Jenkins, "Enrollment in Institutions of Higher Education for Negroes, 1946–1947," *Journal of Negro Education*, 16 (Spring 1947), p. 255.
80. Atkins, "Negro Educational Institutions," p. 145.
81. Turner and Bound, *Closing the Gap*, p. 9.
82. Thompson, "Some Critical Aspects," pp. 518, 519 (italics in the original).
83. Walter R. Chivers, "Traditionalism in Negro Colleges," *The Educational Record*, 25 (April 1944), p. 138.
84. Thompson, "Critical Situation," p. 581.
85. Jenkins, "Availability of Higher Education," p. 462.
86. By contrast, the GI Bill proved a huge boon to religious colleges. The law allowed veterans to use their educational grants at any college, including any religious college, of their choice. As a result, enrollments boomed in Baptist, Lutheran, Methodist and especially Catholic institutions, which schooled over 100,000 veterans. See Edmonson, "Without Comment or Controversy."
87. The best source of systematic information is Turner and Bound, *Closing the Gap*. See also John Bound and Sarah Turner, "Going to War and Going to College: Did World War II and the G.I. Bill Increase Educational Attainment for Returning Veterans?," *Journal of Labor Economics* 20 (October 2002).
88. Turner and Bound, *Closing the Gap*, pp. 5, 32.
89. Similarly, the enforcement of the anti-discrimination provisions of President Roosevelt's 1941 Executive Order 8802, which created the Fair Employment Practices Committee that prohibited racial discrimination in war production industries, led to significant wage gains for blacks in the North but not in the South, where its application was thwarted by effective political opposition—see William J. Collins, "Race, Roosevelt, and Wartime Production: Fair Employment in World War II Labor Markets," *American Economic Review*, 91 (March 2001).
90. A study of postwar education and earnings found that whites with at least one year of college earned $1,300 per year more than individuals whose schooling

stopped at high school. For blacks, the gain was limited to $300—Herman Phillip Miller, *Income Distribution in the United States* (Washington, DC: Government Printing Office, 1966), pp. 145–46.

91. Turner and Bound, *Closing the Gap*, p. 25. "The results of this analysis," they dryly observe, "illustrate some of the pitfalls associated with decentralized federal initiatives." They also conclude that insufficiencies of supply were a more powerful cause of black lags in the South than poor preparation for college. Because the armed forces disproportionately kept out inadequately educated blacks, the average black veteran had a much better than average chance to qualify, especially for the standards applied by black colleges at the time. (pp. 24, 22–23) Mettler has criticized this study for its focus on "formal educational attainment. Therefore, it overlooks the significance of sub-college programs that African American veterans used disproportionately, given that, on average, they had less prior education than white veterans"—Mettler, "Only Good Thing," p. 3. In no respect, though, does this critique invalidate the key findings of Turner and Bound. It also is misleading in placing excessive emphasis on the lack of preparation of blacks for college rather than on the absence of places for African Americans. Turner and Bound demonstrate systematically that the latter cause outweighed the former in the case of access to higher education, as there were many more eligible black veterans than were able to find places at black colleges.
92. U.S. President's Commission on Veterans' Pensions, *Veterans' Benefits in the United States* (Washington, DC: Government Printing Office, 1956), p. 287.
93. Bolte and Harris, *Negro Veterans*, pp. 14–15.
94. Ibid., p. 14; Onkst, "First a Negro," p. 526.
95. Bolte and Harris, *Negro Veterans*, p. 14.
96. Frydl, "GI Bill," p. 256.
97. Cited in ibid., p. 331. Similarly, the VA office in Montgomery, Alabama, told Albright that any proactive efforts on behalf of job training for blacks "might impair the very pleasant working relationship" with local white institutions "which exists at the present time" (p. 332).
98. Cited in Bolte and Harris, *Negro Veterans*, p. 15.
99. Onkst, "First a Negro," p. 530.
100. Frydl, "GI Bill," p. 283.
101. Onkst, "First a Negro," p. 531.
102. Bolte and Harris, *Negro Veterans*, p. 15.
103. A useful overview of its role can be found in Leonard P. Adams, *The Public Employment Service in Transition, 1933–1968* (Ithaca: School of Industrial Relations, Cornell University, 1969); see also Ira Katznelson and Bruce Pietrykowski, "Rebuilding the American State: Evidence from the 1940s," *Studies in American Political Development*, 5 (#2, 1991), pp. 327–32.
104. For a discussion of employment discrimination in the North, see Cohen, *Consumer's Republic*, p. 169.
105. Onkst, "First a Negro," p. 522.

106. Undated SRC report by Harry Wright, cited in ibid., p. 521.
107. Letter of Reuben H. Thompson to the National Farm Labor Union, May 7, 1946, cited in ibid., p. 523.
108. Banks used the Residential Security Maps and the standards provided by the Federal Housing Administration to make such judgments. Often, these practices negatively affected poor whites, but there is no doubt but that they disproportionately disadvantaged black applicants. For discussions, see Desmond King, *Separate and Unequal: Black Americans and the US Federal Government* (Oxford: Clarendon Press, 1995), chapter 6, dealing both with the USES and housing; and Michael Goldfield, *The Color of Politics: Race and the Mainsprings of American Politics* (New York: New Press, 1997), p. 205.
109. E. A. Crawford to H. Boyd Hall of the NAACP, June 13, 1946; cited in Frydl, "GI Bill," p. 313.
110. Cohen, *Consumers' Republic*, p. 171.
111. "GI Loans: Colored Vets Who Borrow Cash Prove Sound Business Investments," *Ebony*, 10 (August 1947), cited in Onkst, "First a Negro," pp. 522–23.
112. A surprisingly generous evaluation, demonstrating just how hard it is to break with the conventionally positive assessments, can be found in an excellent overview of federal government bias against blacks during the nineteenth and twentieth centuries by Linda Faye Williams, *The Constraint of Race: Legacies of White Skin Privilege in America* (University Park: Pennsylvania State University Press, 2003), pp. 112–15. Williams places far less emphasis on the legislation and its official implementation than on the consequences of implementing this, and other "race neutral and 'universal' policies when they are instituted within the context of widespread racial inequality and white advantage" (p. 113).

Chapter 6

1. John Skrentny, *The Minority Rights Revolution* (Cambridge: Harvard University Press, 2002), p. 5.
2. "This was the first time that the term 'affirmative action' had been used concerning race"—Terry H. Anderson, *The Pursuit of Fairness: A History of Affirmative Action* (New York: Oxford University Press, 2004), p. 60. The principal drafters of Executive Order 10925 were Abe Fortas and Arthur Goldberg, both future Supreme Court justices. By adding the term "affirmative action," Taylor drew on "phrases like 'positive effort' and 'affirmative program' [that] had become common currency in the lexicon of civil rights by 1960," and that echoed, probably unintentionally, language deployed by the National Labor Relations Act in 1935. Kennedy's order built on precedents that included President Roosevelt's Committee on Fair Employment Practice and President Eisenhower's Committee on Government Employment Policy, chaired quite assiduously by Vice President Nixon.
3. Four years later, the Civil Rights Act, moreover, seemed to reject any such efforts. Under the language of its Title VII, employers explicitly were not

obliged to redress racial imbalances caused by past discriminatory practices. Further, the law insisted there be a showing that discrimination had been purposeful, ruling out findings of intent by inference. Civil rights leaders took notice that "preferential treatment to right past wrongs is not required," as the general counsel of the Congress on Racial Equality (CORE) put it—Carl Rachlin, cited in Moreno, *From Direct Action to Affirmative Action: Fair Employment Law and Policy in America, 1933–1972* (Baton Rouge: Louisiana State University Press, 1977), p. 226.

4. Johnson to the President, February 14, 1961, VPP/CRF, Box 8, LBJ Library, cited in Hugh Davis Graham, *The Civil Rights Era: Origins and Development of National Policy, 1960–1972* (New York: Oxford University Press, 1990), p. 39 (italics in the original).
5. This is the argument persuasively offered by John Skrentny in *The Ironies of Affirmative Action: Politics, Culture, and Justice in America* (Chicago: University of Chicago Press, 1996), pp. 6–8, 67–110. It is endorsed by Anderson, *Pursuit of Fairness*, pp. 98–99.
6. Writing to *Nation's Business*, Roosevelt indicated that in addition to investigating complaints of discrimination, "we regard our other approach—affirmative action—as important as the . . . correction of violations." Cited in Anderson, *Pursuit of Fairness*, p. 90.
7. For an early report noting the far-reaching intent of the EEOC, see Monroe W. Karmin, "New U.S. Commission Plans Big Push to Open More Posts to Negroes; It Questions Seniority Rules, Calls for 'Creative' Hiring; Line on Sex Bias Is Softer; Beyond Letter of Rights Act," *Wall Street Journal*, October 13, 1965, p. 1.
8. Alfred Blumrosen, a key EEOC figure, hit on the idea of the EEO-1 form quite by chance on a visit to the neighboring PCEEO, the agency that had been created by President Kennedy's executive order on discrimination in employment. "There I discovered a goldmine," boxes of reporting forms. "I saw this as perhaps the most important tool in any program to eliminate employment discrimination. . . . Here at last was a basis for government-initiated programs which were not based on complaints and which could focus on possible potential discriminators effectively"—Cited in Skrentny, *Ironies*, pp. 127–28.
9. Monroe W. Karmin, "Government Gets Set to Withhold Contracts from Some Companies," *Wall Street Journal*, November 9, 1966, p. 1. The first two companies it targeted were the Timken Roller Bearing Company of Ohio and the Mississippi tire plant of Armstrong Rubber.
10. Graham, *The Civil Rights Era*, p. 245.
11. For a discussion of this distinction, see Moreno, *From Direct Action*, pp. 1–2.
12. Tamar Jacoby, *Someone Else's House: America's Unfinished Struggle for Integration* (New York: Free Press, 1998), p. 381. She notes disapprovingly that "In some places, including Philadelphia, the plans were a response to egregious discrimination. But in many cities, no past mistreatment was even charged; it didn't have to be, because justice had been arbitrarily redefined as proportional repre-

sentation. The requirements were said to be 'good-faith' goals, not quotas, although this was a distinction without much difference, since contractors could be barred from federal work if they did not meet them."

13. Mitchell's views can be found in *Opinions of the Attorneys General of the United States*, Vol. 42 (Washington, DC: Government Printing Office, 1975), pp. 405–16, cited in Herman Belz, *Equality Transformed: A Quarter-Century of Affirmative Action* (New Brunswick, NJ: Transaction Publishers, 1991), pp. 36–37. Nixon's record on employment discrimination, however, was very mixed. When, in April 1969, Clifford Alexander, who had been appointed by President Johnson, resigned as chairman of the EEOC, he wrote President Nixon to say, "The public conclusion is inescapable: Vigorous efforts to enforce laws on employment discrimination aren't among the goals of this Administration"—"Chief of Equal Opportunity Unit Resigns; Says Administration Won't Fight Job Bias," *Wall Street Journal*, April 10, 1969, p. 3.
14. *Griggs v Duke Power Company*, 401 U.S. 424 (1971). An earlier federal court decision, *Contractors Association of Eastern Pennsylvania v. Secretary of Labor* (442 F.2d 159; 3d Circuit 1971), had upheld the Philadelphia Plan, endorsing its "color-conscious" and "affirmative action" aspects. This is discussed in Skrentny, *Ironies*, p. 165.
15. William Galston, "Civil Rights and Racial Preferences: A Legal History of Affirmative Action," *Philosophy and Public Policy*, 17 (Winter–Spring 1997), p. 10.
16. *Griggs* was the pivotal employment policy case, just as *Regents of the University of California v. Bakke* established the constitutional standard in higher education seven years later.
17. Cited in Anderson, *Pursuit of Fairness*, p. 129.
18. The picture is not entirely rosy. Black dropout rates are higher than those for whites, and there is a gender imbalance, with African American men disproportionately underrepresented in higher education.
19. See Jack Greenberg, "Affirmative Action in Higher Education: Confronting the Condition and Theory," *Boston College Law Review*, 43 (May 2002), pp. 569–72; Howard Ball, *The Bakke Case: Race, Education, and Affirmative Action* (Lawrence: University Press of Kansas, 2000), p. 3; William G. Bowen and Derek Bok, *The Shape of the River: Long-Term Consequences of Considering Race in College and University Admissions* (Princeton: Princeton University Press, 1998); and Thomas Cross and Robert Bruce Slater, "Only the Onset of Affirmative Action Explains the Explosive Growth in Black Enrollments in Higher Education," *Journal of Blacks in Higher Education*, 23 (Spring 1999), pp. 110–15.
20. In all, I agree with Orlando Patterson's judgment that "For all its imperfections, affirmative action has made a major difference . . . helping to realize, as no other policy has done, the nation's constitutional commitment to the ideals of equality, fairness, and economic integration . . . it is hard to find a program that has brought so much gain to so many at so little cost. It has been the single most important factor accounting for the rise of a significant Afro-American middle class"—Orlando Patterson, *The Ordeal of Integration: Progress and Resentment in*

America's "Racial" Crisis (Washington, DC: Basic Civitas Books, 1998), p. 147. Still, as Jennifer Hochschild has pointed out, many areas of empirical research about affirmative action's performance are missing. The country's debate about norms and legality on the whole has moved ahead more robustly than systematic research to find out what exactly has been happening. For this reason, the work by Bowen and Bok has been particularly welcome—Hochschild, "Affirmative Action as Culture War," in David Theo Goldberg and John Solomos, eds., *The Blackwell Companion to Racial and Ethnic Studies* (Oxford: Blackwell, 2002).

21. Cornel West, "Affirmative Action in Context," in George E. Curry, ed., *The Affirmative Action Debate* (Cambridge: Perseus Books, 1996), p. 31. Of course, some disagree. The National Coalition of Blacks for Reparations in America was formed in late 1987 and early 1988, a goal backed by Michigan congressman John Conyers, Jr., a leading figure in the Black Caucus, and the Reverend Jesse Jackson—Steve Miller, "Jackson to Make Reparations a Priority," *The Washington Times*, September 7, 2001, p. 1. For a defense, see Boris I. Bittker, "The Case for Black Reparations," in Gabriel Chin, ed., *Affirmative Action and the Constitution.* Vol. I: *Affirmative Action Before Constitutional Law, 1964–1977* (New York: Garland Publishing, 1998), pp. 37–71.
22. The term dates to Aristotle, who restricted its use to private exchanges.
23. Jules Coleman, "Moral Theories of Torts: Their Scope and Limits, Part II," *Law & Philosophy*, 2 (#3, 1983), p. 6.
24. Greenberg, "Affirmative Action," p. 555.
25. Nicholas Lemann, "Taking Affirmative Action Apart," *New York Times Magazine*, June 11, 1995, reprinted in Francis J. Beckwith and Todd E. Jones, eds., *Affirmative Action: Social Justice or Reverse Discrimination?* (Amherst, NY: Prometheus Books, 1997), pp. 38, 51.
26. The company agreed to this program in a collective bargaining agreement with the union in the context of having been subject to prosecution for racial discrimination. Before the plan's adoption, fewer than 2 percent of its skilled workers were black, while the area workforce was 39 percent black—Michel Rosenfeld, *Affirmative Action and Justice: A Philosophical and Constitutional Inquiry* (New Haven: Yale University Press, 1991), p. 173. Rosenfeld offers a fine overview of affirmative action jurisprudence through the 1980s (pp. 167–215).
27. *United Steelworkers of America v. Weber*, 442 US 193 (1979), pp. 204, 228–29. For a thoughtful discussion, see Richard Lempert, "The Force of Irony: On the Morality of Affirmative Action and *United Steelworkers v. Weber*," *Ethics*, 95 (October 1994). See also David W. Bishop, "The Affirmative Action Cases: Bakke, Weber, and Fullilove," *Journal of Negro History*, 67 (Autumn 1982). In the 1980 case of *Fullilove v. Klutznick* (448 U.S. 448), the Supreme Court found in favor of the federal government's 10 percent set-aside program to aid minority business enterprise. Writing for the Court, Chief Justice Warren Burger observed that "It is not a constitutional defect in this program that it may disappoint the expectations of nonminority firms" (p. 484).

28. *Firefighters v. Stotts*, 467 U.S. 561 (1984); *Wygant v. Jackson Board of Education*, 476 U.S. 267 (1986); *Local 28, Sheet Metal Workers' International Association v. EEOC*, 478 U.S. 421 (1986); *United States v. Paradise*, 480 U.S. 149 (1987); *Johnson v. Transportation Agency of Santa Clara County*, 480 U.S. 616 (1987). Following these cases, Clarence Thomas, writing from the vantage of the EEOC, conceded reluctantly (if, as it turned out, prematurely, not least because of his own later role on the Supreme Court) that "The legal debate over affirmative action, which has so long and so bitterly divided those who are concerned with civil rights, is behind us, and there is now an opportunity for cooperation and progress"—Clarence Thomas, "Affirmative Action. Goals and Timetables. Too Tough? Not Tough Enough!" *Yale Law and Policy Review*, 5 (Spring–Summer 1987), p. 109. Herman Schwartz, a leading legal supporter of affirmative action, echoed Thomas's assessment in "The 1986 and 1987 Affirmative Action Cases: It's All Over But the Shouting," *Michigan Law Review*, 86 (December 1987). An earlier, more mixed review was provided by Kathleen Sullivan, "Sins of Discrimination: Last Term's Affirmative Action Cases," 100 *Harvard Law Review*, 78 (November 1986).

What linked these cases, irrespective of outcome, was the insistence by the Court on a standard of strict scrutiny to assure that explicitly racial remedies address only "convincing evidence" of prior discrimination. This standard was applied in the 1989 decision to reject a minority set-aside program in Richmond, Virginia, as not meeting this test—*City of Richmond v. J. A. Croson Co.*, 488 U.S. 469 (1989). At the time, it looked as if a severe blow had been dealt to affirmative action, but over the long term this has not proved to be so. A number of cases followed (still in 1989) that either placed restrictions on affirmative action or made it easier for aggrieved whites to challenge existing programs. These decisions reflected a shift in the composition of the Court, as Justice Powell was replaced by Anthony Kennedy, who regularly joined the four justices who had composed the earlier minority bloc in 1980s affirmative action jurisprudence. Yet, just a year later, in *Metro Broadcasting Inc v. FCC*, 497 U.S. 547 (1990), the Court held, in yet another 5–4 decision, that the agency's policy of awarding "enhancements" for minority broadcast management and ownership did not violate equal protection imperatives. A notable reversal for affirmative action came in the next decade in the Federal Fifth Circuit 1996 decision in *Hopwood v. Texas* to outlaw the preferential minority admissions policies of the University of Texas Law School—*Hopwood v. Texas*, 78 F3d 932 (1996).

The most important Supreme Court affirmative action case in the 1990s was *Adarand Constructors, Inc. v. Pena*, 515 U.S. 400 (1995), which overruled *Metro* for its level of scrutiny. What *Adarand* did was to establish "strict scrutiny" as the test required for the constitutional approbation of affirmative action. Justice O'Connor wrote for the 5–4 majority that it is a "basic principle that the Fifth and Fourteenth Amendments to the Constitution protect *persons*, not *groups*. It follows from that principle that all governmental action based on race—a *group* classification long recognized as in most circumstances irrelevant and therefore prohibited—should be subjected to detailed judicial inquiry to ensure that the *personal* right to equal protection of the laws has not been infringed" (italics in the original). With these considerations in mind, she added that "all racial classification, imposed by whatever federal, state, or local governmental actor, must be analyzed by a reviewing court under strict scrutiny. In other words, such classifications are constitutional only if they are narrowly tailored measures that further compelling governmental interests"—*Adarand*, 227.

Perhaps equally important was her rejection of the view expressed by Justices Scalia and Thomas that affirmative action is always precluded. Rather, O'Connor wrote, "The unhappy persistence of both the practice and lingering effects of racial discrimination against minority groups in this country is an unfortunate reality, and government is not disqualified from acting in response to it"—*Adarand*, 237.

29. For the argument that the Court has continued to offer only mixed messages and thus cannot resolve what affirmative action is or should be, see Neal Devins, "*Adarand Constructors, Inc. v. Pena* and the Continuing Irrelevance of Supreme Court Affirmative Action Decisions," 37 *William and Mary Law Review*, 673 (1996).
30. As chairman of EEOC, Thomas had written: "I continue to believe that distributing opportunities on the basis of race or gender, whoever the beneficiaries, turns the law against employment discrimination on its head. Class preferences are an affront to the rights and dignity of individuals. . . . Skin color and gender are truly the least important things about a person in the employment context." Thomas advocated more close attention to employment decisions as they happen, and more assistance to minorities to help themselves rather than what he labeled as "handouts"—Thomas, "Affirmative Action," p. 101, note 3.
31. *New York Times*, June 24, 2003, pp. 1, 23. For an earlier African American polemic against the stigmatizing powers of affirmative action, see Stephen C. Carter, *Reflections of an Affirmative Action Baby* (New York: Basic Books, 1991).
32. *Regents of the University of California v. Bakke*, 438 U.S. 265 (1978), p. 315. Harvard University's admission plan for undergraduates was cited by Powell favorably for the way it counted race as one among a longer list of factors considered when individual applications are weighed.
33. Senator Waitman Willey of West Virginia, *Congressional Globe*, 39th Congress, 1st sess. (1866), p. 397, cited in Eric Shnapper, "Affirmative Action and the Legislative History of the Fourteenth Amendment," 71 *Virginia Law Review*, 753 (1985), p. 763. This article was based on the Amicus brief the author wrote for the NAACP Legal Defense and Educational Fund in the landmark *Bakke* case.
34. *Bakke*, p. 289, note 36.
35. Justice William Brennan observed in *Bakke* that the distinction between the Harvard program of which Justice Powell approved and the Davis plan for special admissions was one of form rather than substance. This argument was made in the more recent Michigan cases by the justices who found in favor of the point system used in undergraduate admissions. A positive evaluation of Justice

Brennan's jurisprudence in this and related cases can be found in Kim Isaac Eisler, "William J. Brennan, Jr.: Judicial Architect of Affirmative Action," *Journal of Blacks in Higher Education*, 17 (Autumn 1997). In all, Ronald Dworkin summarized, the Supreme Court "has now decided, by a vote of five to four, that the Civil Rights Act does not in and of itself bar affirmative action programs, even those, like Davis's, that use explicit quotas. It has decided, by a vote of five to none, that the Constitution permits affirmative action plans, like the Harvard undergraduate plan, that allow race to be taken into account, on an individual by individual basis, in order to achieve a reasonably diverse student body"—Ronald Dworkin, "What Did Bakke Really Decide?" *New York Review of Books*, August 17, 1983, reprinted in Steven M. Cahn, ed., *The Affirmative Action Debate,* 2nd edn (New York: Routledge, 2002), pp. 114–15.

36. Antonin Scalia, "The Disease as Cure: 'In Order to Get Beyond Racism, We Must First Take Account of Race,'" *Washington University Law Quarterly*, 147 (#1, 1979), pp. 153–54, 157.
37. Jacoby, *Someone Else's House*, p. 541.
38. For an overview of these objections, see Greenberg, "Affirmative Action in Higher Education," pp. 580–94.
39. "Negative Action," *Wall Street Journal*, August 23, 1965, p. 8.
40. Nathan Glazer, *Affirmative Discrimination: Ethnic Inequality and Public Policy* (New York: Basic Books, 1975), pp. 58, 75, 197.
41. *Regents of the University of California v. Bakke*, 438 U.S. 265 (1978), p. 2803.
42. Nathan Glazer, *We Are All Multiculturalists Now* (Cambridge: Harvard University Press, 1997), pp. 157, 158.
43. Douglas S. Massey and Nancy Denton, *American Apartheid: Segregation and the Making of the Underclass* (Cambridge: Harvard University Press, 1993).
44. Ronald Dworkin, "Bakke's Case: Are Quotas Unfair?" *New York Review of Books*, November 10, 1977. See also Dworkin, "What Did Bakke Really Decide?" and Vincent Blasi, "*Bakke* as Precedent: Does Mr. Justice Powell Have a Theory?" in Gabriel J. Chin, ed., *Affirmative Action and the Constitution.* Vol. 2: *The Supreme Court "Solves" the Affirmative Action Issue, 1978–1988* (New York: Garland Publishing), 1998, pp. 1–48.
45. Steve Miller, "Jackson to Make Reparations a Priority," *The Washington Times*, September 7, 2001, p. 1.
46. Glazer, *Affirmative Discrimination*, pp. 207–09.
47. *Adarand*, 515 U.S., 273.
48. For a fine discussion, see Michael J. Perry, *We the People: The Fourteenth Amendment and the Supreme Court* (New York: Oxford University Press, 1999), pp. 97–115.
49. *Adarand*, 237.
50. Perry, *We the People*, p. 102 (italics in the original).
51. My Columbia College class, graduating some six hundred students in 1966, had three black members, all of whom came from wealthy families and had attended New England prep schools.

52. *Wall Street Journal*, June 24, 2004, p. A17.
53. Reynolds Farley and Walter R. Allen, *The Color Line and the Quality of Life in America* (New York: Russell Sage Foundation, 1987), pp. 289–90; Melvin L. Oliver and Thomas M. Shapiro, *Black Wealth, White Wealth: A New Perspective on Racial Inequality* (New York: Routledge, 1997), pp. 97–111. A majority of blacks also did not have bank accounts of any kind (compared to one in four whites); only 5 percent owned stocks or mutual funds (compared to 22 percent of whites).
54. For a discussion and a mixed set of conclusions, see Reynolds Farley, *Blacks and Whites: Narrowing the Gap?* (Cambridge: Harvard University Press, 1984).
55. Thomas M. Shapiro, *The Hidden Cost of Being African American: How Wealth Perpetuates Inequality* (New York: Oxford University Press, 2004), pp. 49, 53, 109. See also John Karl Scholz and Kara Levine, "U.S. Black-White Wealth Inequality: A Survey," in Kathryn M. Neckerman, ed., *Social Inequality* (New York: Russell Sage Foundation, 2004), pp. 895–929.
56. See Robert A. Margo, "Explaining Black-White Wage Convergence, 1940–1950," *Industrial and Labor Relations Review*, 48 (April 1995), pp. 470–81; Thomas N. Maloney, "Wage Compression and Wage Inequality Between Black and White Males in the United States, 1940–1960," *Journal of Economic History*, 54 (June 1994), pp. 358–81; and William J. Collins, "African-American Economic Mobility in the 1940s," *Journal of Economic History*, 60 (September 2000), pp. 756–81, and Collins, "Race, Roosevelt, and Wartime Production: Fair Employment in World War II Labor Markets," *American Economic Review*, 91 (March 2001), pp. 272–86.
57. For an important discussion, see Linda Williams, *The Constraint of Choice: The Legacies of White Skin Privilege in America* (University Park: Pennsylvania State University Press, 2003).
58. Thomas, "Affirmative Action Goals and Timetables," p. 109, note 3; Herman Schwartz, "The 1986 and 1987 Affirmative Action Cases: It's All Over But the Shouting," *Michigan Law Review*, 86 (December 1987).
59. By contrast, the point system deployed by the University of Michigan for its undergraduate admissions was struck down by the Court in *Gratz v. Bollinger* in a 6–3 decision. *Grutter v. Bollinger*, finding for Bollinger, was decided by a 5–4 margin. Both rulings were announced on June 23, 2003. For a discussion of the cases by academic leaders at the University of Michigan, see Patricia Gurin, Jeffrey S. Lehman, and Earl Lewis, *Defending Diversity: Affirmative Action at the University of Michigan* (Ann Arbor: University of Michigan Press, 2004). See also the special issue, "Affirmative Action: The Rulings on Admissions Policy at the University of Michigan, June 16, 2003," *The Black Scholar*, 33 (Fall–Winter 2003).
60. These proscriptions supersede judicial rulings favoring affirmative action.
61. For a discussion, see Hochschild, "Affirmative Action." See also Lawrence Bobo and James R. Kluegel, "Opposition to Race Targeting: Self-Interest, Stratification Ideology, or Racial Attitudes?" *American Sociological Review*, 58 (August 1993), pp. 443–64; Lawrence Bobo, "Race, Interests, and Beliefs About

Affirmative Action," *American Behavioral Scientist*, 41 (#7, 1998), pp. 985–1003; James Kluegel and Eliot Smith, "Affirmative Action Attitudes of Self-Interest, Racial Affect, and Stratification Beliefs on Whites Views," *Social Forces*, 61 (1983), pp. 797–825; Howard Schuman, Charlotte Steeh, Larry Bobo, and Maria Krysan, *Racial Attitudes in America* (Cambridge: Harvard University Press, 1997); Charlotte Steeh and Maria Krysan, "The Polls—Trends: Affirmative Action and the Public, 1970–1995," *Public Opinion Quarterly*, 60 (#1, 1996), pp. 128–58; and Gallup Organization, *Affirmative Action: A Gallup Poll Special Report* (Princeton: Gallup Organization, 1995).

62. Morris J. MacGregor, *Integration of the Armed Forces, 1940–1965* (Washington, DC: Center for Military History, U.S. Army, 1981), pp. 216–18.
63. MacGregor, *Integration*, pp. 218–19; Fass, *Outside In*, p. 153.
64. So much so that a recent important study could write that "Affirmative action as governmental policy (both federal and state) is a brand-new phenomenon—except for the preferential programs (such as the Freeman's Bureau aid programs) passed by the Reconstruction Congress from the late 1860s into the 1870s to assist the former slaves of the South. Other than that example, there are no historic precedents for the affirmative action programs, in business, contracting, employment, and higher education, that were created beginning in the mid-1960's"—Howard Ball, *The Bakke Case: Race, Education, and Affirmative Action* (Lawrence: University Press of Kansas, 2000), p. xi.
65. Greenberg, "Affirmative Action," p. 523.
66. James W. Nickel, "Discrimination and Morally Relevant Characteristics," *Analysis*, 32 (1972), reprinted in Cahn, *Affirmative Action Debate.*
67. For a historical and empirical treatment of this issue of the boundaries of harm, see Neil Foley, *The White Scourge: Mexicans, Blacks, and Poor Whites in Texas Cotton Culture* (Berkeley: University of California Press, 1997).
68. For a stimulating discussion of public apologies, see Danielle Celermajer, "Political Apologies: Collective Responsibility and Political Ritual," Ph.D. dissertation, Department of Political Science, Columbia University, 2004.

ACKNOWLEDGMENTS

THE TALMUD TEACHES that debts are not repaid unless they are publicly acknowledged. I am pleased to do so. This book first took shape in a number of public forums. I tested my evidence and arguments in a talk at the Smithsonian Institution, a conference at the Hagley Museum, a workshop series at Harvard University's Kennedy School, and meetings conducted under the auspices of the Social Science Research Council (SSRC) for a project on the middle classes in postwar France, Japan, and the United States.

The SSRC enterprise provided a first venue for me to turn the historical research I had begun on the New Deal toward the topic of affirmative action. At our sessions in Paris in January 1998, in Tokyo in June 1999, and in Charlottesville in April 2000, I had the chance to try out my formulations before talented colleagues, including Patrick Friedenson, Meg Jacobs, William Kelley, Chiara Saraceno, and Margaret Weir. I have tried to take their comments into account. I am particularly beholden to Olivier Zunz, who challenged me to achieve more precision when my paper was turned into "Public Policy and the Middle-Class Racial Divide After the Second World War" for the work entitled *Postwar Social Contracts Under Stress: The Middle Classes of America, Europe, and Japan at the Turn of the Century*, which he edited with Leonard Schoppa and Nobuhiro Hiwatari for the Russell Sage Foundation (2002).

As part of the Weiner Inequality and Social Policy Seminar Series at the Kennedy School in February 2000, I spoke on "Legacies of Universalism: Reflections on the Ironic Precursors of Affirmative Action." After a spirited discussion, Christopher Jencks, Jane Mansbridge, and I continued the conversation at a nearby café. I explained how the talk, based on my contribution to the SSRC venture, was an offshoot of research I had begun for a book on the role the South had played in shaping modern American liberalism in the 1930s and 1940s. They urged me to consider a separate book that would expand my lecture by connecting the history of social policy during that critical era to current understandings and debates about affirmative action. I decided to take their advice. I also appreciate the stimulating questions and observations from other participants who attended the Kennedy School event, among them Katherine Newman, who chaired the series, David Ellwood, Daniel Kryder, Martin Rein, and Sidney Verba.

In February 2004, Jennifer Hochschild and I took one of our customary long walks (this one in Morningside Heights and Manhattanville in West Harlem). With the manuscript well along, she used her keen editorial sensibilities to help me think about vexing issues of structure and content. I also warmly value the information and instruction about the GI Bill that Kathleen Frydl and Suzanne Mettler provided.

Columbia University has been entwined with the development of affirmative action for more than three decades. In 1971, the federal government threatened a punitive response unless it produced an acceptable affirmative action plan. Columbia had to file three plans that year before $13 million in federal aid was released. In June 1977, together with Harvard, Stanford, and the University of Pennsylvania, Columbia filed a brief to the Supreme Court to support the medical school admissions policy at the University of California, Davis. I have learned much about the subjects and period from faculty and students at the university, especially Provost Alan Brinkley (wearing his hat as historian); President Lee Bollinger (formerly at the University of Michigan, where he was the party against whom action had been brought that culminated in 2003 in two landmark Supreme Court decisions elaborating what affirmative action can, and cannot, mean in higher education); Robert Lieberman (whose work on race and social policy in the New Deal helped open the door); and Ronald Krebs (now at the University of Minnesota, and author of a doctoral thesis that includes a fine chapter on African Americans and military service in the twentieth century). I also have profited from the excellent research assistance provided by Benjamin Fishman, Thomas Gorman, and Christina Greer. Sean Farhang, who recently joined the faculty at the University of California, Berkeley, not only provided counsel and assiduous help as he was completing his graduate studies but co-authored with me an American Political Science Association paper, "The Southern Imposition: Congress and Labor in the New Deal and Fair Deal" (2001) that has served as the first draft for chapter 3. I thank him for generously allowing me to draw so substantially on this joint work.

I also owe a particular debt to my colleague Jack Greenberg, who teaches law at Columbia, and was director-counsel of the NAACP Legal Defense and Educational Fund from 1961 to 1984. He attended a seminar at the university in 2001 when I discussed this project. Later, he sent me a reprint of his article on "Affirmative Action in Higher Education: Confronting the Condition and Theory" that had just appeared in the *Boston College Law Review* (May 2002). It was accompanied by a gracious note saying, "This article uses, I hope doesn't misuse, some learning I acquired from you." Actually, quite the reverse is the case. Professor Greenberg's article soon had a big impact on my thinking about affirmative action. His view informs the arguments presented in my closing chapter.

A jewel of an independent publisher, W. W. Norton has offered the gift of two exceptional editors. Roby Harrington, whom I had come to know while collaborating on a project for the American Political Science Association, was my first point of contact. Throughout, despite his heavy administrative responsibilities, he has been a constant source of interest, advice, and quiet prodding. Roby quickly brought Robert Weil into the project. Bob is an extraordinary trade editor, who cares passionately about ideas, history, and the powers of communication. It is impossible for me to exaggerate what a treat it has been to work with both. Neither can I overstate the role played by Gloria Loomis, the first agent I ever have had, whose love of books that tackle themes of public interest is infectious.

I hope Deborah Socolow Katznelson will forgive me for punctuating our New York winter and English Cambridge summer with my reading aloud from drafts of the manuscript. Both the prose and the flow of ideas are a good deal clearer for her sharp advice. The book is dedicated to Leah, our youngest daughter (if only by some two minutes!), a person of uncommon creativity, intellect, and zest for experience.

Finally, I am beholden to E. J. Dionne, Jr., of *The Washington Post.* At the 2002 annual meeting of the American Political Science Association, I described the book I was about to write. E. J. asked the title. I told him. With a wry smile of disapproval, he suggested I name it "When Affirmative Action Was White." Gratefully, I have.

New York
December 2004

Index

Page numbers beginning with 182 refer to notes.